MONSTER OF THEIR OWN MAKING

How the Far Left, the Media, and Politicians are Creating Far-Right Extremists

JACK BUCKBY

BOMBARDIER
BOOKS

A BOMBARDIER BOOKS BOOK
An Imprint of Post Hill Press
ISBN: 978-1-64293-424-3
ISBN (eBook): 978-1-64293-425-0

Monster of Their Own Making:
How the Far Left, the Media, and Politicians are Creating Far-Right Extremists

Author photo by Martina Buckby-Markota

Post Hill Press
New York • Nashville
posthillpress.com

Published in the United States of America

For Cherie

TABLE OF CONTENTS

INTRODUCTION

Everything you think you know about the far right is wrong. A well-coordinated campaign orchestrated by negligent politicians, a complicit media, and the far left has knocked public discourse off kilter. Politics have been toxified, the moderate center has shifted left, and talk of far-right extremism has become shockingly inaccurate.

We're told that the far right poses the greatest threat to our civilized society, and although the claim isn't completely accurate, it's also not totally wrong. It is a believable lie that is based on some fundamental truths, and we must be willing to accept those truths if we are to expose the lie.

Extremists obviously exist and it would be foolish to deny there is no such thing as "the far right," but the matter isn't so clear-cut. It is an issue so complex, so riddled with nuance, and so dangerous to navigate that the extreme left's obsession with labelling such a huge section of society as "far right" is causing real-world damage.

As it stands, the narrative surrounding political extremism is controlled by a network of far-left extremists who offer a subjective and warped view of the issue while profiting from the false narratives they perpetuate. If we are ever to defeat political extremism, we must deal not only with the growing threat of neo-Nazi and far-right terrorists, but we must also reclaim the narrative from dangerous far-left extremists.

Throughout this book, I will explain what conservatives and liberals get right and wrong about the far right, and how activists, writers, commentators, and politicians on both sides of the aisle can work together to stop the reciprocal extremism that is quickly spiraling out of control.

What I have to say might make for some uncomfortable reading. I would ask that readers approach this book with an open mind and understand that everything I say is based on my real-life experience with the real far right. We must all be willing to learn and to accept that our methods might sometimes be counterproductive. That is something I have learned over the years since leaving the far right.

Moreover, readers should understand that at the time of writing this book, I have no political affiliation and any defense of a political party or group in this text is done for the express purpose of identifying hypocrisy and offering a more accurate analysis of what the far right really is. There are groups and individuals referenced throughout this book who I will describe as democratic populists, nationalists, or conservatives who have previously been identified as "far right." *This does not indicate my support for those people or organizations.*

I believe it is in everybody's interests (liberal or conservative) to more accurately categorize these people to offer a clearer view of what the far right actually is—even if you find the views of those people reprehensible.

This book is the culmination of over a decade of learning and real-world experience in the fringes of right-wing politics. It is my goal to deconstruct the current line of thinking about the far right, offer constructive criticism to those who genuinely oppose political extremism, and provide a unique insight into an issue that has been commandeered by dangerous far-left radicals.

CHAPTER ONE

THE PATH TO RADICALIZATION

To solve a problem, we must first understand it.

So, when our political leaders and media class tell us that the far right is growing at an alarming rate, you might be forgiven for expecting those people to have attempted to understand the nature of the problem first. But virtually everyone who makes this claim has either made no attempt to understand it or has drawn extraordinarily inaccurate conclusions as a result of their fundamental misunderstanding of the basics or their own political agenda.

When you start with a fundamental misunderstanding of the basics, any conclusion—or even hypothesis—is bound to be riddled with errors and unrepresentative of what is actually true.

Meanwhile, those who truly understand the nature and motivation of the far right are routinely ignored. I am one of those people. For years, I sat by and watched in horror as radical progressives and extremists assumed control over the political extremism narrative, labelling the wrong people "far right" and advocating policies that would only further radicalize young, white, working-class men toward the extreme fringe of right-wing politics.

Everything we're told about the far right is wrong, and I know because I was *in* the far right.

As a teenager, I was part of the biggest far-right movement in recent British history. I was a member of a nationalist political party with neo-Nazi roots that attracted the votes of a million desperate, working-class British people who had no other option. I have seen the far right from the inside, I understand how they operate, and I can see just how wrong both liberals and conservatives are on this issue.

Throughout this book, I will share with you many of my personal experiences navigating thc world of white nationalist politics in my youth. I will tell the stories of how young men from my home county, including people I called friends, went on to become convicted far-right terrorists and extremists. I will also offer what I believe to be a better and more accurate analysis of what the far right really is, and why the far left finds it advantageous to lie about it.

SKELMERSDALE

I grew up in a town called Skelmersdale in West Lancashire, in the north of England. It's a working-class former mining town that is affectionately known as "Skem." I say affectionately—everyone, including me, moans about how terrible it is. It's the kind of thing you don't mind saying yourself, but I get fiercely defensive if anyone else tells me the place is crap. I had a wonderful childhood, the town was pretty safe, and there were lots of trees and fields. I had a great time.

But, as with so many working-class towns in the north of England, it has fallen into disrepair. Every time I go back to Skem, I see it getting just a little bit worse. The town seems to have resisted the kind of damage done to many parts of East Lancashire, a result of Tony Blair's open-door immigration policy. The only immigration we really saw was a lot of Polish workers who came for the jobs in the factories and warehouses. We grew up making jokes about how Poland must be empty because everyone was living in Skem. There was generally no hatred felt for the Poles; in fact, people often commented on the work ethic of the lads who came there. But that didn't mean there weren't issues.

I remember a protest when I was a child, around 2002. There was a plot of unused land near a school I would eventually become a student at that was earmarked to become a center for asylum-seekers. It was part of a wider plan for more than two thousand asylum-seekers to be housed in centers near airports.[1] Skem was ideal because of its proximity to both Liverpool and Manchester airports. It was also an experimental new town with plenty of empty green land that could be built on.

Parish councilor Irene O'Donnell perfectly summed up the feeling of locals at the time.

> When I heard the news I was horrified. For a start will it be a visual monstrosity, like a Colditz or something?
>
> We are currently opposing the county council's plans to expand the estate because there is too much

1 "Anger over Refugee 'Prisons' Plan," BBC News, February 15, 2002, http://news.bbc.co.uk/1/hi/england/1822083.stm.

> traffic as it is, so the movement of 4000 people per month will not help.
>
> Sadly, we also have to wonder why, if these people are merely asylum seekers, is the place being built up as a virtual prison?
>
> I have to say I'm very skeptical indeed.

We were told it was going to happen whether we liked it or not, and Irene had a point—the proposed plans really did look like a prison. Would any reasonable person want to build such a thing right next to two local schools? And did anyone really care that this was being plonked right in the middle of a working-class community and not next to a private school in an upper-middle-class town?

The government and agencies involved with the plans didn't care how we felt about it, and the only reason it got stopped was because we kept protesting.

I remember being a nine-year-old boy out protesting with what seemed like the entire town. Thousands of people marched around Half-Mile Island, a particularly large roundabout in the center of the town, demanding the plans stop.

The cancellation of the project was a small victory, but this was just one more instance of the government not really caring about the little guy. And over the years, working-class communities in places like Skem just got hurt more and more. Although Skem managed for a long time to avoid the cultural problems that come with mass third world immigration, we *were* hit by economic problems.

Working-class communities started seeing the job market tighten and unemployment rose. The 2008 crash really amplified this effect, so much so that Tony Blair's successor as Labour Prime Minister, Gordon Brown, was forced to pick up the slogan "British Jobs for British Workers" in 2009.[2] He failed, of course, given it was the Labour Party that started the mass immigration project, displaced working class communities, and oversaw an unemployment crisis in traditionally white working-class towns. It was just a slogan, and the Labour Party offered no real concrete proposals to protect British workers. Once again, the politicians proved that they were not only incapable of addressing difficult issues but were unwilling to do so.

Skem was by no means the place to be worst hit by these problems. In fact, everything about the town is remarkably normal. There are other places throughout Lancashire that were hit significantly worse by the crash and experienced higher unemployment, and typically they were the same places affected by the cultural displacement and ghettoization that came from Labour's policy of mass immigration.

It is this political neglect that pushes desperate people toward the far right. It drives some people to madness, some to violence, some to extremism, and some to a feeling of defeat and despondency. Many people just give up on voting, accepting their new life, while others choose much more radical measures to protect themselves against a political elite that doesn't seem to care about them. Throughout this book, and particularly in the concluding chapters, I will explain how we

---

2 Deborah Summers, "Brown Stands By British Jobs for British Workers Remark," *The Guardian*, January 30, 2009, https://www.theguardian.com/politics/2009/jan/30/brown-british-jobs-workers.

can defeat the rise of the far right by addressing the issues on which they capitalize.

When the politicians are willing to address the difficult issues that affect normal people, neo-Nazis and genuine far-right extremists have no ground to stand on. They can't say that they're the only ones willing to listen to the working class, and they can't capitalize on the cultural displacement of working-class English towns.

Until the politicians stop showing contempt for the working class, the far right will continue capitalizing on it and more young men will be drawn to extreme politics. I know, because it's precisely what happened to me when I discovered the British National Party in 2008.

DISCOVERING THE BNP

The BNP was founded in 1982 by former members of the National Front, a white nationalist political party that advocated the forceful deportation of nonwhite people from the UK. The BNP was slightly different, encouraging a policy of voluntary repatriation—something that the Conservative Party advocated just a few decades ago.

After thirty years of campaigning, the BNP became the only political party representing working-class concerns about mass immigration. The established parties had decided that anyone who dared talk about the issue was bigoted, leaving white nationalists as the only people daring to say *maybe we should stop this huge influx of people.* Prime Minister Gordon Brown famously slipped up and proved just how out of touch the Labour Party was when he was caught on a hot mic calling a voter "some bigoted woman."[3]

Gillian Duffy was a sixty-five-year-old lifelong Labour voter who just happened to be walking through her neighborhood in Rochdale when she saw Gordon Brown out on the campaign trail. She told the prime minister that she believed too many people were abusing the education and health system, so much so that people who were genuinely vulnerable could no longer access the services they used to. Brown tried to reassure her that he was cracking down on those who abuse the system, but when Duffy made clear she was referencing Eastern European immigrants, Brown got uncomfortable. She asked, "All these Eastern European what are coming in, where are they flocking from?"

Brown quickly left but his comments were heard on the microphone as he got in the car. It went like this:

> **Brown:** *That was a disaster. Well I just...should never have put me in with that woman. Whose idea was that?*
>
> **Assistant:** *I don't know. I didn't see.*
>
> **Brown:** *It was Sue, I think. It was just ridiculous.*
>
> **Assistant:** *I'm not sure if they [the media] will go with that.*
>
> **Brown:** *They will go with that.*
>
> **Assistant:** *What did she say?*
>
> **Brown:** *Oh everything, she was just a sort of bigoted woman. She said she used to be Labour. I mean, it's just ridiculous.*

---

3 Polly Curtis, "How Gillian Duffy Nipped out for a Loaf—But Left Gordon Brown in a Right Jam," *The Guardian*, April 29, 2010, https://www.theguardian.com/politics/2010/apr/29/gordon-brown-gillian-duffy-bigot.

I'll never forget the response to that. It was shocking. A lot of working-class voters already knew how snobbish the Labour Party, the traditional party of the working class, had become. Those who hadn't realized certainly got the shock of their lives. I just remember laughing my arse off about the "Sue" comment. I wondered who she was, and how much trouble she must have been in after that incident.

But on a more serious note, it reaffirmed to me my belief that if anything was to change in working-class communities, then it would require political action outside the mainstream parties.

I remember seeing Nick Griffin, the leader of the BNP, on the television during what must have been the run up to the 2009 European elections. There was a local TV news report about how the party was expected to win a seat in our region for the first time, and it showed an interview with Griffin discussing his policy pledges. I found it hard to disagree with any of them.

How could I disagree with restricting immigration, reforming the banking system, and putting the British workers first? That was music to every working-class person's ears during the recession.

I went straight to my computer and started researching the party and what it planned to do. I read what the media said about them, and I compared it with what the party actually said. There was a clear disparity, so I felt inclined to believe what members said. A video of a tearful Jewish member of the BNP passionately explaining to an audience at a local branch meeting how hurtful it was for the media to call him a neo-Nazi really made me think. It was shocking. I couldn't believe how wicked these lies were, and I believed the good intentions of the average member of the party. These were good people. Unfortunately, as it would turn out, the good nature of many regular members wasn't really the issue. It was the intention of its leaders.

I'll never forget the first time I publicly mentioned my new political interests. I had seen the phrase "far right" thrown around so much by the press that I just assumed it was the appropriate term for someone like me. And so, when my PE teacher asked me on the last day of school what I was planning on doing with my life, I told her "I'm joining the far right. Not the bad far right. The good far right."

She chuckled nervously, wished me all the best, and I left.

SEEING THE IMPACTS OF MASS NON-EUROPEAN IMMIGRATION

It must have been during the summer between leaving high school and joining the local college that I took a trip to Preston, a city on the other side of Lancashire. This is when I saw the impact of non-European immigration up close for the first time. In the UK, the kind of impact of mass immigration on working-class towns depends on whether that immigration comes from nearby European states or third world countries from further afield. For the most part, the Polish immigrant population in my hometown was decent, hard-working, and very similar to us culturally. But that's not to say there wasn't conflict. Economic issues—namely, job supply—did cause resentment, and to this day, there are around a million Polish people living in the UK.

Non-European immigration is very different. It's a sad fact that with large numbers of non-European migrants comes ghettoization. Towns and cities become divided on racial and religious lines. According to the 2011 census, the native British population made up 83.7 percent of the overall population of Preston. Just 1.3 percent were from Pakistan and 3.7 percent from India,[4] but despite this, entire sections of the city looked unrecognizable. This isn't a mindless or unfair attack on people who aren't white; it is merely an observation. As a young white teenager who grew up in a white Christian town, seeing an entire high street of shop signs written in foreign languages and women wearing burkas was shocking.

I felt like I was in another country.

I knew I wasn't wrong about this. I know to this day that I'm not wrong about this. Western nations must remain identifiably Western if they are to survive. This isn't a matter of hating someone for being different or holding negative feelings about people who weren't born in the same country as me. This is something that runs much deeper.

Western nations are defined by their culture. That is everything from the way the country is governed, the way our economic system works, and the way our children are taught right down to how we treat our neighbors, the kind of pets we keep, and the style of our houses. A culture is a wide-ranging thing, and it defines who we are. What I saw in Preston was not identifiably Western, and the values of many of the people brought into the UK by the post-1997 Labour governments are not identifiably Western either.

---

4 "Preston Census Demographics, United Kingdom," Qpzm Local Stats, http://localstats.co.uk/census-demographics/england/north-west/preston.

Over a period of years, I learned more about how radically different Western values and culture are to the values held by many people coming from countries like Pakistan. And the more I saw the politicians defending mass immigration and continuing to ignore the cultural and economic problems affecting working-class towns, the more committed to the BNP I became.

During the summer between high school and college, I worked at a law firm as a typist. I remember looking for BNP lapel badges on eBay during my lunch breaks. Colleagues saw what I was doing. One just rolled her eyes, but it wasn't really a big deal. The party was polling well and was becoming fairly mainstream. Their softer approach to immigration and repatriation, compared with the National Front, meant people felt more at ease supporting the party. Of course, the United Kingdom Independence Party (UKIP), Nigel Farage's party, was around at the time—but the general feeling among working class voters was that Farage and UKIP were simply "Tory lite." Their NHS policy was vague, they came across as posh, and their policies beyond Brexit didn't seem to chime so well with traditional socialist-leaning Labour voters.

I, along with a large chunk of the voting public, found myself entangled in a political movement with good intentions led by people with bad intentions. This is how extremists on the right of politics operate. They hook you with policies that address real problems. These are issues that are observably causing difficulties within local communities. They are real. Mass immigration was clearly an issue hurting many people no matter how much the politicians tell us diversity is our strength. Muslim rape gangs destroyed the lives of thousands of young girls and their families. That was and is real. And when a party led by genuine extremists is the only political vehicle willing to stand up to these issues, like the BNP was, people are willing to forgive some of their sins. Namely, a history of anti-Semitism and race hate.

WHY WAS I ROBBED OF MY IDENTITY?

A number of major failings by the political establishment, commentators, and the media gave people more reasons to support the BNP; specifically, the denial of the existence of a British people and constant references to the racist views of the party's membership.

I am perfectly willing to say, on the record, that many members of the party were not racist. Plenty *were*, but the average voter and many signed-up members were not. Most supporters I met simply recognized the fact that the native people of Britain and Western Europe are white—an assertion that would be completely uncontroversial if it were made by a Ugandan person stating that native people of their country are black.

It is not an assertion of dominance or superiority, nor is it an attempt at saying nonwhite people should be booted out of the country. It is merely a historic and obvious truth that the majority of people who have populated these islands for the longest period of time are what most people would call "white."

The way in which politicians and members of the press reacted to this simple truth gave credibility to the arguments of the genuine far right. When the establishment denies the very *existence* of a British or European people, and when the politicians say that Britain is a culturally and ethnically neutral place, it gives rise to identity politics and proves the genuine racists right.

"The BBC don't want you to exist!" they say.

Every time I heard that, I became more steadfast in my belief that the media and most political commentators hated me. The most striking example I can remember of this is when Bonnie Greer, an American-British black playwright, took on Nick Griffin on live television in 2009. It was during an episode of *Question Time*, a panel show for elected politicians and commentators, when Greer took Griffin to task and told him there was no such thing as a native British or English person.

Her absolute denial of the existence of an English people was fuel for the fire. Politicians had opened our borders and allowed an influx of people on a scale we've never seen before, the media called anyone who disagreed with it racist, and now we had activists and commentators suggesting English people don't even *exist*.

Whether they realize it or not, far-left activists, progressives, and Marxist ideologues are lending credibility to the arguments of the far right. If the extreme right is right about the politicians denying the very existence of English people, then what else could they be right about?

I brought this topic up a lot when I first became politically conscious. I'd never once before thought about race. It wasn't particularly important or significant to me, and to this day I still don't understand how anyone could harbor a hatred for someone based solely on their race. But nevertheless, it remains true that race does indeed exist, and native Europeans happen to be white. The fact that every single politician made a point of saying there is "no such thing" as a native Brit got under my skin and pushed me further toward racial politics. I was young, I was angry, and I was being told by political leaders that I simply had no identity. As a white man, I'm a citizen of nowhere, and my home country was a culturally neutral space with no native population, just waiting to be enriched and changed.

This is how you make someone who doesn't care about race care about race. Others' denial of what is obviously true just made me double down and ignore the obvious and dangerous flaws of the political movement I'd found myself involved in.

I thought, so what if some of the leaders in this movement did bad things in their past, when the entire political establishment wants to deny my existence as an Englishman? So what if some of the people I know say nasty things about immigrants, when nobody seems to care about the wellbeing of the working class?

Why can't the media and our political establishment see that denying an identity to young white lads is a sure-fire way of *making* them care about race?

DID THE MEDIA EVEN CARE ABOUT ME?

The media became my enemy, and I wasn't the only one who felt that way. During my early days in the BNP, smartphones and social media were still finding their feet. Members of the party would talk positively about the future of alternative media, discussing plans for their own radio stations and online TV stations. I never believed it; I always thought it was pie-in-the-sky thinking and that the traditional media would always maintain its stranglehold over us.

I couldn't have been more wrong!

Resentment for the media has continued to this day and those alternative radio and TV stations did in fact happen. I have been a part of that alternative media revolution and, throughout this book, I will explain the errors made by much of those actively engaged with it—namely, the tendency to drift away from factual reporting toward hyperpartisan sensationalism.

Just the fact that alternative media exists and is engaged in a war with the traditional outlets says that the press was doing something very wrong to begin with, and I will never forget how enraged I felt whenever I saw members of the press calling working-class people like me racist for expressing genuine fears and concerns for our future. I remember the sneering, mocking attitude from reporters when covering the BNP, as if to dismiss millions of working-class people who sympathized with their nationalist policy proposals. During an interview with Sky News, Nick Griffin hit back at a reporter who accused the party of being thuggish by recounting the multiple violent attacks he had received over the years and the thuggish behavior of far-left activists who met the BNP at practically every event they ever held. I felt a great sense of victory when Griffin put the reporter in their place, and every little win we had against the biased press made me prouder to put my name to the party.

It felt like someone was really speaking for me, fighting back against the system and telling the millions of people watching the show about the hypocrisy of those who called working-class, patriotic people "thugs." Did the reporters and the journalists think that constantly demonizing the people at home would work? Did they think they could just brush off millions of people with very real concerns and get rid of the far right?

If they did, then they were naïve at best, or dangerous ideologues at worst.

When the media demonize normal people, at a time when the politicians refuse to represent their interests, they create fertile ground for the far right. It made me even more determined, and it did the same for many others who chose extremism when given the choice between the far right and a media establishment that hated them.

The media outlets have a lot of responsibility for the growth of the far right in Europe and America, and they still have a lot of power to curb that growth. They can't demonize desperate people who joined the BNP anymore, because the BNP is virtually nonexistent—but today, they smear the Brexiteers and the Trump supporters who have finally stood up and asserted themselves. Journalists should know that every time they misrepresent those people, push false narratives, or demonize working-class people, they are arming the far right with the ammunition they need to recruit.

FINDING MY FEET AS A NATIONALIST IN COLLEGE

In the UK, we attend college for two years before we attend university; this happens between the ages of sixteen and eighteen. I started my college studies with a naivete about how my political activity would affect my life. It was shattered one day, near the science block, when somebody from my law class walked past me and muttered "scum" under his breath. I couldn't believe it. I was still a pretty shy young man at this point. I had a small group of friends whom I didn't really spend much time away from, and I hadn't had any altercations with people in college, but this student had clearly heard the rumors and decided he knew enough about me to hate me.

I found during this early time in my political life that most of my political opponents would never take the time to consider why I said what I said. I learned that for most people, a political debate could be relatively civil, there would be little interference in their political events by protesters, and life would largely be normal for them. I would never enjoy those luxuries, and instead I very quickly had to learn that everything I said would be examined through a racism-tinted lens. No matter what I ever did or said I would be accused of being an extremist, and every possible measure would be taken to shout me down or sully my name.

Naturally, it was extremely difficult for me. I had been shy, reserved, and polite my entire life. It never occurred to me that people would not treat me with the same respect I gave them during political discussion, and within a year I found myself becoming an entirely different person. I entered college as a reserved young man, and by the second year, I was an outspoken and angry BNP activist who treated political opponents with the same contempt they had for me.

My politics teacher, Saqib, quizzed me on my political leanings one day. Everyone in class had identified as a Tory, a Liberal Democrat, or a Labourite. I had offered opinions from time to time, but I had never explicitly said in class that I supported the BNP. Saqib was interested and asked me what political affiliation I had, if any. I was sitting next to a girl I'd known since high school, and she chuckled as Saqib asked. She knew it would be difficult for me to say, and it was. I told Saqib, "You'll think I'm racist." He said, "Try me."

I told him the truth. I told him I was a supporter of the BNP, that I thought it was wrong to deny the existence of an English people, and I thought the Labour Party had abandoned the working class. He nodded. I figure he understood my grievances in the same way I understand them now. I suppose he knew that the BNP was filling a void created by a Labour Party that abandoned its principles. He asked me if I knew the history of the BNP, and I told him, "Yes, and I think it's irrelevant."

He sort of pursed his lips and nodded, before telling me, "Jack, I think you're a Tory. You're a Conservative." He was right, it turns out. Well, he was right in a way. I'm not a member of the Conservative Party but I am, for the most part, a conservative.

I soon started taking more pride in my political allegiances. I started wearing the BNP badge I'd found on eBay with pride. I was known by classmates as "the BNP guy," and I started to face up to the fact that my life was going to be more controversial than I'd like.

A local antifascist group came to give a talk at the college one day. I decided to go, wearing my best tweed suit and my BNP badge. I had a feeling they weren't going to like it, but I'd never been face to face with "antifascists" before and honestly didn't know what to expect. I don't know whether the teachers tipped them off about me or whether their hawk eyes really did manage to notice my BNP badge from within the crowd, but just moments before the talk was meant to begin the organizer of the event started shouting at me. "A fascist in a suit is still a fascist!" they said.

Saqib and the other teachers in the room tried to calm them down. They continued protesting about my attendance and insisted they wouldn't go ahead until I was removed. I refused to leave, and the teachers managed to convince them to continue. I'm sure they told them that now would be a good chance to try and convert me, but the presentation didn't come close to changing my mind. I sat through an hour of childish name-calling and wild conspiracy theories. I remember noting down every lie they told, waiting for the Q&A session at the end. When it eventually came and I was the only person with a hand in the air, the presenters thanked everyone, packed up, and tried to leave.

I went in with good intentions, to listen, and I was treated like dirt. That was when I realized I was just scum to them. There I was, a white working-class lad who genuinely just wanted to learn, embarrassed in front of a room of people and called a Nazi and a fascist. Those people didn't know me.

If their intention was to deliver a message of hope, they did the opposite for me. They once again reaffirmed my belief that the political establishment, i.e., those who hold power culturally and in the mainstream political world, didn't like people like me.

And if I was being called a racist, then I had another reason not to believe anyone who called the BNP racist. I didn't think the extreme right really existed because I knew how easily people lied about those things.

Imagine you are a naïve sixteen-year-old being called a fascist by people you have never met and called "scum" by your peers. Would you listen to the politicians and the journalists who tell you to be wary of the far right?

Looking back, I know I was treated with such disdain because people thought I believed something I didn't. I was a member (or, then, just a supporter) of the BNP and therefore I must have been a neo-Nazi who wanted to deport all nonwhite people. No matter how many times I said that wasn't the case, people believed it because that was the common perception (and, to be fair, that was an early BNP policy). I can't help but wonder, however, what might have happened if people had taken the time to listen to what I said rather than put words in my mouth.

If these people were trying to deradicalize me, or to prove me wrong, what made them think their unwavering scorn would do the trick? If I was really the neo-Nazi that they thought I was, wouldn't their hatred just strengthen my convictions? And if I wasn't the monster they alleged me to be, wouldn't treating me that way just push me further away?

Those incidents in college were the first times I experienced real-life confrontation over my politics, and I remained surprised whenever it happened for the rest of my first year studying there. Over time, my shy nature began to change and I began retaliating. I became more radical, angrier, and more vocal every time someone bullied me or suggested I believed something I didn't, to the point where I would go out of my way to be as wildly offensive as I could. If they were offended, I wanted to give them something to be offended about—and if they hated me, I wanted to give them a real reason to hate me. Not only did it push me further away from mainstream thinking (and society), but it gave me reason to become more involved and active within the British far right.

I found a home and a community in the group that accepted me for who I was. At least, that's what I thought at the time.

AN ANTIDOTE TO THE CYCLE OF RADICALIZATION

Much can be done to make the far right less attractive. Measures currently taken by Western governments to do this have proven to be catastrophic failures owing largely to the inability of the metropolitan elite to understand why white, working-class people turn to the far right in the first place. Most conclusions drawn from research into the phenomenon are also inaccurate as a result of a fundamental misunderstanding of what the far right even *is*.

In order to solve the problem, we must first *understand* it—and right now, practically the only people who understand what it means to be far right are the ones who have lived and breathed it.

This, as I will argue throughout the book, is a result of the political center shifting leftwards over a period of decades, combined with a concerted effort by anti-racism groups to inflate their own relevance and importance by creating far-right monsters that don't exist. Nobody understands what the far right really is because so-called anti-racism organizations across America, the UK, and Europe are attributing the label to people who would have been considered centrists or moderate conservatives just ten years ago. There is a dark political agenda behind the far-right witch hunt that makes the problem extremely difficult to solve, but that's exactly the point. For as long as everybody who expresses concern about mass immigration is considered far right, there will always be monsters to slay and money for anti-racism groups to continue their important work.

Likewise, it allows far-left ideologues to shape society however they like with virtually no resistance from big business. Who would want to be seen to endorse neo-Nazis?

The strategy has been so effective that the president of the United States has been labelled a white supremacist and even a neo-Nazi by mainstream journalists and commentators, and 17.4 million British voters were called racist by Labour Party politicians for voting to leave the European Union.

Muddying the waters about far-right extremism is a lucrative industry. It creates well-paying jobs in left-wing think tanks and academia, it allows ideologues to manipulate popular culture, and it makes people with very real concerns keep quiet for fear of being called racist.

All the while, the real far right navigates those muddy waters, hard to distinguish from mainstream conservatives and democratic populists. As long as everyone is a neo-Nazi, it is hard to identify the people who genuinely believe white supremacist and anti-Jewish conspiracy theories.

Are far-left organizations, activists, and politicians really doing justice to their cause when they make it nearly impossible to tackle the extreme-right activists who pose a genuine threat?

It is more likely that, as advocates for social justice and equal rights, the importance of their cause has diminished as society has ditched old prejudices, and they are now looking for new battles to fight. Whether those battles are real is entirely irrelevant to them.

The irrational and hate-filled agenda of far-left activists has drawn the attention of populists and conservatives across the Western world, firing them into a frenzy and creating an entirely new counterculture industry that regularly falls into their opponents' traps without realizing it. Hypocrisy and radicalism amongst the far left are noted by conservatives and populists, but in their fervent opposition and dislike of the left, they have failed to recognize the threat posed by the *real* far right. It is just too easy to dismiss the left's claims that there is a new far-right menace growing ugly heads and reaching its tentacles into popular culture as lunacy because most of what they say *is* insane. That does not mean, however, that the wild claims they make are without any merit at all.

Far-right extremists do exist. They are recruiting and growing their influence, and they are operating under the radar while the radical left and the populist right battle it out between themselves.

It's time conservatives take a step back and critically analyze the situation, as well as their own tactics. In the heat of the debate about which side is more extreme, conservatives are often too quick to either ignore the existence of the real far right or to pin the blame of far-right terror attacks on far-left radicals.

It is easy for conservatives to blame far-right attacks on the far left when the attacker has advocated some left-wing economic policies. But ask yourself this: is a white nationalist inspired by his left-wing economic views or his extreme-right social values when he shoots Jewish or black Christian worshippers?

Failing to even acknowledge that far-right extremists exist—and pointing the finger back at the left—achieves nothing. If anything, it plays right into the hands of left-wing extremists who take great delight in conservatives who look like they are in a constant state of denial. Accepting that far-right extremists exist, and that they are on the extreme end of conservative social values, is not a weakness and it does not mean conservatives are far right. That seems to be the great fear for many conservatives and populists.

Equally, liberals have much to learn. As long as moderate liberals sit back and watch as the radical left takes control of their political narrative, this political divide will continue to grow deeper and wider. The power to stop the far right's profiteering from the madness of the left lies in the hands of liberals who aren't man enough to stand up to bullies on their own side.

If only the people with the power to curb extremism knew they had that power or were willing to put their partisan goals aside and do something good for society. Conservatives and liberals must show willingness to reflect on their tactics amidst this bitter cultural battle, but our politicians and media class must also be willing to consider the possibility that they might have made some mistakes.

I believe, based on my personal experiences and my interaction with far-right terrorists and extremists over the last ten years, that young white men are being systematically radicalized by what I call the three-pronged attack. This is a series of life events that see mostly young, white, working-class men neglected by their elected representatives, smeared and demonized by the national press, and relentlessly attacked by far-left ideologues in practically all areas of their lives.

Neo-Nazis and white supremacists are not created in a void. A cycle of radicalization is allowing a dangerous movement to recruit off the back of political discontentment and a bitter feud between the right and left that has been created by ideologues who want to completely reshape society. Our deradicalization measures are insufficient and fundamentally flawed from the start, our politicians show no desire to address difficult issues, the media just keeps lying about working-class patriots who experience real injustice, and far-left activists keep chucking bricks at those who stand up for themselves.

There is an antidote to this, but it might take listening to a former far-right activist to find it.

CHAPTER TWO

DEFINING THE FAR RIGHT

The prevalent narrative that the West is plagued by a coordinated, active, and booming far-right presence in mainstream politics is a lie. When Democrats in the US or mainstream politicians from any major party in the UK claim that the far right is being normalized and poses a threat to minorities everywhere, they're lying. But they're also not lying.

There is a far-right presence in the West. It's not as big as these people, whom I'll refer to throughout this book generally as *the left*, like to claim—but all the circumstances are ripe for this far-right threat to grow. Despite the ever-expanding presence of far-left politics in all levels of our society, from television shows to our school classrooms, even I as a conservative consider the *real* far right one of the biggest threats the West faces. It is not a threat in and of itself, but rather as a part of an all-encompassing shift toward extreme politics. The far right exists because the far left is growing in size and in influence, and it is compounded by an Islamist threat that the far left seems to be taking sides with. It is a stew of hatred, revenge, ego, and hyperbole—and no side is taking on this threat in any meaningful way.

This book is not designed solely for conservatives to learn, though it is my hope that conservatives might find my argument compelling. Instead, this book is intended to offer a unique insight into the *real* far right. I want those with good intentions who believe in fighting the far right to understand why their perception of "the far right" might be wrong, and how their efforts may be better spent. I want those who think that working-class people who voted for Brexit or Donald Trump are racist to step back and consider the possibility that these people were reacting to a political class who is unwilling to listen to everyday concerns. And, I want those who dedicate their lives to fighting fascism to step back and consider whether they have been targeting the wrong people all this time.

In these vicious, turbulent, and divided times, it is more important than ever for those on the right and the left, if those terms even mean anything anymore, to engage in real discussion about extreme politics and why people are being radicalized. It is equally important that conservatives, populists, and nationalists are willing to accept that while the left has their violent authoritarian radicals, so do we. It might be easy to brush off a school shooter as left-wing because they expressed some socialist leanings, but it is not helpful to do so—particularly if that school shooter had explicitly right-wing views on immigration or national identity.

It is my hope that those who read this book will embark on this journey with me with an open mind.

Let's start by defining the far right.

IT'S ALL A MATTER OF PERSPECTIVE

The term "far right" is largely meaningless. The use of the word "far" implies there is a central point of reference which represents a middle ground in politics. Where that middle ground stands, exactly, is debatable.

The political center in the US has shifted significantly left as Democrats have moved sharply toward extreme political positions. The same is true in the UK. Anyone who takes keen interest in modern politics will be familiar with the prominence of the Black Lives Matter movement, various trans rights groups, extreme-left university societies exerting influence over the education system, and media personalities regularly railing against straight white men.

In 2018, Cassian Harrison, the editor of BBC Four, told an audience at Edinburgh International Television festival that programming should be less white, middle-aged, and male.[5]

The same year, tweets from *New York Times* reporter Sarah Jeong were unearthed that included racist slurs and meanspirited jabs at elderly white men.[6]

One tweet from July 2014 read:

"Oh man it's kind of sick how much joy I get out of being cruel to old white men."

---

5 Toby Young, "Why Is a BBC Executive Calling for the Removal of Middle-Aged White Men from Television?" *The Spectator*, September 1, 2018, https://www.spectator.co.uk/2018/09/why-is-a-bbc-executive-calling-for-the-removal-of-middle-aged-white-men-from-television/.

6 "Sarah Jeong: NY Times Stands By 'Racist Tweets' Reporter," BBC News, August 2, 2018, https://www.bbc.co.uk/news/world-us-canada-45052534.

Another read:

"Are white people genetically predisposed to burn faster in the sun, thus logically being only fit to live underground like grovelling goblins."

And in 2019, British television channel ITV banned all-male comedy writing teams[7]—a culmination of years of left-wing ideologues pushing for radical feminization of television.

This isn't the left-wing politics of old. This isn't normal political commentary. This is hard-left ideological provocation, and it is symptomatic of a once moderate political movement shifting toward the extreme left.

A report from Pew Research, "The Partisan Divide on Political Values Grows Even Wider,"[8] compiles the results of surveys over a period of decades and concluded that politics has become more radical—but it's the left that has shifted further toward extremes.

Specifically, the data found that a declining share of Americans holds a combination of liberal and conservative values. Republicans and Democrats are "further apart ideologically than at any point in more than two decades," showing a continuation of a trend that Pew Research discovered in 2014.

Using a ten-item scale of political values in a questionnaire, Pew's data shows that Republicans have shifted somewhat to

---

7 Ian Youngs, "ITV Bans All-Male Comedy Writing Teams," BBC News, June 18, 2019, https://www.bbc.co.uk/news/entertainment-arts-48668652.

8 "The Partisan Divide on Political Values Grows Even Wider," Pew Research Center, October 5, 2017, http://assets.pewresearch.org/wp-content/uploads/sites/5/2017/10/05162647/10-05-2017-Political-landscape-release.pdf.

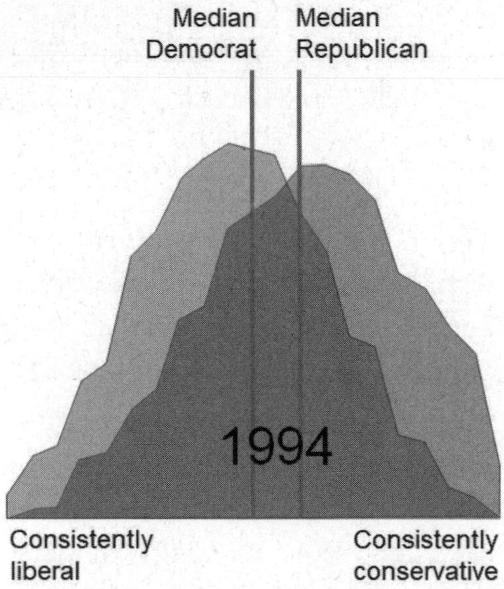
Median
Democrat
Median
Republican
1994
Consistently
liberal
Consistently
conservative

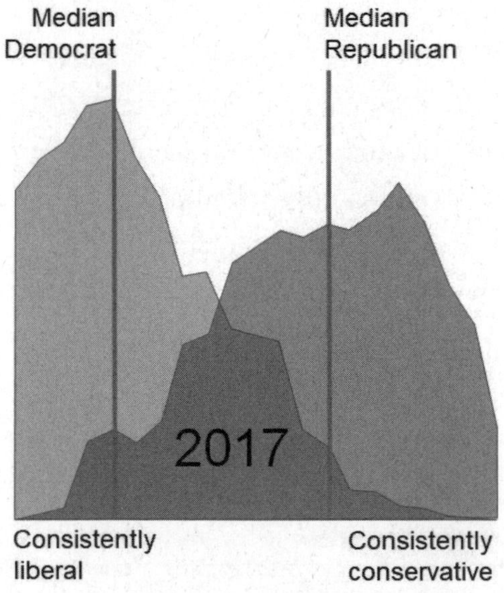
Median
Democrat
Median
Republican
2017
Consistently
liberal
Consistently
conservative

the right while Democrats have moved quite significantly to the left. While Republicans have become more moderate (with regards to minority rights issues), Democrats have adopted an openly socialist political platform that divides society based on race, targets white people as oppressors, and promotes the deplatforming of conservatives (or merely anyone who doesn't subscribe to a far-left social agenda) in education, at work, and online.

When the left moves further left than the right has moved right, the center ground shifts with it. This is visible in the United Kingdom, too. A report by NatCen Social Research and Essex University found that voters had shifted left between the 2010 and 2015 general elections.[9] A lack of any meaningful conservative policies from the Conservative Party also signifies the center ground's shift to the left. While socialist supporters of Labour Party leader Jeremy Corbyn decry the Conservative Party as far right, the Conservatives have embarked on policies that have legalized homosexual marriage, maintained immigration levels in the hundreds of thousands each year (to a country of just 66 million), and campaigned vigorously against "Islamophobia."

This could explain why the term "far right" has become so misused. It requires a central reference point, and that reference point has moved from the center ground of politics to what would have been considered left-of-center in the 1990s or even early 2000s.

---

9 Nicholas Watt, "British Voters Have Shifted to the Left Since Last General Election, Study Says," *The Guardian*, March 20, 2015, https://www.theguardian.com/politics/2015/mar/20/british-voters-left-shift-general-election-labour-thinktank.

Not only is it near impossible to decide what constitutes "far" right anymore, there are differences in opinion over what even constitutes *right.* American and European perspectives on this matter might differ. While the American right, at least until the Trump era, largely constitutes constitutionalists, Christians, and conservatives with a penchant for a free-market economy, the European right is somewhat different. Conservatism existed long before the free market, and much of Europe's nations maintain mixed economies. Here in the United Kingdom, you would be hard pushed to find many right-wing populists who want to dissolve our National Health Service. British academic Matthew Goodwin, a well-known researcher in the field of Euroscepticism and right-wing politics, has longed noted that traditional Labour voters do not share the far-left social views of the modern Labour Party and Jeremy Corbyn supporters. In fact, the working class in Britain are among the most conservative and right wing—at least, socially.

Visit my hometown, or indeed any working-class town that has seen the impact of mass immigration, and you'll see conservative values in action. You'll see, as Goodwin rightly notes,[10] a commitment to *community*, *solidarity*, and *belonging.* Working-class communities lean left on the economy but represent one of the largest socially conservative (or right wing!) voting blocs—if not *the* largest. This is quite unlike the political right of the United States.

---

10 Matthew Goodwin, "Labour's Traditional Voters No Longer Share Its Progressive Values," *The Guardian*, June 23, 2016, https://www.theguardian.com/commentisfree/2016/jun/23/labour-traditional-voters-progressive-values-working-class-ukip.

The American right is decidedly less collectivist, consider socialized healthcare to be theft or forced labor, and value individual rights over the wellbeing of the wider community. To be fair, that doesn't mean the American right doesn't consider the wellbeing of the community to be important—rather, the idea is that by enhancing the rights of the individual, it is possible for people to do more for the community on a voluntary basis.

Although this constitutes quite a major difference in opinion, both positions can reasonably be defined as *right wing*. Working-class patriots who support a National Health Service and a reduction in immigration are unlikely to consider themselves left wing just because they support a government program supported by the public purse. Equally, an American conservative who believes in gay marriage, separation of church and state, no social programs, and a free market economy might not consider themselves left wing because they do not wish to impose socially conservative values on the wider community.

This proves the point that right and left really don't mean much anymore, but to examine the issue of far-right extremism we must find broad definitions. Therefore, in this book I will propose a better definition of the far right. It will take into consideration the transatlantic differences in the meaning of "right" and focus largely on the social values political activists hold.

The term "far right" has been so grossly misused for so many years. It is a term that anyone who rejects far-left social agendas has heard many terms before. Anyone I have told about this book, at the time of writing, have asked me, "Why are you using that word?" I understand the hesitation, and I understand why some might initially misunderstand what I am trying to say. For those who don't want to listen, perhaps they'll never understand—but for those who are willing to go on this journey with me, I hope you will see how reclaiming and clarifying the definition of this term "far right" will be more useful in the long run than simply defending ourselves against baseless accusations at every turn.

Rather than batting away the insults and constantly asserting "I am not far right," I believe that we must stand our ground and recognize the real far right and what it really stands for.

Whenever there has been a mass shooting, attack, or any kind of terrorist incident involving a far-right extremist, you can guarantee that the conservative Twittersphere will immediately become defensive. If the terrorist expresses some solidarity with a socialist cause, conservatives will immediately denounce him as far left. This is unhelpful and not entirely accurate. It is unhelpful because instead of proving that the conservative movement is innocent and pure, it makes its advocates appear feckless, irresponsible, and ideologically motivated. Why deflect blame when we can instead analyze who that person was/is and recognize, as a matter of fact, if they happen to hold socially conservative or nationalist values?

Yes, a far-right terrorist might well have advocated for national *socialist* policies, but is it any more accurate to label a person like this *far left* than it is *right*? Is it reasonable or *honest* to compare a neo-Nazi to a far-left progressive? Can we compare Lena Dunham and Anders Breivik?

Admitting that neo-Nazi extremists are far right is not the same as admitting neo-Nazis and conservatives are the same. It's also not the same as admitting that neo-Nazis and conservatives (or nationalists) are *similar*. In the same way violent extremists in Antifa represent the radical wing of the Democrats/Labour (many of whom are still, believe it or not, decent and moderate people), neo-Nazis and ultra-nationalists represent the radical wing of the European populists and Republicans.

It doesn't mean they are the same, and it also doesn't mean that Neo Nazis and Antifa aren't more similar to one another than they are to the moderates on each side.

The Horseshoe Theory can help me explain this. It asserts that the far left and the far right are closer to one another than they are to the political center—pulling those points down from a horizontal line and into a horseshoe shape.

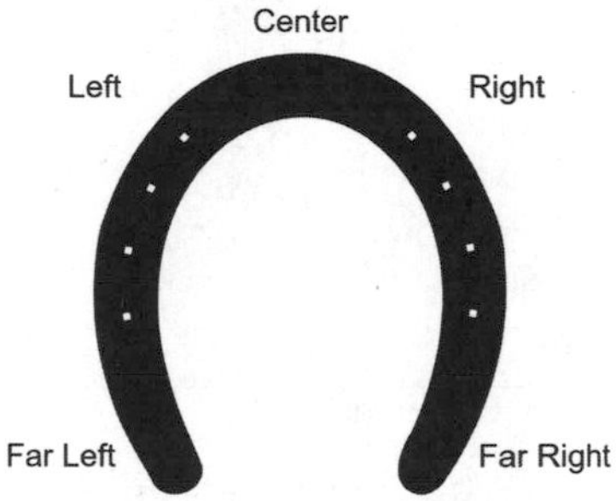

All points on the horseshoe are separate and different. Within each point, there might be multiple political ideologies, multiple groups, and multiple preferred policies. They can, however, all be loosely categorized into each point. Far right is separate from right, though logically it is an extension of right. A far-right line of thinking, in this instance, takes the social political positions from the right and makes them more aggressive.

A concern about uncontrolled immigration under right might become a policy of forced repatriation of nonwhites under far right. These are two *fundamentally different positions*, though one is a natural extension of the other.

Accepting that the far right does exist, therefore, does not mean accepting they are the same as the right generally. Conservatives must break this impasse and be willing to accept that while the far right and the far left might well be united on economic policy in many instances, and might even share views on controlling political dissent, in terms of social policy they are *fundamentally different.*

This can be even better explained with the following visualization.

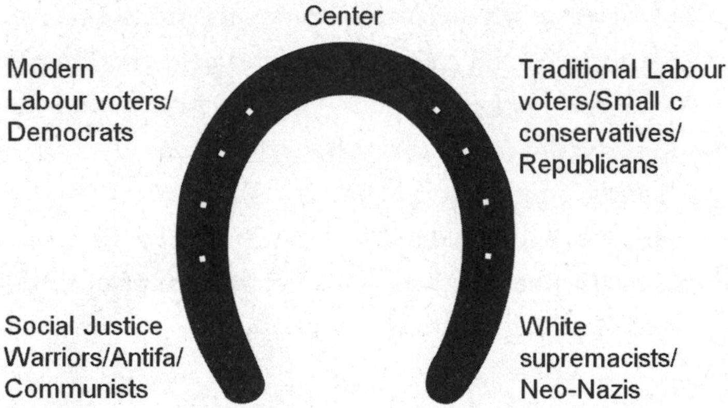

White supremacists and neo-Nazis are closer to social justice warriors and Communists than they are to the political center. That does not make them the same, in the same way that modern Labour voters in the UK and Democrats in the US are not necessarily the same as social justice warriors or Communists.

If we can accept this truth and be willing to accept that a far right *can* exist, we instantly take the power away from the extremists on the social justice left who like to claim the narrative on extremism for themselves. If we—conservatives or indeed anyone who doesn't identify with the far left—are willing to talk openly, honestly and objectively about pollical extremism, then we are one step closer to solving the problem at its root. That means discovering why people become radicalized and who benefits from perpetuating the radicalization of young white men.

This is infinitely more productive than simply denying one is not far right.

It also doesn't put conservatives in a corner. Denying a far-right terrorist is really "right wing" because they expressed some socialist leanings in their social media posts doesn't really protect conservatives much in the first place (you think far-left ideologues care about nuances?), but it also only works for as long as the terrorist does happen to express some socialist values. What happens when a perfectly regular American conservative does something terrible? Suddenly, the argument doesn't work anymore, and only then will conservatives be forced to ask why that person was radicalized in the first place. I would argue that we, regardless of political orientation, must be asking that question *right now*.

With this in mind, we can attempt to define the far right by finding the most extreme variations of right-wing, conservative, or nationalist social policy.

A moderate populist, conservative, or nationalist in Europe or America might advocate strong border security and immigration controls, a sense of national identity and pride, and a deep respect for Christianity. A far-right activist might, therefore, advocate for even stronger border security that extends to the repatriation of non-native people—immigrants or long-settled communities. A far-right activist might also blame non-native people for a dwindling sense of national pride while brushing aside the influence of native far-left ideologues. Specifically, far-right activists might point the finger at the Jewish community for their "over representation" in the undermining of Western civilization while failing to recognize the role that white atheist and Christian far-left ideologues have had in the transformation of our society.

Far-right activists, I would argue, turn national pride into extreme jingoism. Although a conservative, nationalist, or populist might be interested in protecting their own society first, a far-right activist might endorse exclusionary policy that forcefully evicts non-native people regardless of whether they are an asset to society.

It is not radical, far right, or extreme to recognize that a nation has its native people, and that changing the demographic makeup of a nation fundamentally changes the nature of that place. It is, however, radical, far right, and extreme to advocate the forceful ejection of people based entirely on race. At best, this is a knee-jerk reaction to the very real problems that come with mass third-world immigration. At worst, it is blind hatred.

As I said in the opening of this chapter, the best lie is based on the truth. Although it is a lie to suggest that these far-right views are mainstream, it is *true* that they are increasingly common in the United States and Europe. And I fear this is simply going to get worse for as long as we are unwilling or unable to recognize what the far right really is, and why young white boys in particular are being radicalized.

To be clear, I am suggesting that the far right we should *really* be concerned about is a community of white supremacists and neo-Nazis with a radical agenda that is increasingly leading to violence.

I am not talking about decent people with legitimate concerns about jihad, political Islam, mass immigration, or globalism.

This is an extremely important distinction to make. The importance of this distinction will become increasingly clear throughout the book.

I don't like the term *far right*, but because it has such power, we must address it. We must clarify its meaning and chip away at the emotive power behind it. It is one of the most reliable tools of far-left ideologues in the battle for maintaining the moral high-ground, and it is essential if we are ever to regain normal political discourse.

MY FIRST EXPERIENCES WITH THE FAR RIGHT

I remember my first experiences with the far right. It was my first ever BNP meeting. I went along to a pub in St. Helens, Lancashire, to meet what must have been the closest branch to my town. A friend from college decided to come with me. He wasn't supportive, but he was interested. He'd heard what people had said about me and couldn't understand why they'd say it. From what I remember, he also couldn't understand why on earth I was involved with this kind of politics.

I thought it was quite commendable for him to come with me and see for himself what I was advocating. Perhaps he had better foresight than me at the time, because the meeting went exactly how he suspected it would. It was utterly shocking.

I walked into the pub and asked the barman to point me to the BNP meeting. Nobody batted an eyelid—he just pointed to a door at the side of the bar, and I said thanks. It was a large room, the kind usually used for functions and events.

For Americans reading this, old pubs tend to have large rooms with shabby carpets, old wallpaper, and hundreds of wonky and broken chairs that we rent for Christenings and birthday parties. This room was exactly like that, and the BNP meeting was huddled in one corner. There was a table of BNP merchandise and a TV screen hooked up to a battered old laptop.

During the casual meet and greet before proceedings began, things seemed perfectly normal. I introduced my friend from college to some of the men I'd already been speaking to online. They were so delighted to see not just one, but two young people at the meeting. Everyone else was over forty-five, if not fifty.

The guy selling the merchandise seemed perfectly nice, and there were a few others in the audience that I remember thinking were really decent blokes. This was often the case in the BNP. Far left activists as well as establishment conservatives were too easy to smear the average member of the BNP. Many members, like myself, were simply working-class people who had had enough. Most of them, unlike me, had seen Britain's decline over a matter of decades and were desperate for something to change.

But when we all sat down and got ready for the speeches, things started to get weird. The TV screen came on and I saw a photograph of Libyan revolutionary, Muammar Gaddafi. The speech focused on his life and the things he did for his people. It was an attempt at selling Gaddafi's brand of nationalism, and an attempt to prove that ultra-nationalism could work in the UK. The speaker embellished Gaddafi's reign as best he could, selling us on the idea of free homes, free land, and more. A nice thought, of course, but nothing more than that. Unless Britain found itself sitting on some of the biggest oil reserves in the world, it was something that would never realistically happen.

I knew little about Gaddafi at the time. I brushed it off as odd.

The speech came to an end after much nudging and eye rolls from my college friend. Over a pint, I started chatting with a Scouser (for American readers, a Scouser is a person from Liverpool) called Mike. He was running the Liverpool BNP branch at the time, if I remember rightly, and he seemed to want to take me under his wing. Like the organizers of the meeting, he was happy to see young people coming along. He tried to explain ethnic nationalism to me—he asked me if I had a pound in my pocket, whether I'd give it to my struggling child, or to a struggling child I'd never met before. It was hard to argue with the logic. We all know what we'd do.

While I was mingling, somebody asked me about the ring I was wearing on my finger. It was the gold wedding ring of my great-grandfather. He had married my great-grandmother after she'd had children, so we weren't related by blood. He was, however, an influence in my mother's early life and for all intents and purposes, her grandfather. His wedding ring was a family heirloom that my mother gave to me, and I wore it for a number of years.

My step-great-grandfather, Leon, was also Jewish. He had been at Dachau Concentration Camp in Germany during the war but ultimately found himself in England, where he married my grandmother Elsie. It's quite the story, and when asked why I was wearing a wedding ring, I told them.

The tone immediately changed—at least, with some in the room. Mike the Scouser didn't seem all that impressed, and the man chairing the meeting started rattling off something about Zionism. Another man started quizzing me heavily, asking whether I was Jewish, and why I would wear my great-grandfather's ring. I recall one quiet comment that seemed to suggest the Holocaust didn't happen, or that my great-grandfather was a liar. The brother of the man who gave the impassioned speech about Gaddafi was the worst for it. He had been in the audience the entire time, nursing a pint, and from the look in his eye I knew I was in trouble with him.

He and his brother, both well-known anti-Zionist and white nationalist activists in Liverpool, would become fixated on me for quite some time. Their encounter with me, and learning of my Jewish step-great-grandfather, began years of conspiracy theories and rumors that have lasted to this day. It's easy to find articles on anti-Semitic websites about me, suggesting I'm a Jewish infiltrator, a spy, a Zionist shill, or even a government state agent.

For the time I remained in the BNP—and well after—I was told by members of Liverpool BNP that my grandfather was a liar. Some honestly believed the Holocaust was a hoax and tried to educate me. Others seemed to take sick joy in saying horrible things about my grandfather.

Having never met my grandad Leon, it was a weird feeling. It's not like I was defending the legacy of a man who had raised me. But hearing such wicked things said about victims of one of the greatest crimes in history knocked me sick. And it started a prolonged hate campaign against me that was as serious as anything far left activists have ever thrown at me.

I'm sure my writing this book will only serve to aggravate and provoke these men even more. Should the men I'm referring to ever read this, they will no doubt become more certain in their convictions that I was a spy all along. The reality, however, is much different. I was a young man with no world experience and certainly no political experience—and now, I'm a slightly older man who has enough experience to understand what kind of people these men were. And, indeed, why they are the way they are.

Enough people in the BNP told me to ignore them. I knew about the party's history, but I also knew of the efforts to modernize the party platform. The thoroughly decent party members without an extremist bone in their body kept me going, but a nationalist meeting in Preston really made me question whether I could stay.

The meeting was a memorial gathering for the founder of the BNP, the late John Tyndall. He was an eccentric man who flailed his arms around and shouted in an authoritative tone. I don't mean to make the comparison so easily, but his oratory style was not dissimilar to the leader of 1940s Germany.

I forget who had invited me, but I decided to go along and meet others in the movement. Preston had been the city that opened my eyes to how drastically a place can change off the back of an open borders immigration policy, and coming into the city the second time as a British nationalist felt like somewhat of a rebellion. I arrived late at a pub where the event was being held, and I could hear someone speaking as I walked in. A lady at the door asked me to pay a fiver, which entitled me to entrance and a couple of raffle tickets.

As I was walking toward an empty seat, I heard the speaker say something to the effect of "And of course, we know that Hitler was right…." I can't remember the precise context, and I can't remember who was speaking, but I think it's fair to say it's unlikely the speaker was talking about the Führer's views on vegetarianism. My heart sank.

I tried to blend into the background at the meeting, but this was around the time I'd started blogging. I would call myself the "New Nationalist" online, and older figures in the BNP and nationalist circles started to know who I was. I met a lot of people there, many of whom seemed perfectly lovely, others a little eccentric, and others flat-out horrible. But I smiled and, as ever, remained polite throughout.

I was really having no luck blending into the background, so of course I won the bloody raffle. I awkwardly shuffled up to the front of the room to choose a prize from the selection laid out on a table. I saw a copy of *Mein Kampf*, framed Nazi imagery (it was some kind of painting or drawing if I remember rightly), and thankfully, a rather innocuous-looking wooden coat of arms. I had no idea what it represented, but it looked nice, and it didn't have a swastika on it. So that was something. I remember being so glad I was the first to pick the prizes—had I been left with any of the other prizes, I don't know what I'd have done. I'm an awkward person, and I don't think at this time I'd have had the guts to say "no thank you" to a Nazi-themed prize in front of an audience of ultra-nationalists.

I think it was at this meeting when I finally realized what I'd gotten myself into. If a far right exists, and if that term is to mean anything, *then surely it would mean this.*

PURPOSELY MISREPRESENTING THE RIGHT

The main point of contention that people have had when I've told them about this book is my use of the term "far right."

"But Jack, they call *you* far right!" is the typical response I've had, and that's true. I've been called far right all my life. I know how terrible it is being labelled an extremist when you're not, and I would never dream of casually and carelessly using this term to define somebody with legitimate concerns. It is not only inaccurate in many cases to label those vocally opposed to mass immigration as "far right," but it is also immoral.

This term exerts a great amount of power. All it takes is for the words to appear on a single article on Google search results for a person's name and they may never work again. That's no exaggeration—no company in their right mind, in today's climate, would want to hire someone who has been publicly excommunicated from polite society because of perceived racism.

So I'll never use this term without first giving it great thought.

I think it is wrong to completely write off the label. As I've already explained, there is a more accurate definition for this term that we can adopt.

But to apply this more accurate definition, we must examine exactly how far-left ideologues have used this term inaccurately to date. It has been a long process, and one which has been a key part in the shifting of the Overton Window to the left. Regular, nonpolitical members of society now believe that a belief in tighter immigration controls is considered far right. Some do everything they possibly can to avoid people with those opinions, while those who would find themselves within that category might naively accept that they are, in fact, far right. This is untrue and has created real chaos in modern political discourse.

The demonization of Donald Trump and his supporters brought this issue to the attention of millions of people who might have never thought about it previously. From the end of 2015 and the beginning of 2016, Trump went from "a bit eccentric" in the eyes of his detractors to a "far-right extremist." *Observer* columnist and author Nick Cohen in December 2015 told Dave Rubin[11] that, until a few weeks prior, he wouldn't have considered Trump to be on the extreme right. He went on to explain how both the religious extreme right (Islamists included) need to be tackled in the same way as the ideological extreme right (Trump, apparently).

This sums up the problem I'm talking about quite perfectly. Cohen's observation that there are multiple kinds of extreme politics that feed off each other is good. Cohen, in my opinion, is right to say that these multiple sides of extreme politics must be tackled. Where I believe Cohen is wrong is in his analysis of what constitutes far right. In the video interview with Rubin, titled "Nick Cohen on the Rise of Donald Trump and Far-Right Political Parties in Europe," Cohen does more to complicate the cause of tackling extremism than he does to support it. Calling Trump far right or extreme is factually inaccurate, and it labels millions of his supporters far right too. Again, this is inaccurate, but it also pits roughly half of the American population against him and those like him who are too hasty to label people far right.

This continued throughout 2016 and throughout his presidency. CNN published articles pondering whether the President was a fascist,[12] New Europe decried Trump "flirting"

---

11 The Rubin Report, "The Rise of Trump and Far-Right Parties in Europe (Pt. 2) | Nick Cohen | POLITICS | Rubin Report," YouTube video, 16:33, December 10, 2015, https://www.youtube.com/watch?v=1Ydo8AmNqFI.

12 Peter Bergen, "Is Donald Trump a Fascist?" CNN, December 9, 2015, https://edition.cnn.com/2015/12/09/opinions/bergen-is-trump-fascist/index.html.

with the "far right," and Al Jazeera flat-out called him a "far right populist."[13] Mayor of London Sadiq Khan, in 2019, called him a "poster boy for the far right"[14] and compared him to a twentieth century fascist.[15]

And we mustn't forget the disgraceful lie pushed by *The Daily Beast* and others that Trump failed to disavow support from the KKK.[16] A slew of authors have produced literary works that unashamedly compare Trump and his followers to the most radical far-right extremists in the country. Blogger David Neiwert's book, *Alt-America: The Rise of the Radical Right in the Age of Trump*, brazenly features the stars of the American flag wearing white KKK hoods. Ironically, Neiwert was suspended by Twitter for posting the far-right imagery, but these extreme attempts to portray thoroughly decent, normal American people as neo-Nazis must finally be addressed.

Over a period of years, a combined effort by the international media, politicians, and popular personalities has resulted

---

13 Jan-Werner Mueller, "Trump Is a Far Right Populist, Not a Fascist," Al Jazeera America, December 26, 2015, http://america.aljazeera.com/opinions/2015/12/trump-is-a-far-right-populist-not-a-fascist.html.

14 Peter Stubley, "Sadiq Khan Calls Trump 'Poster Boy for the Far-Right' as Row Reignites During UK Visit," *The Independent*, June 4, 2019, https://www.independent.co.uk/news/uk/politics/trump-sadiq-khan-far-right-uk-visit-pod-save-america-interview-a8942936.html.

15 Toby Helm and Mark Townsend, "Donald Trump Is Like a 20th-Century Fascist, Says Sadiq Khan," *The Guardian,* June 1, 2019, https://www.theguardian.com/us-news/2019/jun/01/donald-trump-like-20th-century-fascist-says-sadiq-khan.

16 Gideon Resnick, "Trump Won't Denounce KKK Support," The Daily Beast, April 13, 2017, https://www.thedailybeast.com/trump-wont-denounce-kkk-support.

in the president and his millions of voters being labelled "far right extremists." And then those same people insincerely bemoan the polarization of society.

There is no better way to divide a population than to call 50 percent of it racist.

Think tanks, nonprofits, and other far-left political groups can have great influence, too. When a team of ideologues are given all the time and resources they need to work full-time attacking their political opponents, you can bet they'll make some real inroads. The Southern Poverty Law Center's (SPLC's) Hatewatch project is manned by members of staff and contributors who have hours, days, weeks, and months to spare in their efforts to obsessively stalk political opponents. They produce blog entries about neo-Nazis and real far-right activists and then subtly interweave stories about others who simply don't support an ultra-progressive social agenda. Though they might even include progressives if they happen to suggest Islam is inconsistent with liberal values.

The SPLC has a list of designated hate groups and hate figures in which they include conservatives, counter-jihad activists, and academics alongside the likes of former KKK grand wizard David Duke and holocaust denier David Irving. To put David Horowitz, Frank Gaffney, and Robert B. Spencer on that same list is incomprehensibly unfair and purposely misleading. Activists, authors, and academics who campaign against Islamic radicalism cannot be reasonably compared to white supremacists who deny the Holocaust. But that's exactly why they are on that list. By muddying the waters, it has been made near impossible for normal people outside of the political world to distinguish between neo-Nazis and conservatives. This was done on purpose.

Some ideologues have even gone as far as comparing the atrocities against the Jewish people during the Second World War with the conditions at migrant detention centers on the US/Mexico border. Congresswoman Alexandria Ocasio-Cortez compared migrant detention centers to concentration camps and, when pressured to apologize, she doubled down. Ocasio-Cortez began an online campaign and hashtag, #CloseTheCamps.

I like to call behavior like this "dumbling down." She doubled down because she knew she'd done something dumb. But it was more than dumb—it was a disgraceful attempt at comparing President Trump to Hitler. Conditions in migrant detention centers are hardly comparable to the Hilton or the Ritz, but concentration camps they are not.

Stoneman Douglas High School shooting survivor David Hogg picked up the campaign on his Twitter, too, and soon we saw thousands of people all over America tweeting #CloseTheCamps, as if the United States really had concentration camps operating within its own borders. It is a damn disgrace that these people desecrate the memory of those that truly suffered at the hands of Nazi Germany, but they do it because they know it works. If you say a lie enough times, plenty of people will think it true. Hell, the people saying it might start to think it's true.

We have the same problem in the UK. Far-left organizations operate charitable wings, perform outreach in schools, and lobby Members of Parliament. They pose as counter-extremism think tanks, tell lies to children, and use the money available to them to spend their professional life bullying, mocking, and humiliating people they don't agree with. These shameless organizations, including the likes of HOPE not hate, regularly compare the white nationalists of the National Front, National Action (terrorist group which we'll talk more about later in this book), and BNP to the conservatives like Nigel Farage. They consider me, a former member of the BNP, an extremist beyond the pale.

And they'll stop at nothing to shut us down.

Our politicians are no better. Labour MP David Lammy was dead serious when he tried to lump Nigel Farage in with extremists who have threatened his life. In a tweet on 12th April 2019, Lammy wrote[17]:

> I've received death threats against myself, my wife and my children for standing up to the far-right politics of hate. I will never be cowed, but what a disgraceful way to behave in our democracy. Nigel Farage knows exactly what he's inciting with these dog whistle threats.

This is unhinged. Lammy was quoting a speech Farage made prior to the 2019 European elections, in which he said his new party will put the "fear of God" into MPs.

Farage is a man who, like Lammy, has received death threats. Probably more. He and his family have been attacked while trying to enjoy a dinner together at a pub. I've received

17 David Lammy (@DavidLammy), "I've received death threats against myself, my wife and my children for standing up to the far right politics of hate. I will never be cowed, but what a disgraceful way to behave in our democracy. Nigel Farage knows exactly what he's inciting with these dog whistle threats," April 12, 2019, https://twitter.com/DavidLammy/status/1116665325079158784.

countless death threats, too. Far-left activists have threatened to murder my dogs, to kill me, and to hurt my family. It's extremely common, and if Lammy had any self-awareness at all, he'd know his side is much worse for this kind of behavior.

Nigel Farage, a man who is so wary of being called racist that he calls many of his own voters far right, has even been criticized for using "antisemitic themes" when criticizing George Soros.[18] This is a nonsense.

I'm no fan of Nigel Farage. He has publicly attacked me on national radio for my former membership of the BNP. He has demonized every single BNP voter for many years, failing to recognize the many factors that caused people to vote in this way. I consider his behavior as dangerous and damaging as the name-calling and smears from the far left. In fact, it's probably worse. To be known as "too right wing even for Nigel Farage" is music to the left's ears, and a smear used relentlessly by the press if you happen to be targeted by him.

Farage will do anything to try to avoid the vicious smears and campaigns from the far left. But that doesn't mean he deserves to be attacked and smeared too. He is, without a shadow of a doubt, not a racist man.

But he is "Mr. Brexit," as Trump would say. That's enough for you to be far right, according to Adam Boulton of Sky News. Boulton is a well-known broadcaster on the Sky News channel, and in a tweet on February 20, 2019, he responded to

18 Peter Walker, "Farage Criticised for Using Antisemitic Themes to Criticise Soros," *The Guardian*, May 12, 2019, https://www.theguardian.com/politics/2019/may/12/farage-criticised-for-using-antisemitic-themes-to-criticise-soros.

the former director of communications for the Conservatives (and girlfriend of Boris Johnson), Carrie Symonds.

She wrote:

"Supporting Brexit does not make you far right. Tedious, insulting and just plain wrong to keep stating that it does."

To which he responded:

"Unless you are a Tory in which case it kinda does."

Labour MP Diane Abbott went one further, attacking not just Tory Brexit voters, but Brexit supporters as a whole. During a speech at a Brexit: Unite Against Racism and Hatred event at the Labour Party conference, Abbott said:[19]

"The people that complain about the freedom of movement will not be satisfied because what they really want is to see less foreign-looking people on their streets."

It's not uncommon for Abbott to label people racist, but slamming 17.4 million people for it is a bit rich.

It's easy to think these people are deluded, but in many cases, they're not. Slamming Brexit voters as racist is intentional, not stupid. Making broad and sweeping statements about right-leaning voters and comparing neo-Nazis with academics and voters concerned about the influence of radical Islam is all part of a coordinated and ongoing campaign to shift the center to the left.

And clearly, it is working.

---

19 Lynn Davidson, "'They Want Less Foreign-Looking People' Labour's Shadow Health Secretary Diane Abbott Brands the 17 Million Voters Who Backed Brexit as Racists," *The Sun*, September 27, 2016, https://www.thesun.co.uk/news/1858995/labours-shadow-health-secretary-diane-abbott-brands-the-17million-voters-who-backed-brexit-as-racists/.

For as long as we refuse to wrestle back this "far right" term, it will simply get worse.

Let's not shy away from the term. Let's recognize that there is a real far right. It is small, but it is growing. It is being egged on by far-left ideologues who want nothing more than for the real far right to thrive so they can point and say, "Ha! We were right all along!"

Ideological movements aren't some kind of conspiracy theory. It's easy to assume that nothing this crazy or this evil can exist in the world, but it does. There are people who would rather see young white men radicalized and who would be happy to see working-class towns completely obliterated, if it means fundamentally transforming the basis of British politics and civil society.

For as long as we shy away from this issue, we're just letting them win.

CHAPTER THREE

THE RISE OF THE (REAL) FAR RIGHT

If we apply the more accurate definition of "far right" which I proposed in the previous chapter, the data shows that there is a very real presence of far-right extremism in Western countries—or indeed, across the Anglosphere. Violent attacks and terrorism committed by extreme right wingers are occurring all the time, and it is not in the interest of anybody who cares about maintaining a harmonious society to ignore it. That means conservatives must be willing to face up to this reality, and far-left progressives must be willing to accept that their definition is wrong. Falsely identifying the problem is as dangerous as ignoring it completely.

Claims by the Anti-Defamation League (ADL) truly embodied the effectiveness of basing a lie on the truth. Amidst widespread violence from radical Antifa protestors, it might seem hard to believe that far-right extremism is something even worth thinking about. When Mark Pitcavage, a senior research fellow from the ADL's Center on Extremism, claimed that 74 percent of murders committed by domestic terrorists in the

United States between 2007 and 2017 were right wing,[20] it might seem even more egregious.

It's untrue, but it's also true.

First of all, it's probably not surprising that most figures given by so-called "anti-extremism" think tanks and organizations fail to include the death count from the Islamic terror attack in New York on September 11, 2001. I challenge you to find a left-wing "anti-extremism" organization that doesn't offer data sets specifically post-2001.

The ADL also pads out their stats by including murders committed as part of wider criminal activity that are not necessarily politically motivated. A 2016 report from the ADL admitted "It is common for adherents of extremist movements to commit nonideological acts of violence, which can range from killing a suspected informant to assassinating a rival to acts of violence stemming from traditional criminal motives, such as anger or greed."[21] This admission makes their data significantly less impactful, and while they openly admit that their data includes potentially nonideological murders, they know that this isn't what the national media will focus on. Headlines explicitly state that right wing extremists are killing more people than anyone else, and because a vast majority of readers won't go on to read the report, their job is done. The ADL has successfully influenced public opinion by misleading them while never telling a lie.

---

20 Martin Kaste, "Fact Check: Is Left-Wing Violence Rising?" NPR, June 16, 2017, https://www.npr.org/2017/06/16/533255619/fact-check-is-left-wing-violence-rising?t=1562452963308.

21 Anti-Defamation League, "Murder and Extremism in the United States in 2016," 2017, https://www.adl.org/sites/default/files/documents/MurderAndExtremismInUS2016.pdf.

Misleading the public on this issue is unnecessary if the intention of the report is to offer honest analysis. I would argue that the ADL's motives are less than pure, which is why they misled the public in such a way. Writers of a 2017 report by the *Daily Caller* analyzed the data as best they could. They reported that the ADL had not made the full data set public, but an independent study from the Daily Caller News Foundation analyzed instances where domestic extremists committed murder with "clear ideological motive." Using data from the National Consortium for the Study of Terrorism and Responses to Terrorism, their study found 92 percent of murders were committed by white supremacists and right-wing extremists over a period of ten years.

The Government Accountability Office performed a similar study. It found:[22]

> Since September 12, 2001, the number of fatalities caused by domestic violent extremists has ranged from 1 to 49 in a given year. As shown in figure 2, fatalities resulting from attacks by far right wing violet extremists have exceeded those caused by radical Islamist violent extremists in 10 of the 15 years, and were the same in 3 of the years since September 12, 2001. Of the 85 violent extremist incidents that resulted in death since September 12, 2001, far right wing violent extremist groups were responsible for 62 (73 percent) while radical Islamist violent extremists were responsible for 23 (27 percent).

---

22 Government Accountability Office, "Countering Violent Extremism: Actions Needed to Define Strategy and Assess Progress of Federal Efforts," Report to Congressional Requesters, April 2017, https://www.gao.gov/assets/690/683984.pdf.

But it also found:

> The total number of fatalities is about the same for far right wing violent extremists and radical Islamist violent extremists over the approximately 15-year period (106 and 119, respectively). However, 41 percent of the deaths attributable to radical Islamist violent extremists occurred in a single event—

This is important. The data shows that right-wing violence is significant, but that Islamist violence is typically more dangerous in terms of pure numbers. Those who rely on ADL figures to argue that the far right is the greatest threat to civilization fail to recognize that the West is facing a problem with radicalism and extremism *generally*. Paradoxically, they recognize a reciprocal extremism of far-right and Islamist extremists but don't acknowledge the influence of far-left extremists in this deadly mix.

When the media perpetuates the lie that far-right terrorism is independent of other extremist politics, it is complicit in the continued cycle of radicalization of young white men. When the politicians side with far-left extremists and brush off criticism of their inability to deal with Islamist terror, they are neglecting the people they are elected to represent and serve. When far-left activists use misleading figures to blame the world's problems on young far-right activists, they are advancing their radical politics with no care for those who fall victim along the way.

I should note that these numbers do not reflect the situation here in the United Kingdom. In 2017, there were five extreme-right terror plots recorded by the European Union, and every single one of them happened in the UK. Twenty of all terror suspects who were arrested that year were far right, but 705 arrested terrorists were jihadists.[23] This reflects the growing problem of jihadi violence in Europe, something that the United States has seen in multiple terrorist incidences but which Europe experiences on an almost daily basis. Whether it's jihadi violence, terror attacks, or extremism preached on the streets or in the Mosques, Europe is very much the epicenter of the jihadi civilizational war, and in contrast, far-right terrorism might seem insignificant. But it's not.

Far-right terrorism is a growing threat everywhere in the West, and our current political climate is proving to be fertile ground for the far right to recruit, expand, and grow its sphere of influence. It is encouraging violence, it is warping the minds of young men, and unless we stop viewing data on terror attacks through an ideological lens, nothing will change. There are many ways to interpret the data, but one thing is for sure: the far right is recruiting and growing and will continue to do so unless the fuel they use to recruit is taken from them.

HOW ANDERS BREIVIK SKEWED PERCEPTION OF THE FAR RIGHT

I have spent my whole adult life campaigning against Islamic terror and political violence from the left. So naturally I find the idea of ignoring right-wing violence for political convenience

23 Ben Butcher and Micah Luxen, "How Prevalent Is Far-Right Extremism?" BBC News, March 19, 2019, https://www.bbc.co.uk/news/uk-47626859.

repulsive. There have been some extremely disturbing attacks and mass murders committed by those amongst the extreme right I described in the last chapter, and possibly the most notable in recent years is Anders Breivik.

Breivik is a Norwegian, far-right activist who killed seventy-seven people in a 2011 terror attack in Norway. He killed eight people when he detonated a van bomb in the center of several government buildings in Oslo, Norway's capital city. He killed a further sixty-nine people by shooting them dead on the island of Utøya. The victims were taking part in a summer camp event for the Workers' Youth League, a left-wing youth organization.

Before the attacks, Breivik wrote a manifesto, "2083: A European Declaration of Independence." Writing under the pseudonym Andrew Berwick, Breivik claimed he was heavily influenced by the counter-jihad movement, a political movement with which I have many connections. Breivik referenced anti-Islamist activists and writers Robert Spencer and Pamela Geller, as well as Norwegian blogger Fjordman. He detailed his support for Israel, and his objection to the mass immigration of Muslims into Europe. Strangely, those he made explicit reference to in his manifesto are vocally opposed to political violence.

Something didn't add up.

During his time in prison, Breivik admitted that his 1,518-page manifesto was a ploy to protect ethno-nationalists from the media. He later described himself as a white nationalist and a fascist, and *not* a supporter of the counter-jihad movement. It was all a ploy, it turns out, to protect the real far-right extremists and drag moderate nationalists and conservatives down to the same level as him.

Writing in a letter to the Norwegian press, Breivik said:[24]

> When dealing with media psychopaths, a good way to counter their tactics is to use double-psychology, or at least so I thought. The compendium was, among other things, of a calculated and quite cynical <<gateway-design>> (the 2+?+?=6-approach), created to strengthen the ethnocentrist wing in the contra-jihad movement, by pinning the whole thing on the anti-ethnocentrist wing (many of the leaders are pro-multiculti social democrats or liberalists), while at the same time protecting and strengthening the ethnocentrist-factions. The idea was to manipulate the MSM and others so that they would launch a witch-hunt and send their <<media-rape-squads>> against our opponents. It worked quite well.

Not only did Breivik terrorize a nation and murder seventy-seven innocent people in cold blood, but he contributed toward a skewed narrative that defines a huge section of the American and British public as "far right." This is a narrative perpetuated by far-left activists who benefit politically from the common belief that the far right is lurking around every corner, and by genuine far-right activists who aim to drag as many people into the pits with them in the hope that some become genuinely radicalized.

---

24 Mark Hemingway, "Terrorist Anders Breivik Now Claims He Lied About Pro-Israel Views to Disguise Nazi Beliefs," *The Washington Examiner*, February 23, 2014, https://www.weeklystandard.com/mark-hemingway/terrorist-anders-breivik-now-claims-he-lied-about-pro-israel-views-to-diguise-nazi-beliefs.

RAPE GANGS IN YORKSHIRE AND THE MURDER OF LABOUR MP JO COX

On June 16, 2016, Labour Member of Parliament (MP) for Batley and Spen, Jo Cox, was shot and stabbed to death. Cox had been an MP since the 2015 General Election and was married to Brendan Cox, a former policy director for charity Save the Children who later stepped down over allegations of sexual misconduct.[25]

Cox's murderer, Thomas Mair, was a fifty-two-year-old far-right activist who lived in the local area. He was found to have links to American and British neo-Nazi and white nationalist groups, including National Vanguard and National Front. His internet search history showed that he had spent a great deal of time exploring everything the far right had to offer, from the anti-Jewish conspiracy theories of the Ku Klux Klan to the motivations behind the Anders Breivik murders. Mair collected newspaper clippings about Breivik and searched for information about prominent Jewish people.

He was a textbook example of a white working-class man falling into the realm of conspiracy theory because life could offer him little more. Detective Superintendent Nick Wallen from West Yorkshire Police described him as a "loner in the truest sense of the word" and "a man who never held down a job, never had a girlfriend, never any friends to speak of."

News reports on the day of the murder suggested he might have been connected to fringe anti-Islam group Britain First,

25 Alexandra Topping, "Brendan Cox Resigns from Charities Amid Sexual Assault Claims," *The Guardian*, February 18, 2018, https://www.theguardian.com/politics/2018/feb/18/brendan-cox-resigns-from-charities-amid-sexual-assault-claims.

run by former BNP organizer Paul Golding. Reports said he shouted, "Britain First!" as he stabbed Cox to death. It was later revealed he had shouted "*Put* Britain first" and "This is for Britain!" This was a lone wolf attack committed by a man who felt that he was genuinely putting his country first.

Mair repeatedly refused to defend himself or comment on the attack in the early stages of investigation. In court, his request to address the court was denied by the judge, stating that he had already had multiple opportunities to do so.

The attack came as a shock to the country, obviously. Cox had two young children, and the attack seemed to come from nowhere. She also didn't seem like the natural target for a far-right terrorist, other than the fact she was easily accessible and in the same part of the country as Mair.

Cox was considered a fairly popular local MP, but her constituency had some dark secrets. Batley is just twenty-seven miles northwest of Rotherham, the South Yorkshire town now famous for one of the most shocking cover-ups by British authorities in history. A report commissioned by Rotherham Borough Council, authored by Professor Alexis Jay, found that at least 1,400 young children were trafficked, raped and abused by mostly Muslim men between 1997 and 2013.[26] The Jay report detailed multiple horrific stories of children being seriously abused while the authorities looked the other way. Police literally tore up paperwork relating to child sex

26 "Independent Inquiry into Child Sexual Exploitation in Rotherham (1997-2013," Rotherham Metropolitan Borough Council, 2019, https://www.rotherham.gov.uk/downloads/file/1407/independent_inquiry_cse_in_rotherham.

abuse victims,[27] and former Rotherham MP Denis MacShane admitted he was too much of a "liberal leftie" and didn't do enough to investigate child abuse.

Speaking to the BBC, MacShane said, "I think there was a culture of not wanting to rock the multicultural community boat if I may put it like that."[28]

Despite evidence of widespread abuse coming to light in the 1990s, it took years for real action to be taken. In 2003, a Sexual Exploitation Forum was set up to consider cases of children who had been exploited or who were at risk of being exploited. In 2008, the police launched Operation Central, which investigated groups of Muslim men in the town who were believed to be involved with child abuse. In 2010, they finally convicted five men.

The scandal was huge, it is still ongoing, and there are surrounding Yorkshire towns that have been affected by this same crime. Batley is one of those towns.

Ask anybody who lives on a council estate in Batley and they'll tell you that young girls have been victims of Muslim grooming gangs for years. That's exactly what I did, in fact, in 2016. I went door to door and spoke to local people who told me horror stories.

---

27 "Rotherham Child Sex Abuse: Police 'Ripped Up Files,'" BBC News, November 10, 2014, https://www.bbc.co.uk/news/uk-england-south-yorkshire-29957511.

28 Gordon Rayner, "Dennis MacShane: I Was Too Much of a 'Liberal Leftie' and Should Have Done More to Investigate Child Abuse," *The Telegraph*, August 27, 2014, https://www.telegraph.co.uk/news/uknews/crime/11059643/Denis-MacShane-I-was-too-much-of-a-liberal-leftie-and-should-have-done-more-to-investigate-child-abuse.html.

It was part of my election campaign to replace Jo Cox. Her murder triggered a by-election (special election) to replace her, though the nature of her death meant every major political party in the UK announced they would not be standing in the election to replace her. Had no political party or candidate decided to run in the by-election, and only a Labour candidate registered, a new MP for the Batley and Spen constituency would have been appointed without an election.

I thought this was wrong, and so I announced my candidacy just days after her death. I really didn't think it would be so controversial at the time. A by-election was being held, and there was a possibility that the Labour Party would have the chance to crown a new MP without giving the public a say. My candidacy forced that election to go ahead, and boy, did the press go crazy.

One headline from *The Mirror* read, "Jo Cox's Grieving Colleagues Forced to Contest By-Election Against Far-Right Party in 'Obscene' Move."[29]

I announced my candidacy for a counter-jihad political party called Liberty GB in a video. In it, I explained I was standing not just to ensure the people of Batley were given the opportunity to actually *choose* their next MP, but also to represent the victims of grooming in the area. Nobody seemed to be acknowledging the fact that Jo Cox, during her time as a Labour MP representing the area, had failed to even acknowledge that the problem existed.

29 Dan Bloom, "Jo Cox's Grieving Colleagues Forced to Contest By-Election Against Far-Right Party in 'Obscene' Move," *The Mirror*, June 19, 2016, https://www.mirror.co.uk/news/uk-news/jo-coxs-grieving-colleagues-forced-8230561.

To stand for election in the UK, ten signatures from local people are required. That means knocking on doors in the constituency to find enough people who were willing to sign a piece of paper expressing their desire for you to be a candidate in the upcoming election. I thought this experience would be extremely difficult, and it was. I met some Labour supporters who thought I was the Devil. How *dare* I stand for election after Jo Cox was tragically murdered. No care at all, it seemed, for the victims of grooming gangs in the region I was campaigning for.

But these people were a minority. I have been met with greater hostility in far less controversial elections, and what I actually found was that most of the people I spoke to at the doorstop were aware of the grooming gang problem, and they were even willing to tell me what was happening. On my first day of campaigning, trying to find those first ten signatures, almost everybody I spoke to either knew somebody who had been targeted by these grooming gangs, or had children of their own who had been affected.

The worst story I heard was from the parents of a grown woman who had been a victim of sexual abuse as a young teenager. She had been kidnapped and taken to another city north of Batley. She was held against her will and abused, and after she escaped through a bathroom window and found her way to the nearest police station, she was dropped off back at home in Batley and told they didn't have enough evidence to arrest the men who raped her. The victim struggled with mental health problems for years afterwards and made multiple attempts on her own life. With their permission, I told their story and, surprisingly, I was contacted by the police. They'd seen that people were suddenly willing to speak out about what was happening in Batley, but the family wasn't interested in following up with them. Too many times had the local police told them there simply wasn't enough evidence. The family had lost all faith in the local authorities, and I couldn't blame them.

I was called a racist, an opportunist, and an extremist throughout that election campaign. Labour MP Jack Dromey called my candidacy "obscene."[30] Dromey worked for the National Council for Civil Liberties in the 1970s,[31] an organization that granted affiliate status to the Paedophile Information Exchange (PIE), which campaigned for the abolition of the age of consent.

I will admit, the campaign was uncomfortable. I'm not a naturally outgoing person, and I do get quite anxious approaching people I don't know. I hate knocking on doors, and I hate bothering people. A filmmaker who followed me on my campaign for a TV report picked up on this quite regularly, asking me why I was out on the campaign trail if I hated doing it. Another journalist asked me why I cared about the grooming issue so much, to which I responded, "Why don't you?"

Despite my reservations and anxiety, I was extremely confrontational throughout the campaign. Every time the national press called me a racist, I doubled down. Every time the local Labour Party said I was lying about grooming gangs, I doubled

30 "'Obscene': Far-Right Candidate Criticized over Decision to Run for Slain Jo Cox's Seat," RT, June 20, 2016, https://www.rt.com/uk/347454-right-cox-seat-buckby/.

31 Christopher Hope, "Harriet Harman, Jack Dromey, Patricia Hewitt and the Paedophile Information Exchange," *The Telegraph*, February 24, 2014, https://www.telegraph.co.uk/news/politics/labour/10659100/Harriet-Harman-Jack-Dromey-Patricia-Hewitt-and-the-Paedophile-Information-Exchange.html.

down. I produced a Facebook ad that showed Jo Cox superimposed behind prison bars. When I saw the Labour candidate Tracy Brabin spending her campaign sipping tea and eating cake while I spoke to families of grooming victims, I decided to ice a cake with the words "Muslim Grooming Gangs" and deliver it in person to Brabin's office. She refused to listen, so I figured a cake might be the only language she'd understand. It resulted in a physical scuffle inside the Labour campaign office, with one activist grabbing the cake from my hands and another putting me in a headlock. All I remember was a man's arm around my neck and jam and cake flying everywhere.

It wasn't my finest hour, and I don't look back on some of my tactics with great pride. But I will never apologize for that campaign or for forcing a by-election to take place. It was the right thing to do, and three years later, I was proven right.

Brabin, who won the by-election with 85.8 percent on a tiny 25.8 percent turnout, quietly admitted that Batley does in fact have a problem with grooming after previously telling the media I was just "stirring up hatred" in 2016. In 2019, it was announced that Brabin had worked closely with West Yorkshire Police to secure £1.2 million in special grant funding to aid investigation into historic grooming and child sexual exploitation cases.[32] Brabin completely dismissed this at the time.

In June 2019, it was announced that West Yorkshire police had arrested forty-four people in relation to historical child sex

---

32 Jo Winrow, "Police Secure £1.2m for Investigations into Grooming Cases across West Yorkshire," *Telegraph & Argus*, May 22, 2019, https://www.thetelegraphandargus.co.uk/news/17657456.police-secure-12m-for-investigations-into-grooming-cases-across-west-yorkshire/.

grooming cases in Dewsbury and Batley. As I write this book, all forty-four people arrested have been questioned and released. Investigations continue.

I do not doubt for one moment that Jo Cox's murderer, Thomas Mair, genuinely believed his cowardly act of murderous violence was the right thing to do. Though very much a loner and clearly mentally unstable, Mair is not an isolated case. There are angry people all over this country, particularly in areas like West Yorkshire, who have seen genuine tragedies covered up or ignored by authorities. This isn't an excuse for Mair and others to go out murdering whoever they like, but it *does* mean that genuinely far-right groups can claim legitimacy to their arguments and recruit off the back of these tragedies.

If the authorities ignore the systematic rape of non-Muslim children and the only organizations vocal on this issue are white nationalists, where do the politicians think people are going to turn? Most people will just keep their mouths shut, but some mostly working-class men and boys, fueled by righteous anger, testosterone, and a sense of desperation, will turn to extremism.

NATIONAL ACTION AND THE NEW, YOUNG NEO-NAZIS

Thomas Mair is not unique. In recent years, the UK has seen a resurgence of white supremacist street movements with a distinctly youthful slant. The skinheads of the National Front are long gone, and the old guard of Britain's white nationalist movement are dying off or fading into irrelevance while a new, younger generation of white lads are forming violent gangs and plotting terror attacks.

National Action is the most prominent youth group for white nationalists. It was founded in 2013 by former members of the youth wing of the BNP and quickly grew into one of the most prominent young nationalist organizations. Through the use of striking imagery on its social media accounts, the organization attracted angry young boys and quickly started spreading across British universities. In no time, National Action stickers were being found on university campuses across the UK, and demonstrations started popping up in major cities.

Unlike the youth BNP and similar youth nationalist groups, NA was pitched as cool, young, edgy, and radical. Really radical. Alex Davies, one of the founders of NA, said at a demonstration outside Liverpool Lime Street Station, "We're like the BNP but more radical." Young men who attended these rallies didn't think twice about throwing up a Nazi salute or shouting anti-Semitic slurs on the streets. The veil of respectability had been lost, the attempts made by genuine racists within the BNP to legitimize their cause had failed, and there was no reason to hide it anymore. The Youth BNP group was tragic and cringeworthy, but NA was on the up.

It was the murder of Jo Cox that really brought NA into the national spotlight, though. Until then, the stickers might have easily gone unnoticed. Those who saw them probably didn't know what NA meant and probably didn't search for them online when they got home. Only those who understood this weird world of political extremism knew who they were, until they came out in support of Thomas Mair.

In response to Cox's murder, an NA social media post read, "Only 649 MPs to go!" In a Telegram conversation, members of NA asked who should be "the next MP to be Tommy Maired."[33]

Home Secretary Amber Rudd proscribed NA, making it a terrorist organization. That meant anyone who supported or joined the group after December 16, 2016, was breaking the law. Its members had given speeches calling for the adoption of a "killer instinct" and its propaganda embraced Nazi imagery and targeted Jewish people directly. This was and is a genuinely extreme, far-right group, and it hasn't disappeared. Many young men have been arrested and imprisoned, while others are still out there behind their keyboards, organizing and communicating online.

The comments made by NA members in a Telegram message were revealed during a court case. Details of a conversation among twenty-four-year-old Mark Jones (a former BNP member), twenty-two-year-old Alice Cutter, twenty-three-year-old Garry Jack, and eighteen-year-old Connor Scothern, were read to a jury. It included discussions about how to promote NA, how mixed-race children made them feel sick, and how nonwhites were "subhuman." Cutter was even shown to have entered an online "Miss Hitler" beauty contest, entering under the pseudonym "Buchenwald Princess" in reference to the Nazi concentration camp.

In June 2018, twenty-three-year-old Jack Renshaw from my hometown of Skelmersdale admitted plotting to murder our local MP, Rosie Cooper. In his first day in court, the Old Bailey

---

33 Louie Smith, "Far-Right National Action Suspects' Sick Messages about MP Jo Cox's Murder," *The Mirror*, March 27, 2019, https://www.mirror.co.uk/news/uk-news/far-right-national-action-suspects-14191684.

in London, Renshaw admitted buying a nineteen-inch machete and plotting to murder Cooper in the summer of 2017. He also admitted threatening to kill a police officer. Renshaw denied being a member of National Action, and a jury twice failed to reach a verdict on charges connected with his alleged membership. He had, however, been seen at NA rallies and was known to post about the organization on dummy social media accounts.[34]

In May 2019, Renshaw was jailed for life for preparing to commit an act of terrorism. Judge Justice McGowan said that he had made "detailed arrangements" to commit the act and had been studying Cooper's itinerary. There seemed to be no doubt that Renshaw was serious about killing Cooper.

The nineteen-inch machete that he bought was found hidden in a cupboard in his uncle's house.[35]

As he was sentenced, he made a Nazi salute before being taken away.

From now on, I'm going to stop calling him Renshaw and instead call him Jack. I have a lot more to say about him, because his story is important. I won't be writing about him in a journalistic way, or as someone who merely finds his case interesting from an outside perspective.

I knew Jack.

---

34 Joe Thomas, "Exposed: Extremists Thought to Have Been Involved in Right Wing Liverpool Rally," *Echo*, March 1, 2016, https://www.liverpoolecho.co.uk/news/liverpool-news/exposed-extremists-thought-been-involved-10968899.

35 Nadia Khomami, "Two Members of Banned Neo-Nazi Group National Action Jailed," *The Guardian,* July 18, 2018, https://www.theguardian.com/uk-news/2018/jul/18/neo-nazi-group-national-action-members-jailed.

He was from the same town as me, only a few years younger than me, and at one point, we were involved in the same political campaigns. He wasn't always a monster, and he wasn't always a neo-Nazi.

Jack Renshaw and I shaking hands outside of a pub in Skelmersdale

When I first heard about the plot to kill Rosie Cooper, it was obviously a shock. I've known the name Rosie Cooper for a long time. She was our local MP from 2005, and she made multiple trips to my high school over the years. She wasn't particularly known for doing anything spectacular for the town, if I'm honest. She's a Labour MP after all, and a backbencher—so hardly the most visible politician in the country. But for Jack, she was accessible and local. The idea that somebody could really want to go out and kill Rosie is just insane. I can't imagine the hatred and anger that somebody must feel to want to do that, but Jack was planning it, and I'm amazed to this day that he became the person he did.

When I knew him, Jack was a fairly regular lad. The photo above was taken on a summer day in a pub garden in Skelmersdale. I'm not entirely sure what I was thinking with regards to that hair style, though to be fair I can't really say it's the worst life decision I've ever made. After all, I am seen here shaking hands with a future terrorist.

Jack split his time between his mum's and dad's houses, between Skem and Blackpool if I remember right. He was entirely ordinary to me at the time. His politics weren't too radical, either. Like me, he was concerned about mass immigration and radical Islam. It's incredible how easily young, vulnerable, and directionless lads like Jack can be turned into monsters. He was one of many young men who saw no future for themselves and who found answers in conspiracy theory and pure, unadulterated hatred.

Jack was convicted of threatening to kill a police officer and preparing an act of terrorism in 2018. He was also convicted of inciting a child to engage in sexual activity. During his trial in 2019, it was revealed that Jack had used fake Facebook profiles to solicit sexual photos of boys aged between thirteen and fourteen. I'm afraid I cannot offer any insight into his child sexual offenses, which I find truly perplexing—but I can offer great insight into Jack's radicalization.

I will tell you more about Jack, how we met, and how he became the monster he is in the next chapter.

He wasn't the only person involved with the plot to murder my local MP, though. Thirty-two-year-old Christopher Lythgoe from Warrington, a town in the northwest of England and not very far from Skem, was also jailed for eight years. Twenty-four-year-old Matthew Hankinson from Merseyside, again in the northwest of England, was also found guilty of belonging to NA and was jailed for six years. Hankinson advocated violence against Jews and other ethnic minorities.[36]

Another NA member, Zack Davies, was found guilty in 2015 of attempted murder.[37] Davies attempted to kill an Asian man, Dr. Sarandev Bhambra, in a local supermarket using a machete and a clawhammer. As he attacked Bhambra, he shouted "This is for Lee Rigby" referring to the murder of a British soldier on the streets of London by two Muslim men.

A significant number of others have been through the court system for their involvement with National Action. Adam Thomas and Claudia Patatas, two NA members, named their baby "Adolf" and can be seen in photographs holding a Nazi flag. A counterterrorism police raid on their home in Oxfordshire found Swastika cookie cutters and scatter cushions.[38]

NA was and is a neo-Nazi organization with supporters across the UK. Although it doesn't boast thousands of members, its impact has been quite significant, and I don't believe the British authorities really understand the reach it has. Many of its members and supporters have been found and prosecuted, but most probably never will be. They're

36 Khomami, "Two Members of Banned Neo-Nazi Group."

37 Brian Whelan, "National Action's Zack Davies Guilty of Attempted Murder," Channel 4 News, June 25, 2015, https://www.channel4.com/news/national-actions-zack-davies-guilty-of-attempted-murder.

38 "National Action Trial: Man Trained Daughter to Do Nazi Salute," BBC News, December 14, 2018, https://www.bbc.co.uk/news/uk-england-oxfordshire-46564539.

the keyboard warriors who perpetuate conspiracy theories about the Jews on the internet, and they're all over the world. The online realm of neo-Nazis is extensive and largely misunderstood. While far-left activists scream about the prevalence of neo-Nazis in mainstream society, targeting thoroughly decent and normal people, real neo-Nazis radicalize mostly young white men undetected.

Neo-Nazis are plotting and organizing on Discord servers, 8chan, Telegram chats, and even traditional forums on the internet right now.

RECENT FAR-RIGHT TERRORISM IN THE U.S.

Mass shootings aren't all that commonplace in the UK. If a shooting happens, it'll be with an illegally obtained handgun and one person might fall victim to it. Things are quite different elsewhere, particularly the United States. In recent years, we've seen a spate of far-right shootings that have resulted in huge losses of life.

The Pittsburgh synagogue shooting in October 2018 saw eleven people killed and six injured others during morning Shabbat services. The only suspect, forty-six-year-old Robert Bowers, pleaded not guilty to the crimes. The shooting and his arrest caused a media frenzy surrounding the use of the social media website Gab, a Twitter alternative set up to offer a free platform to anybody regardless of their political views. Of course, the site was quickly adopted by neo-Nazis all over the world who were constantly being booted from Twitter for their extreme views. Gab, a free speech platform, removed only those who directly incited violence.

Bowers, the Pittsburgh shooting suspect, was active on Gab and had made many anti-Semitic and extreme comments online. Reporters revealed that Bowers had posted comments like "jews are the children of satan," railed against "ZOGs" (Zionist Operated Governments), and so on. Article after article revealed the horrific things Bowers said, including the harrowing comment:

"I can't sit by and watch my people get slaughtered. Screw your optics, I'm going in."[39]

Rita Katz, the director of SITE Intelligence Group and a terrorism analyst, revealed some of the most disturbing content Bowers was interacting with on Gab. White supremacists have flocked to the platform ever since it was launched, Katz notes, because they see it as a way of "connecting Jew-wise people"—their words, not hers.

One post, tagged with the "#TreeOfLifeShooting" hashtag, referring to the synagogue where eleven people were killed, asked other users, "What should the future of Jewish people in the West be?"

Thirty-five percent responded "Genocide" and forty-seven percent "Repatriation."

The hashtag #HeroRobertBowers even started trending. There was and is clearly a significant online community who praised what Bowers did.

Anybody familiar with internet culture will know that it is common for people to post sickening things like this

39 Rita Katz, "Inside the Online Cesspool of Anti-Semitism That Housed Robert Bowers," *Politico*, October 29, 2018, https://www.politico.com/magazine/story/2018/10/29/inside-the-online-cesspool-of-anti-semitism-that-housed-robert-bowers-221949.

for a laugh. I don't understand how or why somebody could ever find something like this funny, but the internet is a dark place. That doesn't mean, however, that there aren't people who genuinely believe this. The fact that Bowers (allegedly, at the time of writing) went out and shot these innocent people proves that there are true believers in these sick philosophies. This is what I was talking about in the last section when I said that white supremacists and neo-Nazis are indeed plotting and communicating online all the time. Bowers, if the court finds he did in fact commit this crime, represents the future we face if nothing is done about the root causes of the radicalization of white boys and men in the West.

The Marjory Stoneman Douglas High School shooting, or the Parkland shooting, is another interesting example of how vulnerable young men can easily become radicalized. This instance is quite different from many others, however. I don't really think this is a good example of how the extreme right is winning over the hearts and minds of people, but rather, how mentally challenged or vulnerable people can easily become absorbed in this bizarre and hateful culture.

It is clear that Nikolas Cruz, the gunman who killed seventeen people and injured another seventeen, was extremely vulnerable. He scored under 100 on IQ tests and is reported to have learning difficulties and ADHD. Records from the Broward County Sheriff's office show that law enforcement received forty-five calls about Cruz (or his brother) between 2008 and 2017. The exact number is disputed, but in a press conference, Sheriff Scott Israel said his agency had received twenty-three calls about Cruz or his brother. Either way, the authorities were aware this boy was unstable, and anybody who knew him likely knew too. Unlike committed and knowledgeable white nationalists and neo-Nazis, Cruz was both a supporter of President Donald Trump and espoused racist views about Jewish and black people.

In a private chat, CNN reported, Cruz said "I hate jews, niggers, immigrants,"[40]

White nationalists don't support Donald Trump. Robert Bowers publicly complained that Donald Trump was not a nationalist, but a globalist. He also said he believed Trump is "controlled by Jews."

Cruz was not really an ideologue or a white nationalist. He was a vulnerable young man with learning difficulties—perfect cannon fodder for hard-right ideologues who watched him shoot innocent people from the side lines. I wish the media could see this, but instead, they seemed to take great joy in noting Cruz's support of Trump.

A piece in the *Miami New Times* quotes jailhouse letters written by Cruz sent to a pen pal from the United Kingdom called Miley. It is just one of a multitude of mainstream news articles that attempt to conflate Trump's politics with Cruz's actions. In Cruz's letters, he discussed his belief that liberals are dangerous and that Democrats will take his rights away.

A smart conservative could argue why this is the case, but Cruz is neither smart, nor truly conservative. He is an unstable boy who is parroting what he reads online. His letters offered

---

40 Paul P. Murphy, "Exclusive: Group Chat Messages Show School Shooter Obsessed with Race, Violence and Guns," CNN, February 18, 2018, https://edition.cnn.com/2018/02/16/us/exclusive-school-shooter-instagram-group/index.html.

no real explanation or in depth look at his views, but rather, lines that he could have taken from Gab or Twitter posts. There was nothing of substance, but the *Miami New Times* excitedly connected the dots to, perhaps, try and prove that Trumpism and shooting up a school go hand in hand.

The title gives it away, really—"Jailhouse Letters Show School Shooter Nikolas Cruz Remains a Staunch Trumper Behind Bars."[41]

The author, Bob Norman, excitedly referenced Cruz's support of Ron DeSantis, the Republican governor of Florida, who was campaigning for election at the time the letters were written. Norman also talked about how Cruz was so supportive of Trump that he even placed his favorite red MAGA hat on an urn that contained his mother's ashes.

Any reasonable journalist would recognize this as behavior of a mentally unstable boy with learning difficulties.

This is another example of journalists lying by telling half-truths. Cruz appeared to have racist motivations, but he was little more than a useful idiot to the real far-right ideologues. If journalists really wanted to find a far-right bogeyman to point at, they didn't need to look far.

There was the Charleston church shooting, for instance, in 2015. Dylan Roof was a twenty-one-year-old neo-Nazi and white supremacist who murdered nine black Christians during a service at the Emanuel African Methodist Episcopal Church.

---

41 Bob Norman, "Jailhouse Letters Show School Shooter Nikolas Cruz Remains a Staunch Trumper Behind Bars," *Miami New Times*, April 9, 2019, https://www.miaminewtimes.com/news/from-parkland-school-shooter-nikolas-cruz-writes-of-support-for-donald-trump-ron-desantis-and-gun-rights-11143077.

There was the Charlottesville tragedy, when a woman was mowed down with a car and killed during a neo-Nazi rally. This is possibly the most notable far-right event that has taken place in recent years, with people from all over the United States gathering to express their support for the KKK (or, indeed, what's actually left of it), neo-Nazism, and white supremacy.

And just a few weeks after that *Miami New Times* article was written, the Poway synagogue shooting took place. This, I think, is one of the most disturbing far-right shootings in recent times and one that sums up what I'm trying to say extremely well.

The suspect, John T. Earnest, was a nineteen-year-old young man from San Diego. He was an anti-Semite who, like Bowers, condemned President Trump as a Zionist traitor.

On April 27, 2019, he walked into the Chabad of Poway synagogue in Poway, California. He was wearing a tactical vest with five magazines and (allegedly) immediately shot and killed a sixty-year-old Jewish woman with a semiautomatic rifle. Before entering the next room, he injured Rabbi Yisroel Goldstein. He then fired into a room full of children, injuring a man and his eight-year-old niece. If it wasn't for his gun malfunctioning, more would have died.

What's so scary about this story, apart from the obvious, is that Earnest was seemingly normal in every way. In fact, he was a model student, a talented pianist, and a swimmer on the varsity team. He even made the dean's list at a California State University—twice.

A video posted to YouTube shows a young Earnest playing the piano to an exceptionally high standard. At the end of the video, the uploader attached the following words:

"They have created a world now, where musically gifted, intelligent, talented white kids decide to sacrifice their lives to shoot up a synagogue."

And:

"John Earnest, another victim of the Jewish war on whites."

Earnest used orthodox Christian teachings to justify his anti-Semitism but denied in his own manifesto that he had been inspired by the teachings of his religious parents. Instead, it is much more likely that his views were inspired by an online community. He was a frequenter of the website 8chan, an online message board where extremist content is commonly shared. Any regular internet user would struggle to navigate the site and make much sense of it. The way in which these sites work provides a natural barrier to entry for most users, leaving only the most dedicated internet users to post. For some, posting on the website is entirely innocent and normal. For others, it's a way of sharing neo-Nazi, extremist, and genuinely hateful content.

The YouTube video with the additional commentary was almost certainly uploaded by a supporter of Earnest and a frequenter of sites like 8chan. This is a dedicated community of extremists who feed off one another, compete to say the most shocking things, and reinforce one another's biases in a deadly loop. It's also disturbing to see supporters of Earnest blame his action on the Jews. Their blind hatred for Jewish people leads them to believe that it is, in fact, the action of the Jews that caused Earnest to feel the need to kill Jews. Who can reason with people who think like that?

Instead, I would argue that Earnest was the product of a negligent political class, a complicit media, and far-left ideologues who have left people like him with no reasonable explanation for why white men have suddenly become a target in society. A hostile and extreme political environment is forcing young men into these dark corners of the internet, where even brilliant young minds can be irreparably warped.

CHRISTCHURCH SHOOTING AND PATRICK CRUSIUS

The Christchurch mosque shootings in New Zealand highlighted a problem in conservative rhetoric. A twenty-eight-year-old Australian man, Brenton Harrison Tarrant, was charged with the murder of fifty-one people. Over two attacks on March 15, 2019, he is alleged to have killed fifty-one people. Forty-two were killed at the Al Noor Mosque, seven at the Linwood Islamic Centre, and two at Christchurch Hospital. A further forty-nine people were injured.

The first seventeen minutes of the attack were streamed to Facebook live. Viewers saw him driving to the mosque while he played "Serbia Strong" on the radio. The Serb nationalist song is well known online for being part of a meme known as "Remove Kebab."

I won't describe the attack; you can find the details easily if you aren't familiar with it already. The whole thing played out like some kind of horrific video game. The killer made bizarre online posts, he was known for engaging with far-right material, and his seventy-four-page manifesto focused largely on the demographic replacement of white people in Europe. Just moments before the attacks happened, the manifesto was sent via email to thirty people and shared on 8chan and Twitter.

The killer was clearly a white nationalist and, under the better definition I have proposed in this book, he would easily fit within the "far right" category. Far-left ideologues saw this tragic attack as more fuel for the fire—a new stick with which to beat conservatives.

Conservatives, however, saw the shooter's manifesto as proof he "wasn't really a conservative." A battle ensued. Far-left activists and the press scrambled to connect the shooter with Trump, and label him far right. Meanwhile, conservatives scrambled to prove he wasn't *really* a conservative by picking apart his manifesto.

The first problem with this is that the manifesto was riddled with memes. In it, he claimed black political commentator Candance Owens influenced him, and the video game *Spyro: Year of the Dragon* taught him about ethnonationalism. He even referenced video game YouTuber PewDiePie. It's hard to take something seriously when it contains claims like this. He was clearly trying to cause a bit of chaos, and he definitely did.

There were also serious comments made by the shooter. For instance, he praised China for its lack of diversity. It's easy (or lazy) to read this and immediately label him left wing, but it's just not accurate. In his manifesto, the shooter asked himself a series of questions. Specifically, he asked, "are you right wing?" and "are you left wing?"

"Depending on the definition, sure," he responded to both questions.

He also labelled himself a fascist and described how conservatism was "corporatism in disguise," and that he wants "no part of it."

Like Bowers and Earnest, he also rejected Trump.

Again, it's easy to take this information and conclude that he is left wing. I saw quite a lot of that online for a while after the shooting, in fact. But it's just not true. It is convenient for conservatives to call him a left-wing Communist, but it isn't accurate. It's also unhelpful.

I understand it's a natural survival instinct for many conservatives to want to immediately distance themselves from this horrific shooting, and of course, it's right to do so. It's never nice to be compared to someone who does a terrible thing, especially when that person is nothing like you.

And, it's true to say that the New Zealand shooter is very much *un*like the average American conservative. He said it himself—he saw conservatism as corporatism. He called himself an eco-fascist, and he considered China's lack of diversity a good thing. The average American conservative is a free market capitalist, a Christian, and a supporter of a multiracial, meritocratic society.

This is where the left-wing opinion writers and commentators who attempted to compare the New Zealand shooter to Trump and Trump supporters were wrong.

But the New Zealand shooter wasn't truly left-wing either. Nobody can honestly say that an eco-fascist with socially conservative views and a desire to maintain an ethnically homogenous society is in any way comparable to the average left-wing progressive. The shooter cannot reasonably be defined as far left but *can* be reasonably defined as far right—at least, with modern reference points.

The line between left and right is not very clear, particularly now. And, the belief that to be a "conservative" one must be a Christian and a free market advocate is just wrong. It is,

I'm afraid to say, an American misconception. Conservatism existed before the free market, and it does not strictly apply to Christians. Meet a traditional English small-c conservative, and you'll find nationalist sentiment and support for some socialist economic policies. Conservatism is a tree with many branches, and although the New Zealand shooter was vastly different to the average American conservative who will sit on the free market branch, the shooter is a tiny, fragile twig on an entirely separate branch, sitting closer to the ethnonationalist and ethnopluralist branches/leanings of conservatism. He is, in my opinion, an example of a genuine far-right monster.

Another terrible attack took place during the writing of this book, on August 3, 2019. A man opened fire in a supermarket in Texas, killing over twenty people and injuring dozens of others. The suspect was a twenty-one-year-old white nationalist, identified at the time by the police as Patrick Crusius. Police said that the man had published a racist manifesto, and many conservatives immediately attempted to find anything that could label the man a Democrat, a progressive, or a far-left activist.

The Gateway Pundit misleadingly labelled the El Paso terrorist a "Hardcore Progressive and White Nationalist."[42] Pointing to the alleged shooter's support of universal income and universal healthcare, the article's author suggested that the killer is "without question a progressive."

---

42 Nan McKeeby and Byron McKeeby, "El Paso Terrorist Is a Hardcore Progressive and White Nationalist: Wants Universal Income and Universal Healthcare," The Gateway Pundit, August 4, 2019, https://www.thegatewaypundit.com/2019/08/el-paso-terrorist-is-a-hard-core-progressive-and-white-nationalist-wants-universal-income-and-universal-healthcare/.

I question that. Actually, I wholeheartedly dispute it. This is another thing that I know my American readers might initially disagree with, but I urge you to consider this from a non-American perspective. Right now, there is an insurgent populist movement across Europe, defined by a desire to reduce immigration, protect national identities, fight Islamic terror and extremism, and promote conservative values. Most of the political parties in this movement support universal healthcare. I, as a British conservative, support universal healthcare. Without the National Health Service, I would have either died twice by now or seen my family plunged into tens or hundreds of thousands of pounds of debt. I value our universal healthcare, but the advocacy of universal healthcare does not a progressive make.

This is particularly misleading when the term progressive, in the common lexicon, widely refers to social progressives and SJWs. The alleged shooter, Patrick Crusius, doesn't seem to be the kind of person you'd see at a trans rights or LGBT rally. It is entirely misleading to label him a progressive when he explicitly refers to race mixing as creating "identity problems." He advocated the dividing of America along racial lines, granting territories to each race. This is not a progressive attitude. It is far-right extremism. Again, that's not to say he is a Republican or a normal conservative—but he is also not a progressive. He is far right. A white supremacist.

Perhaps you disagree, and you believe that advocacy for universal healthcare does make him a progressive. And fair enough. That's an American perspective and it's technically not wrong (at least, in America). But ask yourself this: why does his support of universal healthcare even matter when he's clearly motivated by an extreme-right, racist agenda? He didn't kill in the name of universal healthcare. The only reason this is being mentioned is because some conservatives are terrified of being blamed for this horrible, murderous, and cowardly act.

Candace Owens, "conservative" political activist, also got it wrong when she called for a discussion on the "bi-partisan issue of mental health."[43] She's completely missing the point. Maajid Nawaz, a counter-extremism activist and former member of Islamist group Hizb ut-Tahrir, rightly noted her hypocrisy for refusing to acknowledge this was a white supremacist terror attack. It is wrong to label white terror attacks a product of "mental health problems" and not do the same when a Muslim commits an act of terror. It stigmatizes those with mental health issues, too. The sad fact is that there are white supremacist terrorists out there, and they appear to be more active than ever.

Conservatives are making a tactical error by trying to point out that these shooters are not "true" conservatives. I mean, of course they're not.

Going on the defense doesn't work.

If you are a conservative and you condemn the attack, then just condemn the attack. Don't get drawn into a web of explaining how the attacker was really a far-left activist when it's a massive stretch. It makes conservatives look like we're in a state of denial. Mostly because many actually are.

---

43 Candace Owens (@RealCandaceO), "'He was a registered Democrat!' 'But he had Trump-supporting tweets!' Twitter sucks tonight. Can we not make #ElPaso a Left or Right issue and instead mourn a horrible tragedy together as Americans? Maybe for once we can discuss the bi-partisan issue of mental health?" Tweet, August 3, 2019, https://twitter.com/realcandaceo/status/1157839844325937153.

That energy can be better spent analyzing what the far right really is, and why it exists in the first place.

THE THREE-PRONGED ATTACK

The reason I decided to write about far-right extremism isn't because I think it's the biggest danger to Western civilization, but because I think it is *one* piece of a bigger puzzle that nobody seems to be willing to solve. The West faces terrible trouble in the near future thanks to practically uncontrolled migration from countries whose populations hate us and our way of life. I predict growing tensions on the streets of working-class towns because of alien hostile cultures that have divided communities. Far-left attacks on innocent people are more frequent than ever, with people being struck over the head with bike locks and bricks on university campuses and others beaten up and hospitalized for trying to report on protests.

Far-right extremism is not the only threat, and Islamic attacks *are* more deadly on average. But there is an extremely important reason why far-right terrorism needs to be tackled right now, and by people who have an interest in actually putting a stop to it.

Currently, the only outspoken critics of far-right extremism are far-left extremists. These are ideologues who in some instances are paid by the government and in other instances paid for by wealthy benefactors. They work full time, writing blogs, belittling, demeaning, and smearing people. The Insider's Blog from activist group HOPE not hate in the UK is a great example of this. Read it and you'll be presented with analysis of the current events within the "far right" scene in the UK. Each blog entry is written in a sneering tone, discussing personal battles between different members of the far right. You'll also find entries about populists in a clear attempt at blurring the lines between democratic populism and far-right extremism. Their focus on Anne Marie Waters, the leader of For Britain, is representative of this. Love her or hate her, she isn't a neo-Nazi—but the HOPE not hate website might have you believe otherwise.

Waters is a former member of the British Labour Party, a socialist party. She is a feminist, originally from Ireland, a vegan, and an animal welfare activist. She has the support of Morrissey (yes, Morrissey), and has spent her adult life campaigning for our National Health Service. But she committed the crime of pointing out the terrible way much of the Islamic world treats women and children, and suddenly HOPE not hate obsessively began writing about her as if she is somehow on par with Jack Renshaw, the neo-Nazi from my hometown who tried to kill our local MP.

Let me give you another example. Their website wrote about the 2019 leadership election for the British National Party. The party doesn't really have many members anymore, but it's still around, and there were two people running for its leadership. One of the candidates, David Furness, isn't exactly a great orator. And, it's this that HOPE not hate picked up on. Instead of providing an unbiased analysis of what the BNP is, why it is dangerous, and why it exists, they chose to mock and sneer instead. In an article about the leadership election, they referred to Furness as a "bore in a suit" and superimposed the faces of current leadership figures onto the bodies of well-known dodgy dealers from *Only Fools and Horses*, an old British sitcom.[44]

HOPE not hate *could* serve a really important function. It could be a genuinely counter-extremist organization that works to understand why people become radicalized, but instead, they spend their time cracking jokes and behaving like bitchy teenage girls who are out to ruin the lives of the girls they don't like. Even their annual report, the "State of Hate" report (which is usually launched each year in a room full of elected politicians and media figures) is littered with personal opinion and attacks. 2018's report included me, of course, right alongside Britain's most notorious neo-Nazis. The inclusion of me and a host of other people who have simply expressed the view that *mass immigration of people from the third world might not necessarily be a good thing*, could easily be seen as a page-filling exercise, but it's really much more than that. This report, and the work by groups like this, is calculated.

These people know just how terrified the politicians and media are of being called racist, and they have used that to gain influence and power. They have all the money they need, all the public support they need from the politicians, and it all allows them to dedicate their professional lives to defaming political opponents. They're so blatant about it, too. In the last State of Hate report, they simply referred to me as "uncharismatic" and moved on very quickly to personally attack somebody else.

Charming.

---

44 "BNP Leadership Election Is All About the Money," HOPE not hate, July 7, 2017, https://www.hopenothate.org.uk/2019/07/07/bnp-leadership-election-is-all-about-the-money/.

This is why I have taken it upon myself to tackle this issue. Far-right extremism exists, and it isn't properly understood because those in the anti-far-right industry are purposely misrepresenting what it is. They are ideologues through and through who do not care about taking on the challenge of far-right extremism at all. If everyone were to convert to Islam or become communists tomorrow, they'd be out of a job and left to struggle on a job market that doesn't really have much of a demand for Keyboard Warrior graduates with a major in Picking Arguments.

If conservatives, or those who don't subscribe to far-left progressive ideology, do not face up to the issue of far-right extremism, then the ideologues win. As more and more young white boys become radicalized and more violence occurs, the likes of HOPE not hate and the SPLC cash in. Far-left ideologues can claim they were right all along, they'll blame the entire populist/conservative/nationalist movement, and then the far-left wins. Conservatives will never have any influence in popular media ever again, it will become increasingly impossible to host conservative events, and huge sections of society will be forced to shut up or go underground. We're already seeing it happen.

We cannot entrust matters of countering extremism with extremists. We cannot trust ideologues who consider those they are "researching" to be political opponents. Instead, we must address this far-right issue and take it out of the hands of dangerous far-left radicals who openly advocate for open borders and the deconstruction of Western civilization. We must work, in good faith, to solve the problem of young white men becoming radicalized, and the only way to stop it is understanding why it exists in the first place.

In the next three chapters, I will propose a theory. I believe that the radicalization of young, white, working-class men in the UK and America is the result of a three-pronged attack. Young white men are being radicalized by people who profit from their radicalization.

I suggest that a complicit and lazy media class, negligent politicians, and an emboldened far left are creating a new generation of far-right extremists. They are creating the monster they claim to fight by attacking from three angles, surrounding vulnerable people and forcing them underground or way over the top.

CHAPTER FOUR

A NEGLIGENT POLITICAL CLASS

The first part of the three-pronged attack on the white working class comes from the political classes. Modern politicians are, for the most part, completely unrepresentative of society. Political parties frequently nominate candidates completely out of touch with regular life—and when they do nominate someone seemingly "average," they often turn out to be far-left ideologues. Congresswoman Alexandria Ocasio-Cortez was just a humble bartender, but she's also a far-left radical who's wildly unpopular with most of the voting public.

So many politicians have no idea what it's like to be a normal person, getting up early in the morning and catching a bus to go to work, watching the people on the television telling us what to think, trying to raise a couple of kids and keep up with bills.

Worse, those same politicians refuse to even consider the possibility that their policies might be hurting the people they're meant to represent. They refuse to believe that mass immigration might not necessarily be a good thing, and they refuse to even consider changing course. Instead, they align themselves with far-left extremists and double down by calling their own constituents racists.

Emily Thornberry is the Labour Party MP for Islington South and Finsbury in London. In 2014, she was forced to resign from the Labour front bench during a by-election in Rochester and Strood. Upon noticing a house with a white van out front and English flags draped from the windows, Thornberry snapped a photo and made a sneering remark on Twitter. In the UK, the idea of a "white van man" is symbolic of the working class. A working-class man, whether he's a plumber or a builder, might use a white van for work.

A white van man and his family are the backbone of British society. But Thornberry, an elected MP for a party that is traditionally meant to represent the working class, seemed disgusted by the homeowner's very visible support of the England football team.

Dan Ware, the homeowner, said, "I will never forget how insulting Emily Thornberry was to me and Britain's working-class voters when she tweeted a picture of my house in 2014."

A tweet doesn't seem like much, but it was more a manifestation of an out-of-touch politician's hatred for normal people. Thornberry let the mask slip for a minute, and she had to step down from her prominent role in the Labour Party because of it. Of course, these days, she's on the TV all the time. Funnily enough, she was an advocate of remaining in the European Union after the British people (largely the working class) voted to leave in 2016.

There's so much more to this than just their casual disgust of the working class. Mostly left-wing politicians (though there are many so-called "conservatives" who fit in this category, too) are perfectly willing to advocate wildly unpopular immigration policies because they know they're creating a new, more reliable voting demographic. In the UK, politicians ignored the rape of thousands of English girls for decades. In the US, illegal immigration from across the southern border has been left unchecked—and those who have entered the US illegally are being handed out driving licenses and promised access to free healthcare by every Democratic presidential candidate in the 2020 race.

The politicians don't get it. They don't care about regular people—or at least, they're not acting like they care. They are negligent, and for all their talk of wanting to crush the "far right," they're radicalizing young (mostly) men who (rightly) feel like nobody is willing to listen to their concerns about how mass immigration changes communities and impacts the job market.

As long as politicians claim to represent the working class while categorically failing to address the social problems that come with a policy of state-sponsored multiculturalism and mass immigration, young men will feel completely ignored. Dismissing uncomfortable topics because it might make for difficult TV news interviews breeds anger. Some people put their head down, mutter under their breath, and get on with their life knowing that the politicians just don't care about them. Others get angry and become more politically aware, but know they're facing many years of activism before anything really changes. I couldn't tell you how many times I've heard activists tell me that they only remain politically active out of a sense of duty and believe their efforts ultimately will come to nothing because the politicians just don't care.

A small minority, but I believe a minority that is growing in size, turns to more radical measures to make their point.

The negligence of our politicians is a monumental failing of our political system and every politician who refuses to listen to their constituents deserves to lose their job immediately. What they are doing is dangerous, and the story of Jack Renshaw shows why.

BLACKPOOL AND THE RAPE OF BRITISH GIRLS

In the last chapter, I introduced you to Jack Renshaw. He's a young man who, at the age of twenty-three, was convicted of preparing an act of terrorism and threatening to kill a police officer. He is an avowed neo-Nazi who gave a Hitler salute as he was jailed for planning to kill Labour MP Rosie Cooper.

I can't remember the first time I met him, but I do remember that we met through our mutual interest in a campaign in the seaside town of Blackpool relating to the death of a young girl. This was very much the case that dragged me into politics, and it was the same with Jack.

In the town's heyday, Blackpool was a thriving seaside resort where working-class families would go for summertime holidays or fun days out. These days, it's a town hit by poverty and mass immigration. It's a town that has changed for the worse, and it's also where a fourteen-year-old girl named Charlene Downes went missing after falling victim to a grooming gang in the area.

Charlene disappeared in 2003, and to this day her body has not been found. She is presumed dead. Her case was one of the very first instances reported of the grooming and rape of young non-Muslim girls by predominantly Muslim men in England. A 2003 police report, which wasn't publicized at the time, found that children as young as eleven in Blackpool were being targeted by Muslim pedophiles who owned takeaway and kebab shops in the town. The men were using cigarettes, alcohol, and food to groom young girls from poor backgrounds. At least sixty girls were reported to have been groomed and/or raped by workers at Blackpool takeaways around the time Downes went missing, and it is reported that the findings were suppressed for "reasons of political correctness."[45]

The Charlene Downes story is shocking not just because she was the victim of grooming gangs in the town. During the trial of the two men who were believed to have killed Downes, Iyad Albattikhi and Mohammed Reveshi, undercover recordings suggested that her body had been chopped up and disposed of in the back of a kebab shop they owned. Newspapers ran the story of a young girl who had been "chopped up" and "put into kebabs," triggering the circulation of wild rumors that drunk kebab shop frequenters had eaten Charlene. It's the most shocking story that, ultimately, may not actually be true. In recent years, ongoing investigations have shone a light on the poor quality of the audio used to make the case that the two suspects disposed of her body in this way.

New investigations suggest the murderer could in fact be a white British man, and that opens up an entirely different can

45 James Tozer, "Police 'Hid' Abuse of 60 Girls by Asian Takeaway Workers Linked to Murder of 14-Year-Old," *The Daily Mail*, April 7, 2011, https://www.dailymail.co.uk/news/article-1374443/Police-hid-abuse-60-girls-Asian-takeaway-workers-linked-Charlene-Downes-murder.html.

of worms. The people of Blackpool know the history of these two men.

It is possible that Reveshi and Albattikhi are innocent. Many would dispute that and remain convinced that they committed the crime, but whether they killed her or not, it remains true that Reveshi admitted to a police officer before Charlene went missing that he had watched soft porn in a bedroom in his property with two nine-year-old girls. Home videos taken by Reveshi were shown in a 2019 television documentary about the case, in which he filmed teenage girls in his garden, describing their "beautiful legs." In 2011, Reveshi's business partner Albattikhi was convicted of assault after he headbutted an eighteen-year-old girl.[46]

And the grooming gang issue in Blackpool remains. Charlene was a victim of it.

While the grooming and rape of young girls in Blackpool was committed predominantly by gangs of Muslim men, nobody really knows what happened to Charlene Downes and who was responsible for her murder. That didn't matter to the British National Party, of course.

Back in 2011, I went to Blackpool for a "Justice for Charlene" demonstration. It was the same protest movement that pulled Jack Renshaw into nationalist politics.

I drove there in my 1996 Renault Clio, my first car, which I was really proud of at the time. I still miss that thing, actually. It's the furthest I'd driven at the time, on the other side of my

---

46 Sam Chadderton, "Blackburn Man Jailed for Attack on Girl," *The Lancashire Telegraph*, June 20, 2011, https://www.lancashiretelegraph.co.uk/news/9094908.blackburn-man-jailed-for-attack-on-girl/.

county, and I was pretty nervous. I'm a generally shy person, and even more so back then. Politics toughened me up, but the idea of driving to a protest and meeting people I'd never met before was genuinely scary. But I felt compelled to go. I had to. Who else was going to stand up for British girls? If nobody else was willing to, wouldn't it be wrong for me to just stay at home and do nothing?

I parked in a multi-story car park in Blackpool, and I was running late. I dashed to where the protest was taking place and thankfully managed to introduce myself to a few people, grab some leaflets, and get going. We walked along the promenade by the sea, handing out leaflets to passersby and people dining in the beer gardens of restaurants and pubs on the front.

A lot of people there were shocked to see me, and some were even a little skeptical. The British National Party's protests were predominantly attended by middle-aged white men and women. Young people didn't typically turn up, and some immediately thought I was a plant. That's a theme that you'll hear a lot throughout the rest of this book, as I share my stories from inside this world. The fear of government plants and media spies is widespread and not unfounded.

I wanted to fit in as best I could, and I suppose this was the first time I found myself influenced by older people in this movement. While handing out leaflets, some chuckled about handing one to a black or Asian couple. It didn't really make much sense to me at the time—after all, the leaflets were calling for justice for Charlene Downes. But the nature of the BNP, being accused (falsely, I believed) of racism, meant handing leaflets to nonwhite people was kind of ironic. And it became a game of "who could give the most leaflets to nonwhite people."

While navigating my way around the chairs in a packed beer garden, handing leaflets to everybody I could, I happened to give one to a black lady enjoying a drink in the sunshine. I went back to the team of fellow canvassers and chuckled alongside them—I'd just taken part in their daft game and I felt like I was a part of the crowd. The suspicion gradually disappeared, people seemed more accepting, and we gathered with the other teams and arranged to go to a memorial service for Charlene.

I offered a lift to one woman who hadn't driven into town, and we walked back to my car to head to the service. We chatted a lot on that short drive, and she was genuinely kind and compassionate. She'd stood for the BNP before and she wanted to help me find my way around this new world of politics. She took me under her wing, and to this day I don't believe she held genuine hatred in her heart. She was one of many working-class people who had seen their hometowns completely and utterly transformed, and it was people like her that made me believe everything the press said about the BNP were just plain lies. The good faith of so many people couldn't possibly have been taken advantage of, surely? There was no way that the BNP's leadership were exactly what the press were saying, and the members just didn't know it, I thought. I was wrong.

We arrived at the memorial service for Charlene, where her family made some statements, there were prayers, and the leader of the BNP, Nick Griffin, said some words too. It was the first time I'd ever seen him in person, and I was excited to meet him and shake his hand. We took a photo together, and I briefly introduced myself to him.

That was the photo we took.

Things were wrapping up at this point and we didn't speak for long, but Griffin and I kept in touch and this served as a springboard for me to become more active in the party. My experience with the thoroughly decent people who were at that protest reaffirmed my belief that everything the press was saying was wrong, and that what we were doing was right.

No politicians seemed to be talking about the issues we were campaigning about, so how could we be wrong? If Blackpool's MP was nowhere to be seen on this issue, then wasn't it right we should be out protesting on the streets?

There was a lot of controversy surrounding the BNP's involvement with Charlene's campaign. Soon enough, a street protest organization called the English Defence League got on board and protested the lack of action and the perceived injustices in the case. It was huge, and many people decried the involvement from the far right—but looking back, I can't help but wonder what those critics really expected to happen.

Not a single mainstream political party in the UK was willing to address this issue. It was completely ignored. Elected councilors ignored the ongoing grooming and rape of English and non-Muslim girls, and the only people who seemed willing to talk about the issue were far-right organizations and parties. This is how negligent politicians—people who are meant to be *representative* of their constituents—allowed far-right extremists to recruit perfectly normal, decent people.

This isn't hyperbole. The failure of elected politicians to take on cases like Charlene's across other parts of England is well-documented, and excellently summarized in the book *Easy Meat* by Peter McLoughlin. In his book, he notes that when the parliamentary committee reported on instances of localized grooming cases back in 2013, two councils were singled out for having failed particularly badly. A Home Affairs Select Committee Report read:

> Both Rochdale and Rotherham councils were inexcusably slow to realise that the widespread, organised sexual abuse of children, many of them in the care of the local authority, was taking place on their doorstep… That it took so long for anybody, at any level from the Chief Executive downward, to look at reports of young girls with multiple, middle-aged "boyfriends", hanging around takeaways, drinking

> and taking drugs, and to think that it might be worth investigating further, is shocking.[47]

There was no political will from the politicians at a local level, or at a national level, to tackle this problem.

In an interview with BBC Radio 4 on October 19th, 2018, former chief crown prosecutor for North-West England Nazir Afzal showed just how little the government cared about this issue.

He said:

> You may not know this, but back in 2008 the Home Office sent a circular to all police forces in the country saying 'as far as these young girls who are being exploited in towns and cities, we believe they have made an informed choice about their sexual behaviour and therefore it is not for you police officers to get involved in.'

That's exactly the kind of thing that breeds discontentment and anger among working-class voters, particularly when this happens almost exclusively in working-class areas.

When monsters live on the same street as you, your daughter or sister isn't safe to be outside alone, and the politicians don't want to do anything about it (or blame the girls), you bet that's going to radicalize young white men. Did the politicians in Westminster ever think what it must be like to have a young girl in their family groomed, drugged, and raped by gangs of people from alien cultures and no desire to integrate into

47 Home Affairs Select Committee Report, op. cit., p. 27, https://publications.parliament.uk/pa/cm201314/cmselect/cmhaff/68/68i.pdf.

regular British life? These people are monsters, but they didn't live on the same streets as the politicians.

So, is it any wonder that when a far-right political party took up the Charlene Downes case and fought for justice for her family, young lads like me and Jack Renshaw got involved? Is it really a surprise to anybody that young, angry white lads would turn to this realm of politics to try and do something about the horrible crimes being committed?

Over the years, I realized that the BNP profited from the issue. It's clear now that the Downes case isn't so cut and dry, and we might never know what really happened—but the thousands of other cases of this happening to young girls meant that the protest was brimming with righteous anger. It was a long journey for me, realizing that while the main parties clearly didn't care, the likes of Nick Griffin saw the case as political gold. I don't doubt for a moment that he cared about the young rape victims—but I do recognize this was a great opportunity to recruit, and recruit he did.

I'm still fighting to raise awareness in whatever way I can about the abuse of young girls. My election campaign in Batley and Spen was by far the most politically significant thing I've done on that issue, and it was purely the result of me being young, hot-headed, and angry. For me, my anger and resentment of politicians who seemed unwilling to do anything about the rape of young children culminated in me running an extremely controversial and angry political campaign. But it wasn't the same for other young men.

I've learned to control my anger and look at things differently. The likes of Jack Renshaw, however, just carried on down that rabbit hole, becoming more extreme along the way. It's sadly a common story.

THE TRANSFORMATION OF PENNSYLVANIA AND WORKING-CLASS AMERICA

I didn't talk about the United States in the last section because I'm aware the issue of Muslim grooming gangs is mostly confined to Europe. But the issue of mass immigration and the transformation of towns and cities is relevant on both sides of the Atlantic. Both Europe and the United States have seen whole towns and cities fundamentally transformed by mass immigration, and it doesn't affect the rich.

The city of Hazleton in Pennsylvania is a sorry tale of a city that was once a coal powerhouse, a shining example of a working American city, that has been fundamentally transformed without the permission or consultation of residents to a majority-immigrant/Hispanic/Latino city. A series of measures taken by Mayor Lou Barletta in 2006 were slammed as racist at the time, and ever since, the transformation of the city has been hailed a great success. Not by the residents who were chased out, and not by Mayor Barletta, but by the overwhelmingly left-wing press and Democratic advocacy groups.

Mayor Barletta had attempted to crack down on the hiring of illegal immigrants in the city early on, after council members passed the Illegal Immigration Relief Act. The measure was designed to stop local businesses from hiring illegal immigrants over local people, as well as renting properties to illegal immigrants. The legislation would create a fine of one hundred dollars for every illegal immigrant that was hired or rented to. Not a huge fine, in the grand scheme of things. Companies save huge sums of money by hiring illegals, and a measly fine is barely enough to make these unethical employers sit up and listen—but that doesn't mean Barletta wasn't slammed as racist and every other kind of "ist" you can think of.

In 2018, Barletta gave an interview to Tucker Carlson on Fox News.[48] He explained how in the year 2000, the "English as a second language" program in the Hazleton area school district had a budget of just $500. Five years later, it had increased to $1.5 million. That's a huge change, and it's a huge reallocation of local taxpayer's money. When huge groups of new immigrants are taken in, a lot changes. The local community looks different, the stores are different, the schools are different, and the local government's budget looks different. It's not about race and it's not about hatred, it's about local people having a say over how their local government works and the kind of city or town they live in. The people of Hazleton had no choice, and it has changed beyond all recognition.

The Hispanic/Latino population of Hazleton increased from 4.9 percent in 2000 to over 54 percent in 2017.

More than anything, a change like this dislocates the local community, breeds resentment and anger, and changes the very nature of working-class America. European Americans—or even American citizens whose families have been in the country for generations already—are being replaced by new immigrants who don't all necessarily want to fit in or abide by the law. A small quantity of immigrants who want to adapt to the American way of life are usually welcomed with open arms by Democrats and Republicans alike, but the huge numbers that Hazleton has seen over the years are quite different.

---

48 "Hazleton 'Transformed Forever': Tucker, GOP Rep Talk Mass Demographic Changes via Liberal Immigration Policies," Fox News, March 27, 2018, https://insider.foxnews.com/2018/03/27/tucker-carlson-illegal-immigration-hazleton-transformed-hispanic-illegal-immigration-lou.

Most of the Hispanic/Latino immigrant population in Hazleton come from the Dominican Republic. With the change in the local population came a change in local culture, with some immigrants completely unaware of local laws and customs. Crime generally has increased, and many immigrants seem to show little to no regard for the law.

Illegal parties are taking place in private properties across Hazleton, where immigrants gather to illegally purchase and consume alcohol. The property owners have no state licenses, and the parties are hosted entirely for the immigrant communities who live parallel lives. Jeff Cusat, the mayor of Hazleton since 2016, said he won't "put up with this stuff" and, "I've been saying for years, we need to inform the people moving here from the Dominican Republican what our local laws are."[49]

In a piece published by the North Jersey Record, as part of a series focusing on the issues that Trump-voting regions care about, local people explained how they felt about their new neighbors. Following a major police bust of an illegal Dominican gathering, a fifty-four-year-old FedEx warehouse security guard said, "The town has turned into garbage."

Even a native of Puerto Rico who moved to Hazleton with her husband from New York told the North Jersey Record that the "quality of life has gone down."

Local people don't invent concerns. They respond to them. The rapid change of this town has not been overwhelmingly accepted, and why should it have been? The politicians were very keen for it to happen, but what about the people? Not only do the politicians seem to want to avoid listening in

49 Shon Gables, "Friday Morning News Brief," North Jersey, November 20, 2011, https://eu.northjersey.com/story/news/columnists/mike-kelly/2018/10/10/us-immigration-divide-stands-hazleton-pa/13812330.

the first place, they regularly attack other politicians who *are* willing to listen. As I write this book, former vice president Joe Biden is taking aim at President Trump, heavily implying that he supports white supremacy.

On his campaign trail, and even in his first video announcing his candidacy, Biden suggested that Trump was enabling or supporting white supremacists. Following the El Paso shooting in August 2019, he even suggested that the president's message denouncing white supremacy was disingenuous.

Biden's not the only one guilty of it. Every single major candidate for president on the Democrat side implies or says outright that the President is racist, seemingly forgetting that half of the country voted for him. Candidate Kamala Harris told CNN that it was "no longer really a debatable point" that President Trump encourages white supremacy.[50]

When they attack the president and suggest his policy of wanting to curb illegal immigration and straighten out normal immigration laws is "racist," they are alienating themselves from half of the American population. They are calling the nonimmigrant population of Hazleton racists, and they are doing everything in their quite substantial power to completely delegitimize any honest concern about immigration levels.

Meanwhile, American people are suffering. Illegal immigration, and even legal immigration in so many cases, is transforming the face of American towns and cities, hurting job opportunities for citizens, and aiding the drug crisis.

---

50 Ian Schwartz, "Kamala Harris: 'No Longer a Debatable Point' That Trump Is a White Supremacist, Has No Empathy," *RealClear Politics*, August 9, 2019, https://www.realclearpolitics.com/video/2019/08/09/kamala_harris_no_longer_a_debatable_point_that_trump_is_a_white_supremacist_possesses_hate.html.

Politicians so willingly use the issue of child separation at the border as a stick to beat President Trump with, despite the practice being implemented during the Obama administration. The fact that children are separated from criminal parents who get arrested every day in America is completely ignored, while politicians suggest illegal immigrants should be given special rights to break the law without being separated from their children. Equally, the issue of child trafficking by illegals at the border seems to be completely ignored because it's just too good an opportunity to attack Trump and his voters to miss. Some go as far as suggesting that the president is operating "concentration camps" at the border (I'm of course talking about freshman gobshite Congresswoman Alexandria Ocasio-Cortez). The fact that anybody in these "concentration camps" is free to go if they decide to go back to Mexico is, again, ignored.

The concept of sanctuary cities is fiercely defended by most or all of the Democratic Party, too.

Meanwhile, Americans are left behind. The victims of illegal immigration are ignored or brushed aside. The only politicians willing to represent these people are some Republicans in Congress, though there are still plenty of elected officials in the Republican Party who would side with the out-of-touch and negligent Democrats on this issue.

In the summer of 2019, Immigration and Customs Enforcement officials and workers from the Pacific Northwest issued a press release that contained details of cases of rape and murder committed by illegal aliens protected by sanctuary city laws.[51]

---

51 Jack Buckby, "ICE Releases Chilling List of Rapists and Murderers Protected by Sanctuary Laws," *The Western Journal*, June 26, 2019, https://www.westernjournal.com/ice-releases-chilling-list-rapists-murderers-protected-sanctuary-laws/.

One of the most disturbing examples given was the story of illegal alien Francisco Carranza-Ramirez, who raped a wheelchair-bound woman from Seattle twice. Carranza-Ramirez was expected to self-deport back to Mexico after serving time in prison and being released. Although he did, in fact, go back to Mexico, he assaulted the same victim in Seattle once again before doing so.

Another example involved illegal alien Rosalio Ramos-Ramos. An immigration detainer requested by ICE was denied, and when released from a jail in Washington, he went on to murder and dismember a victim.

ICE detailed many instances when current sanctuary city laws allowed illegal criminals to roam free and murder, assault, and rape innocent people. That is not to say every immigrant entering the United States is a criminal, or even that every illegal alien is intending to hurt somebody—but for every person that is hurt by an illegal alien who should never have been allowed into this country, the politicians have blood on their hands. Every single politician who defended laws that stopped ICE from detaining these murderers and rapists has been complicit in these tragedies, and in the radicalization of American people who are tired of having their legitimate concerns ignored.

It should come as no surprise that in Pennsylvania, a state that has seen its fair share of mass immigration (both legal and illegal), genuine far-right activists are out recruiting and campaigning. In 2018, federal prosecutors charged six people, all members of the "Aryan Strike Force," with drug and weapons offenses.[52] The white supremacist and neo-Nazi group was believed to have

---

52 John Beauge, "Two Purported Aryan Strikeforce Members Agree to Plead Guilty," *Pennsylvania Real-Time News*, January 30, 2019, https://www.pennlive.com/news/2018/03/two_purported_aryan_strikeforc.html.

been plotting a suicide attack at a far-left protest. Prosecutors said that one of the group's members, who was terminally ill, was willing to hide an explosive device in an oxygen tank and blow himself up.

Also in Pennsylvania, in 2016, a branch of the KKK began recruiting and received press attention when a regional newspaper accidentally promoted one of their flyers. In an article about KKK recruitment, *The Press Enterprise* published a flyer that had been distributed to hundreds of homes, leading people to believe the paper was advertising the group.

The leader of the Pennsylvania state chapter of the National Socialist Movement, a group that dates back to the 1970s, told *The Washington Post* that meetings happen every month, and that there's "more collaboration." Again, this is nowhere near on the same level as the thousands of Antifa protestors out on the street bashing people's face in with bricks, but it's concerning, nonetheless. The circumstances are just right for angry young white lads to be taken in by these groups, either online or in person. There's never been a better time, because as long as Antifa are out there calling for the death of white men, there will be recruiting material for young white men who want to see the death of the Jews who, they say, pull the strings of organizations like Antifa.

It seems to me that there is quite a significant difference between the far right in the UK and in the US, though. In the UK, the far right typically organizes on a group level in pretty much the same way they always have. Sure, more young members of far right and neo-Nazi groups are communicating online (and some may never even leave their house and talk to someone else on their wavelength), but they still typically get together for nationalist meetings, bootcamp sessions, or pub meetups. I expect this is partly cultural and partly geographical. The UK is much smaller than the US, and it's really not all that hard to travel to the other side of the country and back in a single day.

In the US, it's quite different. The country is much bigger, and neo-Nazis have further to go to rally, protest, or organize. That's what made the Charlottesville rally in 2017 so disturbing. It's a sight nobody had really seen since the days of the KKK, and even though it drew only hundreds, it showed that this strain of far-right extremism isn't going away. Those hundreds at the Charlottesville rally represented a much larger community of people who communicate entirely online.

I still find it utterly amazing that there are some people who just flat out deny the existence of the far right just because it means the far left are (sort of) right about something. Neo-Nazis and real far-right extremists are very prominent online, and the recent ruling that Andrew Anglin must pay out $14 million in damages to a Jewish woman is all the evidence you should need.[53] Anglin, perhaps one of the most well-known neo-Nazi trolls on the internet, subjected Tanya Gersh to years of intimidation and harassment after publishing her personal information on the Daily Stormer website. His army of neo-Nazi trolls went after the woman. She received voicemails from people telling her to kill herself, and saying that people will take pleasure in her pain.

53 Mallory Simon and Sara Sidner, "Neo-Nazi Website Founder Ordered to Pay $14M for Troll Storm," CNN, August 8, 2019, https://edition.cnn.com/2019/08/08/us/montana-jewish-woman-federal-judgment-neo-nazi-soh/index.html.

The case was picked up by the SPLC and taken to court on Gersh's behalf. Again, we can't allow the fact that the left was right about something cloud our vision here. These online trolls exist, and they do terrible things. I've been at the receiving end of this in the past, and I know how difficult it can be. There is a cult-like group of neo-Nazis online, most or many from the US, who can't organize in real life and instead spend their time subjecting their political opponents to pure terror in their everyday lives.

The fact that these neo-Nazis organize predominantly online is what made the Charlottesville "Unite the Right" rally in 2017 so surprising. Hundreds of neo-Nazis turned up, along with some regular old conservatives who were duped into attending under the "unite the right" message, and you know the rest. It descended into violence—largely because of the massive violent Antifa presence who didn't seem to realize that turning up in opposition to these things is the worst way to deal with the problem. That's not to say the neo-Nazis were without fault, but it's very commonly the case that violence at right-wing or far-right events is triggered by aggressive counter-protesters. That being said, there's plenty of footage of Unite the Right attendees mindlessly knocking the crap out of people over politics. Livestream footage from the event shows a number of white nationalists physically attacking an older man who announced he was a representative of the SPLC. I'm no fan of the SPLC for reasons I've explained, but the violence against the man was clearly unwarranted.

The murder of one person and injuring of two dozen others by Alex Fields, a neo-Nazi who drove a car into a crowd of people during the protest, has no doubt set back American neo-Nazis' desire to assemble publicly. But it won't stop them continuing to recruit online. For as long as politicians continue ignoring very real concerns about mass immigration or illegal immigration and smearing those who are willing to stand up for the regular people who are concerned about it, these far-right extremists will gain power. It doesn't matter how many people are hurt by them along the way, because when the politicians are so unimaginably negligent and refuse to represent the concerns of the people who elect them, conspiracy theorists and extremists start to make sense.

The power of political negligence is evident in the election of Donald Trump in 2016. Here we had a man who echoed the kind of policy proposals coming out of the populists in Europe, appealing to Americans. It doesn't really make much sense. Populists in Europe tend to be more collectivist, concerned about national identity, and even happy to pay into benefit systems and universal healthcare. Quite different from the American right. Trump seemed to echo this collectivist, culturist rhetoric and it somehow worked. The American people had been let down so badly, and the very identity of America was so clearly under threat from the most radical incarnation of the Democratic Party yet, that European populism came to their shores and they welcomed it with open arms.

And how did the left respond? By calling Trump and his supporters Nazis.

The Democratic Party and far-left ideologues in the United States should thank their lucky stars that Donald Trump is as moderate as he is. He doesn't want to close America's borders completely, he isn't a racist or a white supremacist, and he's been a donor to multiple Democratic campaigns over the years. And America is faring well with him in charge.

Had he lost that election and Hillary Clinton won, the likes of Alexandria Ocasio-Cortez and her "squad" of feminist congressional windbags would have notably more power than they do now. That would have disenfranchised the American working class even further, and who knows what kind of traction neo-Nazis could have gained. Donald Trump is a relief valve—he took that bubbling anger from working class America who were being smeared by the political class, and he took action. He started giving people the change they had been asking for, spoke up for those without a voice, and helped steady the righteous anger from the forgotten people of America. He also fought back against far-left ideologues, though that war is nowhere near over.

Had Trump not done that, the far left would have something real to worry about. A bigger, stronger, angrier class of people who would have had nowhere to turn but the real far right.

Smear and abuse good people at your peril. It quickly creates monsters.

WELFARE AND POVERTY

The negligence of politicians, particularly in the UK, can be seen in the shocking state of employment. The Conservative government touts figures suggesting employment is higher than ever, conveniently ignoring the issue of underemployment.

Official employment figures consider those working under a "zero-hour contract"—meaning they are not guaranteed a set number of hours at work every week—to be officially employed. Receive three hours of work every week and the government considers you gainfully employed and free from trouble. And if you need to claim benefits to supplement your income because you're unable to find full-time employment, the Conservative government's Universal Credit system is there to help—in theory. In practice, not so much.

Universal Credit was a system implemented by the Tory government that was designed to streamline the welfare system, combining six different benefits and tax credits. In theory, it's simpler than the individual benefits and credits—in practice, it has hit the poorest really hard. The rollout of the new system was controversial, flawed, and left many struggling people with no income at all. It led to the rise of the use of food banks in many of the most impoverished parts of Britain.

Hartlepool, a town in the northeast of England hit hard by unemployment, was one of the towns chosen to test the scheme. At the time of writing, there are at least seven food banks and charities now operating in the town providing essential food and services to people who spend weeks and months with no income at all, waiting for Universal Credit payments to kick in.

The town is one of the most unemployed parts of Britain. In 2017, it was briefly the most unemployed part of the country, moving to the second most unemployed shortly after. It has also been at the receiving end of major spending cuts. Local spending was slashed by 33 percent between 2010 and 2017. Funding from the central government is also expected to drop by 45 percent by 2020. Meanwhile, crime is increasing, a local police station was shut down to save money, and local people are taking to the streets to take law enforcement into their own hands. Robberies are up, burglaries are up, drug use is up, and child poverty is worse than ever.

Between January and December 2017, data showed that 29.2 percent of households were workless,[54] 27.1 percent of children lived in workless households.[55] 2019 data showed that, after housing costs, 36 percent of all children in Hartlepool were living in poverty.[56]

This is still an overwhelmingly white English town, seemingly forgotten by the politicians—in particular, the Labour Party. Negligence from the politicians here meant that in 2015, Labour met its biggest challenge yet when the United Kingdom Independence Party (not traditionally a working-class party, but one that was willing to talk about immigration) came within just a few thousand votes of taking the seat from Labour. It is quite exceptional for anyone but Labour, the Tories, or the Liberal Democrats to win a seat in the Westminster Parliament.

Poverty in the United Kingdom hasn't gone unnoticed, either. The UK government might not want you to know about it, but the United Nations has been reporting on it for some time. In 2018, a report by the UN's Special Rapporteur

---

54 Bob Watson, "Households by combined economic activity status of household members by local authority: Table A1 LA," Office for National Statistics, July 30, 2019, https://www.ons.gov.uk/employmentandlabourmarket/peoplenotinwork/unemployment/datasets/householdsbycombinedeconomicactivitystatusofhouseholdmembersbylocalauthoritytablea1la.

55 ONS Annual Population Survey—households by combined economic activity status.

56 You can download the data underneath the "local data" section, by clicking "North East: Parliamentary Constituencies" and then choosing Hartlepool. http://www.endchildpoverty.org.uk/poverty-in-your-area-2019/.

on Extreme Poverty and Human Rights, Philip Alston, found the British government was in a "state of denial" about the impact of austerity policies on the poor.[57] The report found that Universal Credit was a good idea in principle, but that it was "fast falling into universal discredit."

Although arguably wrong in his analysis of Brexit, Alston did note that while the UK government had told him there was no extreme poverty in the UK, the British people feel differently. Hearing the testimonies of people Alston met during his time in the UK, the story seemed quite different. Perhaps he visited Hartlepool, where families are left without any meaningful job opportunities and rely on local food banks for cans of beans to feed their kids. I'm not exaggerating.

Alston's report noted that 14 million people in the UK—a fifth of our population—live in poverty. Four million of those people were over 50 percent below the poverty line[58], and 1.5 million of those are destitute and unable to afford basic essentials.[59] The Conservative government appears unwilling to admit this problem and continues celebrating its "success" with regards to employment. The Labour Party might well pretend they can do better, but Labour governments of the past have opened up the borders to millions of immigrants who

---

57 Philip Alston, "Statement on Visit to the United Kingdom," November 16, 2018, https://www.ohchr.org/Documents/Issues/Poverty/EOM_GB_16Nov2018.pdf.

58 Social Metrics Commission, "A New Measure of Poverty for the UK," September 17, 2018,https://socialmetricscommission.org.uk/wp-content/uploads/2019/07/SMC_measuring-poverty-201809_full-report.pdf.

59 Suzanne Fitzpatrick et al., "Destitution in the UK 2018," June 7, 2018, https://www.jrf.org.uk/report/destitution-uk-2018, 2–3.

have had an adverse effect on the job market and allocation of government funds.

So when British people learn that benefit claims by foreign nationals increased by over 40 percent between 2008 and 2013,[60] EU migrants claimed over £4 billion a year in benefits as of 2018,[61] and migrants from Africa, Bangladesh, Pakistan and Eastern Europe are more likely than Brits to claim benefits,[62] is it any wonder they get angry?

MASS IMMIGRATION AND THE COMPLACENCY OF MILLIONAIRE POLITICIANS

The negligence shown by politicians manifests itself largely in policies relating to immigration and the support of foreign nationals in the UK and the US. Although the conversation about immigration in the US seems to focus largely on illegal immigration over the southern border (at least for now), in the UK it's a wider and more complex issue.

---

60 Jack Doyle, "Number of Foreigners Claiming UK Benefits Leaps 41% in 5 Years: More Than 400,000 Now Handed Payouts That Cost Tax payers Billions Each Year," *The Daily Mail*, August 28, 2013, https://www.dailymail.co.uk/news/article-2405053/Foreigners-UK-benefits-leaps-41-5-years-400k-handed-payouts.html?fbclid=IwAR0kGW8U_L_FBZCaKhPxlCMOGFs2VACuDvoMiJ6LPdWi0bOvmDEBFi6y0KE.

61 David Wooding, "Migrants Benefits Bill: EU Migrants in Britain Claimed More Than £4bn a Year in Benefits," *The Sun*, March 11, 2018, https://www.thesun.co.uk/news/5776790/eu-migrants-in-britain-claimed-more-than-4bn-of-handouts-in-a-year/.

62 Anil Dawar, "Migrants 'Milking' Benefits System: Foreigners More Likely to Claim Handouts," Express, July 21, 2015, https://www.express.co.uk/news/uk/592541/Migrants-milking-benefits-system-Foreigners-more-likely-to-claim-handouts.

Between 1997 and 2010, net annual immigration into the UK quadrupled. The population increased by over 2.2 million. Labour Prime Minister Tony Blair opened the floodgates, and immigration into the UK has remained in the hundreds of thousands every year since. It has proven extremely unpopular, and the Tories have been promising to bring those numbers down to the "tens of thousands" since around 2010. They haven't succeeded.

That resulted in the immigration issue being closely tied with Brexit, and one of the driving factors behind the vote to leave the EU. However, the issue of immigration goes well beyond the EU, with most immigrants coming from outside of Europe.

With no change to our immigration policy in sight, voters have limited options to choose from if they want to vote for someone willing to change it. For a long time, voters turned to the BNP. Today, they turn to UKIP, the Brexit Party, and For Britain. Knowing just how difficult it is for new parties to break into Westminster—or just being conscious that nothing ever seems to change—some turn to more extreme politics and organizations to express their anger.

One of my favorite documentaries ever made is called *The Battle for Barking*. I don't love the documentary because it fills me with hope and optimism, or anything like that. I think it is an incredible piece of work that documented an election race that sums up the problem with political negligence perfectly. It was a film that followed BNP leader Nick Griffin during the 2010 General Election, where he was running for the Barking constituency. I was in college during the 2010 General Election, and I felt quite positive that Griffin was in with a good chance of winning the seat. People with more political experience knew that it was much more likely he could have come a strong second to Labour, eating into their majority and giving then-prime minister Gordon Brown a good political kicking.

In the end, Griffin came third. The Labour Party expertly mobilized the immigrant vote in the constituency and increased turnout so much that the white working-class people desperately voting for change and hoping the BNP would deliver it were crushed. Once again, the politicians told white residents that their views were abhorrent, and immigrants were more important. I'm sorry if that sounds brash, but it's true. Labour MP for Barking Margaret Hodge relied on the immigrant community to hold that seat, and her attitude throughout the documentary showed her contempt for concerned English people in her constituency. It also showed just how far detached she was from normal life, wrapped up in her millionaire lifestyle.

I remember a particular line from Griffin in the film that sums the issue up really well. Referencing Barking's radically changing demographics, the film maker asked why Griffin and his voters were opposed to it. "Because we were never asked," he responded.

And we weren't.

Barking is in the east end of London. A few decades ago, it was a bustling, British, Cockney part of London. Today it is one of the most multicultural parts of London, struggling with poverty, crime, and drugs. The white British people who stayed in the area have seen their community change around them, and they weren't ever asked if they were happy for it to change. In the documentary, Hodge knocked at the door of a voter to warn them about the threat of the BNP. A white woman answered the door and said:

"I think, not to do with race, colour, or creed, but we are having far too many immigrants…who can't get a job in England because they can't speak our language, we've got people here who can speak our language and they can't get jobs."

As she tells Hodge about her concerns, the lady's granddaughter appears around the door. She's mixed race.

Hodge tells her:

"The only thing I'd say to you is what we don't want is the BNP here. So even if you get cross with us…"

To which the voter responds with a long "hmm" and says:

"I don't know. I think whatever government is in, somebody's got to be brave enough…we are actually an island and there's only so many people we can retain anyway."

That's not the answer Hodge was hoping for. When a woman said that she would consider voting BNP while her mixed-race granddaughter stands beside her, you know something's not right.

Could it be that the British people didn't want to open the borders in the first place and would have said no if we were asked back in 1997?

It's the complacency of these politicians that really gets to me and that can easily push people to extremism. Hodge thought that she could knock on every door in Barking and convince them the BNP were dangerous, not realizing that it was her own party and its policies that were making the BNP so attractive.

I always tell people who watch this film to compare two particular scenes. The first is in a pub in Barking, where local

BNP activists are gathered to kickstart the election campaign. "Put something in the bucket!" an activist shouts as a bucket is passed around the pub and people put in handfuls of coins. These were people with not very much to give, offering what they could to try and make the campaign a success. They wanted to see real change in Barking, they wanted to see jobs come back to the area, and they wanted to stem the tide of mass immigration that had changed their community.

Compare that to the scene when Margaret Hodge is on the phone to one of her handlers in the Labour Party, in the back of her private car being driven by a chauffeur. Laughing, she's heard saying "What a bastard!" She's talking about Griffin's announcement that he'll be running against her.

"I've gotta turn the threat into an opportunity, this is my current state of mind you know," she said.

"Can I just, I mean, it would be great to meet…Can I just do the two immediate asks? One is, whatever I do, I need money, in a way that I didn't before. So what I'm after at the moment is sort of big donors, who give you know, a lot of money each."

"150? Yep."

The call ends.

Hodge is a millionaire with a family company that paid 0.01 percent tax on £2.1 billion of business in 2011.[63] She doesn't have to live amongst the crime and the drugs in Barking, and

63 Helia Ebrahimi, "Margaret Hodge's Family Company Pays Just 0.01pc Tax on £2.1bn of Business Generated in the UK," *The Telegraph*, November 9, 2012, https://www.telegraph.co.uk/finance/businesslatestnews/9668396/Margaret-Hodges-family-company-pays-just-0.01pc-tax-on-2.1bn-of-business-generated-in-the-UK.html.

her job allows her to see only the positive side of immigration. That is, meeting nice people on the doorstep and occasionally dealing with local issues for politically engaged immigrants who just want to get on in life and do well. Either she is completely unaware of the problems people face in the worst parts of Barking, or she doesn't care.

The difference between Hodge's fundraising style and the BNP's methods says it all. One campaign saw people with nothing giving as much as they could; the other saw Hodge calling in favors from her rich friends for what seemed to be a donation of £150,000. Which is interesting, given the spending limits in 2010 were around £30,000[64] (depending on the number of electors in each constituency). Whatever the 150 reference was, we know Hodge was seeking big money from her handlers—and we know it was easy for her to get.

If that doesn't show you how out of touch and negligent the politicians are, I don't know what does.

It's overshadowed only, perhaps, by the admission of Tony Blair's former speech writer and advisor Andrew Neather that the Labour government only opened the borders to "rub the Right's nose in diversity."[65]

Criminal negligence or orchestrated sabotage? You decide.

---

64 Isobel White, "Regulation of Candidates' Campaign Expenditure: The Long and the Short of It…" House of Commons Library, January 14, 2015, https://commonslibrary.parliament.uk/parliament-and-elections/elections-elections/regulation-of-candidates-campaign-expenditure-the-long-and-the-short-of-it/.

65 Tom Whitehead, "Labour Wanted Mass Immigration to Make UK More Multicultural, Says Former Adviser," *The Telegraph*, October 23, 2009, https://www.telegraph.co.uk/news/uknews/law-and-order/6418456/Labour-wanted-mass-immigration-to-make-UK-more-multicultural-says-former-adviser.html.

CHAPTER FIVE

A COMPLICIT MEDIA

The smearing and sneering attitude from establishment media outlets form the second part of the three-pronged attack that I believe is radicalizing predominantly young white men. After being ignored by the politicians, the forgotten people of America and Britain turn to the media to see if the issues they're concerned about are being reported on, or even advocated for by those with louder and more powerful voices. But they don't find anything like that. In fact, they find themselves at the receiving end of constant vitriolic abuse from entitled and snobbish (overwhelmingly) left-wing journalists.

In theory, the press could offer a voice that these people desperately need. Newspapers, news channels, and radio shows could provide an outlet for the people to vent their anger and make the politicians listen, but it's not happening. At least, it's not happening enough, or on behalf of *everybody*. The press appears to be acting as a check against the politicians, but only for the middle and upper classes. In the UK, the newspapers, radio shows, and TV shows take the politicians to task over Brexit because middle-class viewers and readers didn't vote for it. In America, they poke fun at Donald Trump's fake tan, call him and his supporters Nazis, and advocate for welfare and healthcare for illegal immigrants—because rich white families don't have to live near them.

I don't like conspiracy theories, and I don't like to try and attribute a common goal to a huge group of people working for different media companies and with different editorial positions. I would say, however, that there is a general direction in which the media collectively seems to be travelling. Western media outlets, for the most part, advocate for far-left political groups, organizations, and politicians. They dismiss the concerns of the working class and they try and silence anyone who even dares to try and stick up for the working class.

We saw that when former home secretary Jack Straw was criticized for saying the Pakistani community in Britain needs to "think much more clearly" about why the grooming of children is happening. He suggested that some Pakistani men saw white girls as "easy meat" and it was a national scandal. But this is something the working-class communities of Britain *know to be true* and had been wanting to hear for some time.

Jon Snow, a news presenter for Channel 4, showed his true colors in 2019 when he bemoaned the presence of white people at a Brexit rally on live television, saying:

"It has been the most extraordinary day. A day which has seen—I've never seen so many white people in one place. It's an extraordinary story,"

In August 2019, Ivanka Trump tweeted her opposition to white supremacy, labelling it an "evil that must be destroyed." A former CNN host responded with, "Fuck you Ivanka…Fuck you and your entire white supremacist family."[66]

66 Reza Aslan (@rezaaslan), "Fuck you Ivanka. Seriously. Fuck you and your entire white supremacist family," tweet, August 4, 2019, https://twitter.com/rezaaslan/status/1158095043804033024.

And when the media tries to portray Hazleton, Pennsylvania as a success story for immigration,[67] you just know these people (as a whole) feel nothing but contempt for the white working class. *To hell with their concerns. Screw their misfortune. We've got a diversity program to get on with and we'll stomp on anyone who tries to disrupt it.*

The media is utterly failing. It is representing the views of the wealthy elite and the far-left ideologues who now dominate our institutions. The regular people are just left behind, constantly smeared and derided by the modern church ladies who consider a crude joke a hate crime and the mere presence of white people *problematic*.

HERE'S WHERE THE MEDIA GOES WRONG

When it comes to the media's role in the three-pronged attack, there are a few key things that need to be addressed. The first is the usage of the term "far right." As a whole, Western media outlets seem unwilling to consider the possibility that their understanding of the term is wrong. If I was a glass-half-full kind of guy, I'd say the media just hasn't realized their mistake and has a lot to learn. But I'm not a glass-half-full kind of guy, and I think the glass has long since been knocked over and smashed.

Widespread use of the term "far right" shows just how little the media class, in general, understands the nuances in the ideological right. We're somehow expected to know the difference

67 Octavio Blanco, "How Latinos Are Saving This Former Pennsylvania Mining Town," CNN, September 2, 2016, https://money.cnn.com/2016/09/02/news/economy/hazleton-pa-latino-immigrant/index.html.

between intersectional genderfluidity and transfeminism, but these people seem to be blind to the difference between Israel-supporting conservatives or populists who are concerned about Islamic extremism, and far-right neo-Nazis who want to exterminate the Jews and forcefully repatriate all nonwhite people to their countries of ethnic origin.

The conflation between populists and neo-Nazis happens in American, British, and European press all the time. I've lost count of how many times President Trump has been referred to as far right. No matter how disagreeable one might find his position on illegal immigration (though frankly it's shocking there are people who advocate *for* illegal immigration), it is objectively inaccurate to refer to this man as far right, a white supremacist, or a neo-Nazi. His daughter converted to Judaism and his grandkids are Jewish, for Christ's sake. He's also disavowed white nationalism and the extreme right on multiple occasions—more than he's really ever needed to—not that anyone really cares. In fact, the press has repeatedly claimed that Trump hasn't disavowed white nationalism and white nationalists when he has.

The President is no secret Nazi. He has reduced black and Hispanic unemployment significantly, and he's very vocal about it. Far-right extremists don't like black and Hispanic people, and they won't pretend to like them to win favor. So, when Guardian writer Paul Jackson claims Trump "is the archetypal far-right charismatic leader,"[68] he's talking out of his arse. When

68 Paul Jackson, "Donald Trump Is the Archetypal Far-Right Charismatic Leader. But His Magic Won't Last," *The Guardian*, July 19, 2019, https://www.theguardian.com/commentisfree/2019/jul/19/donald-trump-archetypal-far-right-charismatic-leader.

Ishaan Tharoor writes "Trump's racism cements his party's place among the West's far right" for *The Washington Post*,[69] he's either being purposely disingenuous, or he's stupid. The total lack of understanding about what the far right really is is dangerous.

It's clear that the British media is equally oblivious to the difference between populists and far-right extremists. Their coverage of Katie Hopkins, Tommy Robinson, and even Nigel Farage makes that point.

Katie Hopkins shot to fame on British reality TV for her controversial opinions on pretty much everything, but she soon became a columnist, journalist, and political pundit. In recent years, she's moved toward counter-jihad populism, though she has maintained the forked tongue that made her famous in the first place. It would be fair to call her rude, aggressive, and angry—but a Nazi or "far right" she is not. You wouldn't think that reading the British (or even American) press, though. Ever since President Trump tweeted about her, it's difficult to find any article from mainstream outlets that doesn't call her "far right." But so far, Hopkins hasn't advocated the forceful deportation of nonwhite people, anti-Jewish conspiracy theories, or white supremacy. Until she does any of that, it's factually inaccurate to call her far right. Populist or nationalist loudmouth, maybe, but not far right.

The same goes for Tommy Robinson, the anti-Islam activist who became famous when he founded the English Defence

---

69 Ishaan Tharoor, "Trump's Racism Cements His Party's Place Among the West's Far Right," *The Washington Post*, July 15, 2019, https://www.washingtonpost.com/world/2019/07/16/trumps-racism-cements-his-partys-place-among-wests-far-right/.

League in 2009. The EDL was a street movement set up by working class lads in response to the increasing presence of Islamic radicals in the town of Luton. With local knowledge of Muslim men dealing drugs, grooming young girls, and preparing acts of terror, Robinson and others started protesting in the street. And there was violence. For years, the organization demonstrated against extreme Islam, and Robinson grew more and more popular with disenfranchised working-class people who saw (and still see) him as one of few people willing to speak out about radical Islam.

Robinson has a criminal record as long as your arm, which I obviously can't and won't defend. But that doesn't make him far right. Nor does his objection to Islam. The press, as well as advocacy groups like HOPE not hate, constantly use this "far right" term to describe Robinson, despite him growing up in one of the most diverse areas of the country, his closest friends being black, and him previously being convicted of assaulting a neo-Nazi who turned up to one of his rallies. Robinson has made it clear over and over again that he has no objection to nonwhite people living in Britain, and he's an avowed Zionist. He's the worst far-right extremist I've ever met.

I'm not defending either Hopkins or Robinson, but it's important to make it clear that you can't just call people who say controversial things "far right," no matter how much you might dislike them.

It's easy to label people who object to Islam or who want stricter immigration controls "far right." It shuts down the argument pretty quick, puts those people immediately on the defensive, diverts the discussion, and makes it easier for left-wing narratives to win. If you call someone a Nazi, then why would anyone ever want to listen to that Nazi ever again? It's an easy and powerful way of winning the argument, and that's why the politicians and members of the press so frequently do it. The politicians create this narrative, the media supports that narrative, and then the far-left ideologues and lackeys for the state enforce the narrative by violent force. But that's one for the next chapter.

This combination of willful deception of readers and viewers and the ignorance of quite important differences between different ideologies on the right is a driving force behind the emboldening of far-left ideologues *and* the disenfranchisement of the white working class. When you call everyone who opposes mass immigration and Islamization a Nazi, you make it impossible to even have a sensible discussion about these topics. You also make it far more likely that young lads will just embrace the neo-Nazis you're trying to fight.

So, the media, in general (yes, I'm generalizing here—the issue is so prevalent that it's really pointless talking about individual journalists) uses the term "far right" too widely. The term is attributed to people who simply are not far right. It is used as a weapon, and this irresponsible labelling of populists and nationalists as extremists is muddying the waters and making it impossible to actually identify and tackle the *real* far right.

When we can't tell the difference between a Tommy Robinson supporter who wants the government to do something about grooming gangs and a neo-Nazi who wants to murder an MP, then I think we're in deep trouble.

The press also seems unwilling to ask *why* young white men are turning to the far right in the first place. Any time there's a protest on the streets, the media jumps to call the protesters racist. They'll even send someone out with a camera to find the least eloquent member of the crowd and portray every single protester as a drunk hooligan or a fool. That's not to say drunk hooligans don't exist (in fact, you'll find plenty of them in any protest against mass immigration or Islamic extremism), but that doesn't mean the issue is made up.

Is it any wonder that the working class isn't interested in watching CNN or reading *The Guardian* when any discussion of illegal or mass immigration is automatically deemed racist or extreme?

Finding the least eloquent member of the crowd and portraying the entire group as thick is a common tactic, and it's not something the left does exclusively. The right does it a lot too, and I'm no fan of it. But when the press endorses this kind of behavior, it shows off the worst kind of snobbery. Not only does it show just how little middle-class members of the press think about the working classes of Britain and America, but it shows the lengths they'll go to in order to perpetuate the stereotype that normal, working-class people are stupid. I'll never forget the way the media covered the Tea Party back in the day. I was in college during the Tea Party protests, and I was first introduced to the way the media covered these patriots by my teacher.

The "journalist" found any member of the crowd who couldn't articulate themselves quite as well as a politician, asked them tough questions, and posted a compilation on YouTube for the world to watch and laugh. I thought it was despicable. There's a reason why not everyone is a politician. Some people have damn good reasons to support the political cause they do, but just don't have the skills to articulate themselves professionally. Let's not pretend that's exclusive to one side.

If the media class is unwilling to ask why young people are turning toward right-wing groups, and even more unwilling to ask why some young people are turning to *far-right* groups, then what is the point in their reports? What do reports about right-wing radicalism actually achieve, other than pushing negative stereotypes?

It's not just a matter of being unwilling to ask questions, either. It's a matter of refusing to engage with working class people at all. Unless they can get them on camera making a tit of themselves, the media doesn't seem interested. It infuriates me as a working-class person that whenever Brexit is discussed on the TV, all I see are millionaires, businessmen, and posh Tory boys who have never worked a day in their lives.

I'd suggest they put me on instead, but to be fair, I've pulled the odd controversial stunt or two on national television in the past. They're tactics that I no longer support, but which I engaged with at the time for all the right reasons. Over the years, I've obviously grown up a lot and found better ways to release my anger. I don't think shock tactics are as useful as I once thought they were, but regardless, my antics have meant that the TV networks are reluctant to put me back on camera. But there's no reason why the media shouldn't engage with other people *like* me on the issue of Brexit.

I won't name names, but the media seems particularly fond of putting a trust-fund Tory boy, from a wealthy family and who has never had a proper job in his life on the TV to talk about Brexit. He's young, he's privileged, and he's completely unrelatable. Instead, the television networks and news shows could offer a more well-rounded view of the Brexit issue if they invited working-class people to offer their views. After all, it was we, the working class, who overwhelmingly voted for Brexit in the first place—and we're not just a bunch of apes who sit around eating junk food and watching reality TV all day. We do have brains, and we might just shock people with our knowledge, insight, and opinions on Brexit.

INADVERTENTLY LENDING CREDIBILITY TO THE FAR RIGHT

This total inability to accurately define the far right (or even try), and the constant smearing of people who *aren't* far right, is inadvertently lending credibility *to* the far right. I think I'm being very generous when I say "inadvertently," as it could be argued it's in the media's interests to perpetuate the myth that everyone to the right of Jeremy Corbyn or Alexandria Ocasio-Cortez is "far right."

For argument's sake, let's say the media class isn't intentionally doing it. Here's how they're inadvertently lending credibility to the real far right.

Working class people aren't stupid. Political commentators writing for the newspapers, outraged columnists, and disingenuous far-left ideologues given airtime might think they can win people over to the left by smearing everyone as Nazis, but people don't buy it. You can shout about the mean and nasty racists who want stricter immigration controls all you like—it doesn't mean people are going to stop caring about mass/illegal immigration. When communities are being irreversibly changed, the job market hurt, and children raped by gangs of men who have no interest in assimilating to Western culture and ideals, people are going to shout from the rooftops about their problems.

Calling people racist doesn't mean the flaws of state-sponsored multiculturalism and mass immigration are solved. I know it's not nice to admit there might be problems that come along with immigration, and that not every single immigrant is an angel, but facts are facts and working-class people are hurting.

So, when the media lies, lies, and lies, why should anyone ever believe them when they say a party, a person, or an organization is racist? Think about it. When the BNP was at its height in the UK, the media was calling them racist at every possible opportunity. But when the media is calling everyone racist, and not even trying to understand the legitimate concerns of working people, why would anyone believe them? This lends credibility to the far right.

The media is the boy who cried wolf, and nobody believes him anymore.

That's one of the main reasons why I refused to believe that the BNP was racist when I was a teenager. The people I met, at least for the most part and for the first little while, were thoroughly decent. Before I was exposed to the hierarchy of the party where I met some real crackpots, loonies, and extremists, the average members were just like people from my hometown. They were mums and grandmas and dads and grandfathers who just wanted better for their kids and grandkids. Why would I believe the media over these people who, like me, had simply sought out a political home that was willing to take them in and stand alongside them?

I'm not saying that in hindsight the media was completely right. I really don't want to give much credit to the mainstream outlets at all. They weren't wrong about Griffin and a lot (but not all) of the people running the party, but they were wrong about most of the members. It was the demonization of BNP voters, members, and even some of its organizers and candidates that was totally wrong. Had the media been clearer, perhaps more people would have listened to them. But they weren't, and their smearing meant people like me (and a million others who voted for them in 2009) ignored them and went with our guts. After all, there was no one else to support.

It was only when I started attending the pretty serious nationalist events that I started to realize I was wrong. I should never have gotten this far into this mad world, but the media's warnings meant nothing, and I soon found myself at a meeting of the BNP and other members of its European party, the Alliance of European National Movements.

European parties are collections of different political parties represented in the European Parliament, united by their similar ideologies and political goals. The event I attended was the official launch of the group that took place at a hotel in Merseyside. I was surprised when I was told where it was being held, as nationalist meetings were usually held at grotty old pubs and the venue details very secretive. Most of the time, you don't even know where the event is being held, and you have to meet people at a rendezvous point to get the details on the day. Sadly, this is true even for regular right-wing and conservative events, owing to the obsessive nature of Antifa. The minute a venue is leaked, Antifa will shut it down—that is, if the venue hasn't rejected you themselves already.

But this time, the event was being held at an upscale hotel, and it turned out the only reason it happened was because the event was booked under the French variation of the name Alliance of European National Movements. All the venue owners knew was that it had something to do with the EU, so when Nick Griffin walked in the venue, I'll never forget the faces of the staff and the servers. Jaws literally dropped, and I spent the rest of the day worried our drinks were being spiked.

The event was the usual combination of mingling and listening to speeches. Some of the people I'd seen at that first BNP meeting in St. Helens were there, along with plenty of faces I'd seen online. At the time, there were a few popular online forums where people would chat, and I'd managed to amass quite a large number of Facebook friends from the BNP membership. Some of the people I met that day were thoroughly lovely. I had great conversations over a beer and cigarettes in the beautiful hotel grounds. But others were decidedly more hostile.

I saw raised eyebrows, a few hushed whispers and glances in my direction, and even a couple of people flat out asking why I'd come. It was around this time that the rumors of me being a "Jewish spy" had been circulating. It wasn't helped by the fact I'd recently asked the party's membership line whether I could use a fake address for my membership, as I didn't want my parents' address to be put on the system. Mike the Scouser, whom I'd first met at the St. Helens meeting, had heard about it and told others to be wary of me. The fact I didn't want to give away my address might have been a red flag if I was a grown adult, but I was in my late teens at this point and still living with my parents. My reluctance to make my address known, combined with the rumors of me being a Jewish Zionist plant, meant that I'd become the focus of a pretty nasty hate campaign.

Regardless, Griffin still liked me and so I stayed at the event. Honestly, I shrugged off the weird hostility toward me as all a bit silly. Again, I didn't have any reason to believe the media, so I gave those who had been really quite unpleasant to me the benefit of the doubt. I just saw it as a daft misunderstanding—and one that Griffin just told me to ignore. I was beginning to learn that bickering was simply a fact of life in this weird political world.

It was actually during this event that I gave my first ever political speech. I was asked if I wanted to say a few words about an organization I was setting up for university students, and I accepted. I remember quickly scrawling notes onto the back of a drink menu, excited to give my first ever speech but also extremely nervous. I was to announce to a room full of people my organization, the National Culturists. It was a short-lived youth group I tried to set up based off the ideas of Dr. John Press, a Republican who was then the leader of the Brooklyn chapter of the Tea Party. His book, *Culturism*, explained how national identity can be preserved and maintained by respecting national culture and rejecting racism. I had developed an online campaign for the National Culturists called "Love Culture, Hate Racism" that I was going to announce on stage. And I did.

I told the room that I knew people there weren't racist and that I wasn't racist, which is why the slogan "Love Culture, Hate Racism" makes perfect sense. The room laughed. I know most of the people laughing did so because of the irony. They'd been called racists for years, so supporting a slogan like this was funny. It's also comical to turn that word round on the left, which is something I expressed during the speech. But looking back, some years later, I think plenty in the room were also laughing because it would have just been so disingenuous. There were people in that room who were real racists. That didn't occur to me at the time.

At this point, I should have known very well what I'd gotten myself involved with, but I was still blissfully unaware. The media were liars, and the people I'd met were lovely, so why would I think negatively of a room full of people willing to lend me their ear and give me a chance to have my say?

During lunch, I mingled in the hotel grounds. I spoke to some representatives of other political parties across Europe and was introduced to a man called Bruno Gollnisch. I was told he was a prominent member of the Front National in France, the populist party led by Marine Le Pen. Despite the party being founded by Marine's father, a man who has been (fairly) accused of anti-Semitism for years, it had successfully modernized and was promoted a more modern nationalism. For that reason, I didn't think twice about snapping a photo with him.

But I didn't really know who Gollnisch was. Had I known that in 2007 he was sentenced to a three-month prison sentence on probation for saying the following, I wouldn't have been so keen to take a photo with him:

> I do not question the existence of concentration camps but historians could discuss the number of deaths. As to the existence of gas chambers, it is up to historians to speak their minds ("de se déterminer").[70]

I won't call Gollnisch a Holocaust denier, because that's a big accusation to throw at someone. And, I suppose, technically he didn't. But a comment like that really makes me queasy, and it's usually only the Holocaust deniers who say things like this.

A lot of other things completely went over my head, too. One of the biggest parties represented at the conference was Jobbik, a Hungarian nationalist party that's riddled with anti-Semites and extremists. The people I met at the conference seemed perfectly normal to me. I didn't hear anything anti-Semitic or radical, though I suppose I wouldn't in polite company. It didn't even occur to me that anybody there might have been the slightest bit radical, because again, why should I have ever believed the media?

If I, an intelligent young lad, could have sat through a conference like that and met some of the most notorious and famous radical nationalists in Europe without for a moment thinking that I was surrounding myself with extremists, then clearly there's some failure somewhere. Granted, it was probably partly a failure on my part. I could have done better research.

---

70 Bruno Gollnisch, "Négationnisme: Gollnisch Persiste," L'Obs, October 13, 2004, https://www.nouvelobs.com/societe/20041012.OBS8819/negationnisme-gollnisch-persiste.html.

I'm not sure how much I would have believed had I looked these people up online first, though. I'd already heard a lot about how the BNP was racist, and people voting for the BNP were racist, so why would I believe any news articles saying Gollnisch was racist, or Jobbik was racist?

I'm not sure if anyone in the press has ever stopped to think how calling everyone racist is devaluing the meaning of the word. I'm sure many of these people do what they do to try and stop the growth of the extreme right, but I'd argue they're aiding it.

When the media can't be trusted, people will look elsewhere for answers. I found answers from the BNP, and today, young lads are finding answers on 8Chan and white supremacist forums. White nationalists, anti-Semites, and conspiracy theorists seem to have all the answers, and when the media lacks credibility in the eyes of normal people, there's more reason to believe them. Especially when you're an angry young teenager.

Let's say you're a seventeen-year-old boy looking for answers. You see the unmitigated political chaos on the news, the congresswomen calling the president a white supremacist, the Republicans fighting back against Antifa and an increasingly radical Democratic Party, and a media who just seems to want to demonize middle America. Are you going to listen to the talking suits on the TV and the journalists with dyed-green armpit hair and their pronouns in their Twitter bio—or are you going to listen to young white nationalists like Nick Fuentes on the internet, who poke fun with memes and make edgy jokes? The latter seems more fun because the people doing it are relatable, and the media's already made it pretty clear they're not interested in engaging with mean old racists.

INVENTING MONSTERS

The media is not only lending credibility to the far right, but they are *inventing* monsters all the time. I don't just mean they are creating new radicals, either. I'm saying that it is common for members of the press to simply lie about conservatives, nationalists, and populists to create monsters the public should hate. That means calling people Nazis or "far right" when the claim is objectively and verifiably untrue.

It's bad enough that the politicians are unrepresentative and negligent, and the media complicit in that negligence—but these same people are creating the monsters they write about. They lend credibility to the far right without even realizing it, they push young men into their arms, and then they attribute some of the worst possible labels to innocent people. Anyone at the receiving end of being called a Nazi will know how gut-wrenching a feeling it is the first time you hear it.

With regards to the press telling lies like that, it's astonishing that so many people seem to have forgotten that lesson we were all taught as children: don't believe everything the newspapers tell you. Every word about the "far right" from mainstream media outlets seems to be treated as gospel, and the way in which the media demonizes and smears working class people is having a hand in the radicalization of young white men. Call everyone a racist and a Nazi, and what reason do vulnerable and angry white lads have not to just...become a racist and a Nazi?

President Trump has been at the receiving end of these media attacks for years, and whether or not you like him, there's no denying that the media has told plain lies about him. He was condemned over and over again by pundits, newspapers, news anchors, reporters, and online commentators for refusing to condemn white supremacy. In August 2017, NBC News reported "Trump Must Condemn Hate Groups His Political Rise Energized" and referred to his "slow response to the deadly white-nationalist attack in Charlottesville."[71] For the Associated Press News site that same month, Julie Pace asked, "Why won't Donald Trump condemn white nationalism?"[72]

In August 2018, Bloomberg published a piece initially titled "Trump Still Fails to Condemn Racism a Year After Charlottesville" (though the title of the piece has since changed to "Trump Stays True to Himself on Charlottesville Anniversary."[73]) But writer Timothy O'Brien still doesn't mince his words in the subtitle, which reads "The president's support of racist causes is right in line with a lifetime of race-baiting and fomenting division."

In April 2019, BuzzFeed News claimed "Trump Defended the Charlottesville White Supremacists—Again."[74]

---

71 Benjy Sarlin, "Trump Must Confront Hate Groups His Political Rise Energized, Experts Say," NBC News, August 14, 2017, https://www.nbcnews.com/politics/donald-trump/trump-must-confront-hate-groups-his-political-rise-energized-advocates-n792671.

72 Julie Pace, "Analysis: Why Won't Donald Trump Condemn White Nationalism?" AP News, August 13, 2017, https://apnews.com/7d824d4df86649fd98c4ba63a8015d0c.

73 Timothy L. O'Brien, "Trump Stays True to Himself on Charlottesville Anniversary," Bloomberg, August 12, 2018, https://www.bloomberg.com/opinion/articles/2018-08-12/trump-still-fails-to-condemn-racism-a-year-after-charlottesville.

74 Otillia Steadman, "Trump Defended the Charlottesville White Supremacists—Again," BuzzFeed, April 26, 2019, https://buzzfeednews.com/article/otilliasteadman/trump-charlottesville-defend-white-supremacists.

In August 2019, after the El Paso shooting, *The Washington Examiner* called on Trump to condemn the evil of white nationalism.[75]

The average reader might be fooled, and that's the problem, really. Most people won't research every claim themselves. But it's so easy to refute these wild accusations. BuzzFeed's claim that Trump defended Charlottesville white supremacists is based on the following quote from the president:

"People were there protesting the taking down of the monument of Robert E. Lee—everybody knows that."

This is factually correct. The Charlottesville rally was named "Unite the Right." It was a rally organized by white supremacists in an attempt to fool regular conservatives into appearing alongside them. Some young conservatives were fooled and turned up to protest the removal of the Robert E. Lee statue. Those naïve protesters ended up at the same protest as white nationalists. If BuzzFeed really knew as much about the far right as they claim, they'd know that it's a common tactic for white supremacists and anti-Semites to try and trip up conservatives and drag them down to their level. Just like Anders Breivik admitted. For some of them it's a game; an attempt to distract themselves from their own miserable lives. For others it's a tactic—they want conservatives to feel what it's like to be sidelined as a white nationalist and ultimately get on board because they have no other option.

Trump explained all this in a press conference after Charlottesville, telling reporters in the crowd:

---

75 "Trump Must Name and Condemn the Evil of White Nationalism," *The Washington Examiner*, August 5, 2019, https://www.washingtonexaminer.com/opinion/editorials/trump-must-name-and-condemn-the-evil-of-white-nationalism.

> Excuse me, they didn't put themselves down as neo-Nazis, and you had some very bad people in that group. But you also had people that were very fine people on both sides. You had people in that group—excuse me, excuse me, I saw the same pictures you did. You had people in that group that were there to protest the taking down of, to them, a very, very important statue and the renaming of a park from Robert E. Lee to another name.

And if that wasn't clear enough, he also said, "I'm not talking about the neo-Nazis and white nationalists because they should be condemned totally."

Despite this, the media ran with the story that Trump called white nationalists "very fine people."[76]

Trump was right when he said people were out there protesting about the removal of a statue. He also made it clear that the white nationalists who were also there should be condemned.

As for his lack of condemnation on other occasions...I almost feel like I'm wasting my time going over this. The president has condemned white nationalism, racism, white supremacy, anti-Semitism, and violence so many times. He did it after Charlottesville, he did it immediately after he was endorsed by David Duke (funny the uproar wasn't quite the same when Duke endorsed 2020 Democratic presidential candidate Tulsi Gabbard), and he did it after the El Paso shooting. And all the other times in between. I remember *watching* the press conference in which Trump condemned Duke and seeing news stories for days after claiming he hadn't.

---

76 Michelle Goldberg, "Trump Is a White Nationalist Who Inspires Terrorism," *The New York Times*, August 5, 2019, https://www.nytimes.com/2019/08/05/opinion/trump-white-supremacy.html.

For anyone unfamiliar with this story, I encourage you to look it up. Search the terms "Trump very fine people" and compare it with what he said at the press conference. The op-eds and reports you'll find are shocking. These are pieces written by ideologues spewing faux-righteousness and pure vitriol and hate into these pieces because they saw an opportunity to take try and take down a man they hate.

You see it even on the rare occasions when members of the media class picked up those condemnations. They still found ways to make out he's the Devil incarnate or that he's just lying. In August 2019, QZ reported "Trump Condemns the White Supremacists He Inspires."[77]

So much of the establishment media, and even new media, outlets just don't care about telling the truth anymore. They'll just call Trump a neo-fascist or a white supremacist because everyone else does. On July 18th, 2019, popular tech journalism website, Gizmodo, took to Facebook to write, "Last night, the most popular dictionary word was 'racism' after President Trump's neo-fascist rally."[78]

They don't even try to hide their bias or their hatred.

We saw this same level of vitriol, designed to invent a monster that just isn't there, when the press dogpiled the

---

77 Ephrat Livni, "Trump Finally Condemns the White Supremacists He Inspires," Quartz, August 5, 2019, https://qz.com/1681650/trump-condemns-the-white-supremacists-he-inspires/.

78 Matt Novak, "Top Searches on Merriam-Webster Include 'Fascism' and 'Racism' After President Trump's Latest Rally," Gizmodo, Julay 18, 2019, https://www.facebook.com/gizmodo/posts/last-night-the-most-popular-dictionary-search-was-racism-after-president-trumps-/10157485408378967/.

Covington kids. It showed that they really don't care who you are. You could be the leader of the free world, or a high school student—the media is perfectly willing to distort facts to create a false narrative, sell papers, get clicks, and get more eyes on the failing TV news networks.

In January 2018, high school students from the Covington Catholic High School in Kentucky were outside the Lincoln Memorial, wearing MAGA hats. They were confronted by Nathan Phillips, an indigenous man who began chanting and banging a drum in front of the kids.

The story the press peddled was the one Phillips told, not the one the teenagers told. Phillips's story was considered more credible, and they ran with it. He alleged that the teenagers surrounded him and mobbed him, chanted "Build that wall," and were generally provocative.

Phillips changed his story multiple times as more video footage of the incident was released. He made his claims as wild as he could, but gradually walked them back as the evidence started proving him to be a liar.

The *New York Times* reported "Boys in 'Make America Great Again' Hats Mob Native Elder at Indigenous Peoples March,"[79] but it just wasn't true. One of the teenagers, Nick Sandmann, also became the focus of media attention for simply smiling. In the footage, Sandmann could be seen smirking as Phillips inexplicably banged a drum at him.

---

79 Sarah Mervosh, "Viral Video Shows Boys in 'Make America Great Again' Hats Surrounding Native Elder," *The New York Times*, January 19, 2019, https://www.nytimes.com/2019/01/19/us/covington-catholic-high-school-nathan-phillips.html.

Sandmann released a statement as new footage was revealed, explaining what really happened:

> At no time did I hear any student chant anything other than the school spirit chants…I did not witness or hear any students chant "build that wall" or anything hateful or racist at any time. Assertions to the contrary are simply false. Our chants were loud because we wanted to drown out the hateful comments that were being shouted at us by the protestors.
>
> After a few minutes of chanting, the Native American protestors, who I hadn't previously noticed, approached our group. The Native American protestors had drums and were accompanied by at least one person with a camera…
>
> The protestor everyone has seen in the video began playing his drum as he waded into the crowd, which parted for him. I did not see anyone try to block his path. He locked eyes with me and approached me, coming within inches of my face. He played his drum the entire time he was in my face.
>
> I never interacted with this protestor. I did not speak to him. I did not make any hand gestures or other aggressive moves. I believed that by remaining motionless and calm, I was helping to diffuse the situation. I said a silent prayer that the situation would not get out of hand.

Constant reports about Sandmann committing the crime of smiling meant he quickly became the focus of several media faces and contributors.

Saturday Night Live writer Sarah Beattie wrote on Twitter, "I will blow whoever manages to punch that maga kid in the face."

Author, commentator, and former CNN host Reza Aslan tweeted a photo of Sandmann's face and wrote, "Honest question. Have you ever seen a more punchable face than this kid's?"[80]

CNN employee Bakari Sellers also took to Twitter to say, "He is deplorable. Some ppl can also be punched in the face."

CNN did not respond to requests for comment.

Did high school student Nick Sandmann deserve this? And was he the monster the media portrayed him to be? The way in which he was treated, and the lies told about him, prompted a $275 million lawsuit for false and defamatory media coverage. The suit was only thrown out because the characterizations about Sandmann in the papers were considered "opinions," which are protected speech under the First Amendment. Even if the claims were false—which they verifiably were.

The media gets away with clear defamation and making a high school boy a target for online bullies, and members of the media endorse punching the kid, and we're meant to believe nothing sinister is going on?

The media establishment, whether they realize it or not, is a key part of the three-pronged attack on working class people that is resulting in the radicalization of young white men. Like the politicians, the press regularly distorts facts regarding the far right, suggesting the movement is bigger than it is and throwing moderate conservatives, Christians, nationalists, populists, and

---

80 Aslan (@rezaaslan), "Honest question. Have you ever seen a more punchable face than this kid's?" tweet, January 19, 2019, https://twitter.com/rezaaslan/status/1086806539552284672.

counter-jihad activists into the same political sphere as violent neo-Nazis.

They create monsters who don't exist, and I've been a victim of this myself. I don't like to call myself a victim, but being called a Nazi and a far-right extremist by the media isn't exactly a walk in the park. In 2017, I found out that I'd been the focus of an undercover documentary and that a journalist had been covertly filming and recording me for six months.

I was driving through a town near Luton when I got the email with the news. I don't know why, but I had a bad feeling. I used my BlackBerry as a GPS when I was driving, so I'd see email notifications and a tiny snippet of the contents. I can't remember what I saw, but I remember the notification filling me with dread. I'd usually just wait until I was home to read the emails, but this time, I pulled into a car park to read it.

It was an email from a television company called Hard Cash Productions. The email told me that my friend, Hazel Brown, had been secretly recording me for a documentary called *Undercover: Inside Britain's New Far Right*.

I felt sick. In 2017, I had long left behind my involvement with the BNP. I had been talking, for some years, about the dangers of the real far right. But here was this production crew who had produced an entire film designed to make me and others look like extremists. And the worst part was that the journalist was somebody I had come to know, and quite like! She presented herself as a care worker. She was from London and she had come along to a campaign launch event for Anne Marie Waters. At the time, Waters was running to become the next leader of the United Kingdom Independence Party, and I was heavily involved in the running of her campaign. Hazel had come along as a supporter, told us she was new to the scene, and we took her under our wing. She was a nice girl, and over the six months we knew her, she met lots of Anne Marie's supporters and people within the wider populist movement.

She met gay men, she met lesbians, she met immigrants, she met people of various racial backgrounds, she even met Muslims who were involved with our cause. Hazel was embraced by everyone, treated with respect, and I even took her to one side to tell her who to avoid. On the morning of the UKIP conference when the results of the leadership election were to be announced, Hazel and I sat in a hotel drinking some champagne (it was a big day!) and I told her who the white supremacists and neo-Nazis were, how to identify them, and who to avoid. I went out of my way to make sure this girl wasn't pulled into those circles as I'd seen many other young people, and it seemed like she was listening.

But that footage was never used in the documentary. I never saw or heard from "Hazel" ever again, but the documentary they produced really didn't achieve much. They got nothing on me. I'm an open book, so they were never going to find anything. But that didn't stop them trying to present me as a far-right extremist.

The same goes for Anne Marie Waters. All they caught her saying were a few swear words. Everything else were things both Anne Marie and I were willing to say publicly. Regardless, they used footage of her and I during the UKIP leadership campaign alongside footage of other decidedly more "far right" people to try and paint us as extremists the public should be scared of. Interestingly, Hard Cash chose to work with Nick Lowles and Matthew Collins of HOPE not hate. This wasn't an honest exposure of Britain's far right. If that's something they were interested in, I'd have been happy to cooperate with them and show them what the British public (and government) should really fear. The fact that they chose to omit footage where I warned of the real far right in Britain speaks volumes to their intentions.

I've experienced this a lot over the years. My first ever interview with "real" media was with *Vice*, when I was still in the BNP. My naivete is so obvious in that interview, and I cringe every time someone mentions it. In it, I praise Nick Griffin while at the same time explaining that the BNP should focus on culture, not race. The piece labelled me the "Boy Wonder of the Far Right," a title I've probably lost now that I'm the ripe old age of twenty-seven. In the piece, they included a photograph of me wearing a suit and a satchel in the middle of Liverpool city center, taken by an unknown photographer. I remember when it was taken, actually—a random person passed me in the street, took the photo, and then quickly moved along. But the picture, and the *Vice* piece, established me as some sort of "racist hipster" that *Esquire Magazine* eventually picked up on.

During my 2014 election campaign in the South East, *Esquire Magazine* accompanied me on a day of action. We did a photo shoot and from what I could tell, the intention was to pitch me as a far-right hipster. Canadian magazine Maclean's had done a piece about me in 2013, describing me as an "unlikely far-right trailblazer." They said I was "neither old, nor angry, nor square." A French radio station had made a documentary about me and a girl I was close with at the time, noting that I was young, cool, and friends with hipsters who disagreed with me.

Esquire seemed to want to do their own piece, and I was all in favor of it. I knew they'd try and stitch me up, but I was willing to fight back, and I did. The writer followed me around all day, acting friendly and even trying to appear like he was on my side. When a Muslim woman walked past with her daughter, both wearing face coverings, he pointed and pretended to be shocked or disgusted. I knew what he was doing.

That day he witnessed a far-left activist kick down our stall. He also saw some Muslim women take me aside and quietly tell me they'd be voting for me, because they came to England expecting freedom and instead nothing had changed, and they were still controlled by the men in their community.

At the end of the day, the journalist took me to a pub where he interviewed me. He tried to get me to drink, but I didn't. The questions started off fairly normal: asking me about my upbringing, how I got into politics, all that stuff. Then he started accusing me of being far right, giving me examples of things I'd said, looking for hidden meanings in comments I'd written online or said in speeches. He tried and tried to get me to say something racist, but I said nothing of the sort. He became visibly more annoyed and aggressive as he realized he wasn't going to get me to say anything extreme or racist. I was shocked he was so convinced I was some kind of monster, or that he wanted to paint me as some kind of monster. I'd hoped that instead, the interview might have served to show people what I really think, and that it's possible to be young, to speak up, and to be patriotic.

The reason this interview sticks in my mind is because he eventually started shouting. He tried to argue with me, and I stayed calm, collected, and sober. It's no wonder he wanted me to drink. I think the anger was partly a result of him thinking I was a slippery Nazi, too clever to accidentally spill the beans and show my true self, and partly because he knew the piece wouldn't get published and he wouldn't get his commission. After all, a piece about a Nazi hipster doesn't sell unless the Nazi hipster says something a Nazi would say. Needless to say, he stormed out of the pub angry, the piece never got published, and I never bloody managed to get a hold of the cool photos they'd taken of me that day.

This happened to me again in 2017 when a documentary maker reached out to me about participating in a film on Britain's populists. I don't remember the pitch exactly, but I always quiz anyone who wants to film me quite extensively. I made it clear I wouldn't appear alongside neo-Nazis, and I was told that wouldn't happen. We met at my house in Bedfordshire, which was unusual for me. I would never usually let the press anywhere near my home, but I was moving a week later and figured it was safe. The host spent the first ten minutes examining my living room, noting the giant map of the British Empire on my wall, quizzing me about some of the left-wing books on my shelf, and trying to get a feel for who I was. He told me multiple times that I was nothing like he'd expected me to be. That seems to be a common theme when I meet journalists.

We took a drive to a manor house nearby where we filmed on the grounds, and it was all a pretty normal discussion. He asked me why I'm concerned about mass immigration and Muslim immigration. I gave him, as always, entirely reasonable responses. He didn't get what he needed, so at the end he asked me, "What would you say if I told you I was a Muslim"? I just shrugged.

I think that's what sealed the deal. I knew right then and there that the footage wouldn't be used, and it wasn't. In fact, I spent the next year or two wondering where the documentary he promised was. He'd told me it was going to be released on PBS, I kept an eye out, and nothing ever appeared. Until the writing of this chapter. I stumbled upon a promotional clip on Twitter for a documentary called *Britain's Ultra Nationalists.* I immediately recognized the face and checked out the site.

The first trailer starts with a clip of Anne Marie Waters, the Irish lesbian feminist who leads the For Britain party. An ultra-nationalist she is not. He goes on to speak to some other people in right-wing political circles in the UK, many of them just angry working-class lads. I recognized most of them, and while I don't like the aggressive approach of some of the lads he spoke to, I wouldn't call them ultra-nationalists. They would be Labour voters if it wasn't for the immigration problem. They are literally just angry working-class people who have seen their communities change, and they're lashing out in anger over it. They're not far right, neo-Nazis, or ultra-nationalist.

Then, the clip shows him speaking to *real* neo-Nazis and ultra-nationalists. I won't give these people the satisfaction of naming them, but anyone familiar with British politics will recognize them immediately.

I found it interesting that the presenter, journalist Aron Tori, had chosen to put neo-Nazis in the same production as people like Anne Marie Waters. At best it's intellectually lazy, at worst it's disingenuous and scheming. Interestingly, I seem to have been cut from the film. He didn't get anything radical enough from me.

That's a common theme with the press, I've noticed. I've had outbursts with the press in the past and been at the center of a few national controversies, but I've never said anything a neo-Nazi would say, because I'm not a neo-Nazi. But the media seems to be working off the theory that Neo Nazis keep their views secret, and with enough prodding and probing, a good question can reveal them. The truth is that Britain's neo-Nazis, white supremacists, and far-right extremists will tell you exactly who they are without any prodding and poking.

Nobody seems to want to believe that, though. Instead, the media still seems invested in this tactic of inventing monsters the public should be scared of. They'll make anyone they can into a Nazi, and if they can't find anything you've ever said to misrepresent, they'll just ignore you and move onto the next person they can.

Whether it is malicious misrepresentation of normal people, one big honest mistake, or just sheer ignorance, it all plays into the hands of the far right. It leaves normal people wondering *who* exactly the press is serving, and why.

The far right claims to know the answer to that question, and with no other answers available, it gives them just enough credibility to continue gaining ground. Until the media gives people a voice, there will be an ideological and political fightback against them that will just get uglier and uglier.

CHAPTER SIX

AN EMBOLDENED FAR LEFT

The third and final part of the three-pronged attack comes from an emboldened and radical far left, and throughout this chapter, I will explain the role they play in reinforcing the negative feelings many working-class people have about the media and politicians.

It's important to understand that an entire class of demotivated, tired, unhappy, and despondent people has been created by politicians failing to represent the interests of the people who put them there, and a media class that shows no willingness to engage with the people left behind. The working class of Britain are left without representation and nobody to turn to for help. Middle America might be (right now) represented by a populist president trying to keep promises he made during his election campaign, but the Democratic Party is more radical than ever before, and more willing to work against the President and the Republican Party to stop Trump voters getting anything even *close* to what they hoped for when they voted in 2016. If they succeed, the normal people of

America who voted for change will be denied the change they asked for.

The political class and the media have shown clear bias, and they've told tens of millions of people that their concerns don't matter. That's enough to drive people crazy as it is, but the truth is most people just put their heads down and get on with their lives. People just tune out of politics and don't vote. You'll hear it at the doorstep if you ever go out and campaign in working class areas. I couldn't tell you the amount of times someone has said to me "I won't vote for you or anyone else, because you're all the same." A member of my own family asked me just days ago why she should ever vote again if her vote to leave the European Union isn't going to be respected. And these people are right.

As I've previously explained, during my election campaign in Batley I went door-knocking in one of the poorest parts of the region. It was a council estate badly neglected by the local authorities and suffering from a major unemployment issue. I spoke to local people, and the question I got from almost everyone was "Why should I trust you?" It happened so many times that I eventually just started saying, "Good point—I wouldn't trust me either." And why should I? Every single time a politician has promised to represent the voters, they've lied. And then the media dogpiles you, calls working class people racists and bigots, and that's that.

Most people tune out. Some people get angry and take to the streets, forming street organizations like the EDL or becoming political commentators like I did. But it's the people who stay quiet who particularly interest me, and who I think are the most susceptible to radicalization when the final part of the three-pronged attack is added to the mix. The final part of this attack is an emboldened far left, taking the form of street activism, harassment campaigns, boycotts, social engineering and mass hysteria.

When you're let down by the politicians, smeared by the press, you might take to the streets to protest. When you're then physically attacked by gangs of far-left activists, that's enough to make most people snap. These far-left activists might hit you over the head and crack open your skull with a weapon, take photos of you to find out who you are, contact your employer and harass them until you get fired, write appalling lies about you online, and do everything in their power to have you cast out from civil society. The people typically targeted in this way are the ones who are willing to fight back against the political system, though in some instances otherwise politically inactive people might be targeted for an "offensive" tweet or quip made during the workday.

Far-left activists are everywhere. They are the all-seeing eye for the media and the politicians, and they strike fear into the hearts of so many because they can be exceptionally powerful. That's not because they're particularly intelligent or special, but because the media and the politicians have their back, and they don't face any backlash for doing what they do.

Throwing a brick through someone's window, cracking their head open with a bike lock, or harassing employers until they fire the person you don't like is all very well and good when you're fighting "Nazis."

The motivation behind this obsessive behavior is debated. I believe that these people are looking for some kind of identity and community. As we have been taught to care less about our national identity and care more about diversity and inclusion, the British people have slowly forgotten what it means to be English and European. Similarly, American citizens have been told over and over that they are a nation of immigrants and should be welcoming to everybody. The truth is that America is a nation of settlers—European settlers—with a government and society based on European traditions. The West has been robbed of its identity, and we have been told that we are a wasteland devoid of any culture until new immigrants arrive and enrich us with theirs.

When you believe that your ancestors were pure evil and the West built on racism, fascism and hatred, and when you believe that you have no identity of your own, the community found within "anti-fascist" networks can be a breath of fresh air. Just like a girl at school might find kinship with the feminists who dye their armpit hair green, people old and young are organizing under the banner of anti-fascism and making it their goal to destroy the lives of "racists" everywhere. I think it's all a matter of community and identity, but they're also being motivated by well-funded advocacy groups that give them their ammunition.

As well as the media pumping out articles telling activists which mean old racist to target next, far-left organizations like the SPLC in the US and HOPE not hate are publishing biased reports and material that misrepresents the issue of the far right. These reports, which are portrayed as academic but regularly include personal remarks and attacks, are then used by politicians and the press to perpetuate false narratives on far-right extremism. It gets individuals and organizations targeted by feral mobs of "anti-fascists" who have nothing better to do.

For all their talk of community "cohesion," these far-left organizations play a key role in the demonization of the white working class. And when far-left activists take to the street to attack people who have already been let down by the politicians and the media, it reinforces their perception that nobody cares about them. Who could blame them?

This is exactly how you create a far-right extremist, and that's exactly what's happening today in America, Britain, and continental Europe.

Here in the UK, the working classes have traditionally turned to the left to be represented. Whether it's a trade union or the left-wing Labour Party, working class people would typically lean left to provide a check and balance to the right-wing capitalists in the Conservative Party. It's a political balance that has long ensured that businesses take care of their employees, and that employees don't milk the system so much that businesses can't thrive. But today, the political left doesn't really care about representing the white working class. Instead, left-wing activists seem to care more about avocados and pop-up cocktail bars than the plight of working people—if they're white, that is. Today's left-wing activists will never shy away from calling someone who suggests we might have to address Muslim grooming gangs a "racist."

In America, the political left serves only as a polarizing force that does nothing but prod and poke Republican or Christian families. They'll campaign against Christianity while promoting Islam, and they'll sneer and mock white lads for their "toxic masculinity."

Dogpiling the white working class is not a wise strategy if you're *honestly* trying to create a cohesive and harmonious society.

John F. Kennedy was right when he said, "Those who make peaceful revolution impossible will make violent revolution inevitable."

IGNORING REALITY AND CONTROLLING THE PARAMETERS OF DISCUSSION

The story of Hazleton, Pennsylvania sums up the three-pronged attack very well. The politicians (well, mostly the Democrats) refused to consider the interests of the people of the town who were concerned about illegal immigration. Then, the media attempted to portray the transformation of the town as positive. Finally, far-left ideologues and activists attacked their former mayor for his "racism." As part of their "Ten Scariest Republicans Heading to Congress" series, Right Wing Watch wrote a profile of former Hazleton mayor Lou Barletta, accusing him of "anti-immigrant zealotry" for his opposition to illegal immigration.[81] The report quoted Barletta saying "I will get rid of the illegal people. It's this simple: They must leave" as if telling people who entered the country illegally that they must go is shocking or somehow unreasonable.

Search "Lou Barletta racist" on Twitter, and the vitriol and hatred being expressed toward the man is incredible. My own cursory search found tweets calling Barletta an "American Nazi lover" and suggestions he had committed "racist attacks on POC."

---

81 Miranda Blue, "Meet Lou Barletta: America's Anti-Immigrant Mayor Heads to Congress," Right Wing Watch, November 11, 2010, https://www.rightwingwatch.org/post/meet-lou-barletta-americas-anti-immigrant-mayor-heads-to-congress/.

Barletta wasn't the only one to be ganged up on by these rabid ideologues, either. Fox News host Tucker Carlson was called "racist"[82] for detailing the hypocrisy of politicians who are happy to see the demographics of Hazleton change while their own towns and cities stay the same. "Diversity for thee, but not for me" he said during a segment. Is he wrong? In America and Britain, the people who push diversity program the most vigorously tend to be the ones who live in gated communities and send their kids to private schools. But Tucker's just a terrible racist for pointing that out.

When they make these wild, unsubstantiated and, let's face it, false accusations about Barletta and Carlson, they're making the same accusations about the people of Hazleton who had very real concerns about their city. Imagine your roof is caving in, and the builders, the housing association, and the local government all tell you it is fine. You know something is very wrong but the only people who can possibly help you refuse to even acknowledge there's a problem, and to top it off, there's a bunch of rabid lunatics at your front door screaming at you to stop complaining about it.

I'm not exaggerating when I call them rabid lunatics. I don't want to put people off by using language like this, as it is my hope that people who hold left-wing political views could read this book and seriously think about what I have to say. I just can't think of any other way to describe these people. They

---

82 Michal Kranz, "People Are Calling Tucker Carlson Out on Twitter for His Segment Criticizing 'Changing Demographics in America,'" *Business Insider*, March 21, 2018, https://www.businessinsider.com/tucker-carlson-changing-american-demographics-segment-slammed-twitter-2018-3?r=US&IR=T.

are mentally unstable, and most people will only ever realize the extent of this problem when they become a victim of one of their hate campaigns. Far-left activism goes way beyond online name-calling. These ideologues ignore reality and then use whatever means possible to control the parameters of discussion. They decide what you can and cannot say, and the media and politicians enforce their rules.

Leaving aside boycott culture, which everybody should be perfectly aware of by now, far-left ideologues are willing to stoop as low as celebrating the firing of a Christian doctor because he doesn't believe it is possible to change sex. In July 2019, Dr. David Mackereth hit the headlines when he was sacked for saying he wouldn't call a six-foot-tall bearded man "madam."[83] He claimed using transgender pronouns was "a ritual denial of an obvious truth" but regardless, did not refuse treatment to anybody and cared for all patients in the same way. His firing was widely celebrated online, and trans activist Munroe Bergdorf appeared next to him on a morning television show repeatedly calling the mild-mannered and polite Christian man a "bigot."

If he's a bigot, then 90 percent of people who live on council estates in Britain are downright evil—because in general, I can't imagine they would choose to be as polite as Mackereth was to Bergdorf during that exchange. Most people believe the trans agenda has gone too far, but far-left ideologues know they can

83 Ewan Somerville, "Doctor Sacked for Refusing to Refer to Transgender Woman as 'She,'" *Independent*, July 10, 2019, https://www.independent.co.uk/news/uk/home-news/christian-doctor-trans-woman-sacked-gender-pronouns-universal-credit-a8999176.html.

keep abusing decent people because the media just lets them get away with it.

Bergdorf is a good example of how trans activists are, as a whole, part of a wider movement that aims to vilify straight, white, Christian men. In 2017, she was fired by L'Oréal after it was revealed she had claimed all white people are racist. Facts don't matter to Bergdorf or people like her; they care more about vilifying white people because it advances their radical cause. They want nothing less than the total transformation of society, and if that means throwing white people under the bus (or laughing when a Christian doctor can no longer treat his patients), then so be it.

Open and vocal hatred of white people has been a popular theme amongst the far left (and, increasingly, the left) for some time now. In 2015, the Welfare and Diversity officer for Goldsmiths University in London, Bahar Mustafa, stepped down from her role after being arrested for a tweet in which she endorsed the murder of white men. Mustafa had tweeted the hashtag #KillAllWhiteMen and was accused of creating a hostile environment for other members of staff.[84] The story really blew up at the time and was one of the first times that far-left extremism on university campuses was exposed to the general population. Readers of national newspapers saw photos

84 Euan McClelland, "Student Diversity Officer Who Allegedly Tweeted 'Kill All White Men' Quits Over Claim She Bullied Union President," *The Daily Mail*, November 20, 2015, https://www.dailymail.co.uk/news/article-3327413/Student-diversity-officer-allegedly-tweeted-kill-white-men-set-quit-claim-bullied-union-president.html.

of Mustafa pretending to cry in front of a poster tacked to a door that read "No white-cis-men pls."

The #KillAllWhiteMen campaign continues to this day, and any university student will tell you how prevalent this kind of thinking is on campus and in the student societies.

Dare to challenge this obviously insane rhetoric, however, and you'll be told your white privilege means you don't qualify for an opinion. White privilege is the notion that any white person is inherently privileged, no matter their upbringing. Ethnic minority people, according to the theory, face ongoing prejudice in society that inhibits their ability to get and hold down a well-paying job, get ahead in society, or be represented in the media and popular culture. It asserts that a black man from a wealthy suburb in the south of England faces greater struggles than a white boy who grew up on a council estate in Liverpool. It is nonsense, but it is a theory peddled widely not just by university students, but by professors too.

So, when a young, working-class white lad who studies and works hard to get a place at university is later met with accusations of racism and prejudice, that's a sure-fire way to breed resentment against people he might otherwise have had no problem with. I don't want to start parroting tired old talking points, but it is almost as if these ideologues *want* to be victims. If that's the case, I would again argue that this is a matter of people searching for an identity.

When British and American politicians so regularly disregard the idea of assimilation or integration and encourage new arrivals to fully embrace the culture of the lands from which they came, they are unknowingly segregating society and destroying the common bonds that keep our society together.

Without that common identity to bind us together, society more easily fragments into competing groups and the minorities go to war with the majority. Soon enough, young white boys who grow up without a pot to piss in end up being labelled privileged oppressors and, boy, does that make those young men angry. As a white, working-class man who grew up in a terraced house in a former mining town, it definitely made me angry. My parents gave me everything they could, but we were by no means wealthy, and I've never had anything handed to me on a plate. I've worked my entire life, made my own money, and never relied on my parents the same way a middle-class child might have done. But during my time at the University of Liverpool (and into my adulthood), I've been shrugged off as a privileged oppressor who just wants to stop black and brown people from getting ahead. It's not just offensive, and it's not just wrong—it's a kind of psychological warfare that makes people like me angry. Someone less stable than me would have seriously lashed out under that kind of pressure, and many young men I know have done exactly that.

The vindictive nature of these activists has been clear to me for a long time, but when I received a phone call from the FBI to tell me they were investigating a tip that I was a terrorist planning on committing an attack in the United States, I learned just how nasty the far left can really get. I was walking out of the Channel Four studios after appearing on a live segment on the news when my then-fiancée called me. She told me that the FBI had been in contact with her, investigating tips that I was a terrorist and our relationship a sham to obtain a Green Card. She told me to expect a call from the FBI any moment, and sure enough, they called.

It was totally surreal. For the next forty minutes or so, my relationship with my now-wife was put under scrutiny, I answered questions about my political activity, and thankfully the FBI agent saw sense. They told me they believed this was a false tip (seemingly from a far-left activist), and that was that. It would have been fine, had my visa waiver travel to the United States not been cancelled. I was later denied a tourist visa and a journalist visa, and effectively banned from entering the United States to see my wife.

After years of battling for an answer for why this had happened—and a lawsuit—it seems that the tip that I was a terrorist was understood to be fake. However, the tip that I was engaged to a US citizen was enough to cause all these problems, stop me from being able to enter the United States, and turn my relationship with my wife upside-down for years. It was a vindictive and evil act that risked my relationship with my wife, and the person who submitted the false tip knew it.

At the time the tip was submitted, we were both the target of a hate campaign from far-left activists in New York City who had taken issue with my wife's support of presidential candidate Donald Trump. She had been working at a theater in Manhattan but was soon fired and dropped by her agent after catty burlesque dancers and fellow performers spread rumors that she was a neo-Nazi. They drove my Republican wife out of New York City, destroyed years of hard work building her career, and separated us by thousands of miles at the worst possible time. My young sister-in-law was in the hospital with leukemia, and not only was I unable to visit her, my wife couldn't work and contribute toward the enormous cost of her treatment.

These ideologues justify their actions by claiming that we are Nazis, without even considering the possibility that their judgment might be wrong.

Insane hate campaigns like this happen all the time, but you don't hear about them because A) they're complicated, and B) they happen to people without any public presence. Employers are harassed until they fire employees because it's not worth the trouble. I've personally known people fired from jobs as receptionists, cooks, and office administrators after being exposed as Trump supporters or conservatives. "Anti-fascist" activists go out of their way to identify people who make comments online or who appear at protests. They'll find out everything about you, tweet your address, and do everything in their power to stop you making any money.

If the activists don't do it for you, your employer might just do it of their own accord. Hostility toward Trump voters is deep-rooted in major brands across the West, including social media company Facebook. Palmer Luckey, a virtual reality expert and Facebook executive, was booted from the company after he donated $10,000 to an anti-Hillary Clinton group.[85] It took just six months for him to be fired, but not before CEO Mark Zuckerberg pressured Luckey to announce his support for the Libertarian presidential candidate Gary Johnson, despite his clear support for Trump.

Business owners aren't safe from these people, either. The recent case of Jessica Yaniv, a transgender woman from Canada,

---

85 Kirsten Grind and Keach Hagey, "Top Facebook VR Exec May Have Been Fired for His Trump Support," MarketWatch, November 11, 2018, https://www.marketwatch.com/story/top-facebook-vr-exec-may-have-been-fired-for-his-trump-support-2018-11-11.

is particularly troubling. Yaniv went out of her way to find multiple local salons that offered ladies waxing services. When informing the salons that she was transgender and had male genitalia, she was politely denied service. There are a couple of reasons why a business would reasonably deny Yaniv service. One is that female workers might be uncomfortable dealing with male genitalia. Another is that waxing male genitalia is obviously very different from waxing female genitalia, and it's unlikely the people at the salon have the experience required to do it properly. Despite this, Yaniv filed a human rights complaint against the company and put them out of business very quickly. Yaniv's response to their closing down was that they hadn't been open very long anyway.

What do these ideologues want to happen to those who don't conform to their extremist worldview? If they find out where you work, they'll campaign to get you fired. If you start your own company, they'll bombard your social media pages with one-star reviews and expose you as a "racist" until you're shut down. And do you think they'd be happy for you to live off government welfare? If they had it their way, there would be no chance government money would be spent on racists down on their luck. So what if you were out on the street? What if you found yourself jobless and homeless? Do you think they'd spare a dollar for you on the street or buy you a sandwich?

HOSTILITY TOWARD WHITE MEN IN EDUCATION

The sight of the UC Berkeley campus set on fire when Milo Yiannopoulos was due to give a speech in 2017 was hard to ignore, even for those who are otherwise nonpolitical. Up until then, the violence from Antifa was largely buried by the press and seen only by those in the midst of political protests. But the footage of a university set on fire by Antifa in opposition to a planned speech shows just how extreme the average university campus has become. This is true in both the UK and America, and it's not new.

It started in the '60s, but January 15, 1987, was a real turning point. Five hundred protesters walked side by side with Jesse Jackson through the main entrance of Stanford University chanting "Hey hey, ho ho, Western Civ has got to go." It was a protest in opposition to a humanities course at the school called "Western Culture." The protests forced the university to replace it with a course called "Cultures, Ideas, and Values." Ever since, universities have been increasingly dedicated to promoting "diversity" at the behest of extremist student organizations and pressure groups. I put "diversity" in quotes because it's never really been about empowering nonwhite people, who enjoy all the same rights and privileges as white people, but instead about putting down white people. Diversity simply means fewer whites, and when that's constantly celebrated, it doesn't exactly help race relations. It worsens them. Universities are no longer meritocratic, and students are being divided on racial and religious lines.

The abandoning of the study of Western culture and the sidelining of white people—in particular, white men—has created a void where common values once existed. Students are united by nothing and divided by much. On any campus in Britain or America, you'll find a plethora of far-left student societies: militant LGBTQ groups, Marxist societies, and so forth. You'll struggle to find any that embrace traditional European culture. In fact, I don't think any exist. I tried to set one up at the University of Liverpool and was met with extreme hostility and even violence. My intention was to form a culturist society called the National Culturists. Our literature celebrated culture and rejected race hatred. This was during my time in the BNP, but not long before I decided I'd had enough and left.

Every university student is assigned a professor who guides you through your studies. I had left university during my first year for medical reasons and returned the year later to complete my first year of study, and before my return I'd informed my professor of my intentions to set up the society. He didn't seem particularly impressed, and it later turned out he definitely *wasn't.* I was eventually expelled from the University of Liverpool on political grounds, as I explained in full in my book *A Paradoxical Alliance.* When I was expelled from the university, I was given copies of the emails between lecturers at the school, all about me. In them, my professor expressed his concern about the student society I was planning on setting up. Other professors discussed options to "get rid" of me, and one even claimed they had removed me from their class for upsetting other students. That was a lie. I definitely did upset other students, but I was never removed from any class. In fact, it was a miracle if I actually turned up to a class in the first place. Every time I stepped foot out of my student accommodation, I was met with hostility.

The class that the professor might have been talking about was a politics seminar that I remember quite well, because a girl raised her hand and asked the professor what a referendum was. I was surprised that somebody without even a basic understanding of our political system had first of all managed to pass a politics class in college (which comes before university, in the UK), and secondly ended up in a university politics class.

During the seminar, the topic of multiculturalism came up. The girl made the argument that Britain is a multicultural nation. I responded by asserting a nation is culturist in its very nature, and that multiculturalism is an invention that denies the existence of a unique British cultural identity. She got extremely agitated; upset, even. That was no doubt the class my professor was talking about, but I certainly wasn't asked to leave.

That was considered controversial, somehow. I honestly wasn't prepared for people to be so incapable of having their worldview challenged, and I wasn't expecting university to be a place where I'd be shunned or ostracized for disagreeing with somebody. But that's exactly what happened.

The hatred toward me was something I'd never experienced before. I'd seen it on occasion during my time in college, before university, but it wasn't quite the same as this. It was the day I found posters of me in the university library that made me realize just how intense the hatred people felt toward me was. The posters compared me to mass murderer Anders Breivik, and asked students "Is this the kind of person you want on campus?" I was still a relatively reserved person at this point, extremely polite and considerate, and nice to everyone I met. I was (and still am!) an advocate for peace. All I cared about was promoting everything good about British culture and representing the interests of working-class people while I was at it. University should have been an ideal place for me to do that, to get politically active, to engage in discussion and debate, and to connect with likeminded people. But those posters made me realize that was never going to happen.

I took it off the notice board and found the librarian's office. They directed me to the university's administrators, and an extremely nice woman took me into a room and asked me about them. She seemed genuinely taken aback and concerned, and to her credit, she did what she could to stop it. But there's only so much she really could have done…which is why the posters just kept going up. In no time, everyone knew who I was. I was the guy who supported Anders Breivik.

Days later, outside that same library, I was approached by another student who I later learned was an active member of the local Labour Party. He asked, "Are you Jack Buckby?" I hesitantly responded, "Yes," to which he said, "I've been following your work" and lunged toward me. When a number of other young men started surrounding me and threatening me, I brushed them off and started walking away. They became more aggressive, so I made the decision to get to the library quickly, where I alerted the librarian and took cover in their office. I could have tried to be the big man and started throwing punches, but with a gang of lads following me, it didn't make much sense. That, and I would have been portrayed as the aggressor had I hurt any of them.

The librarian thought I was mental. The idea of a gang of lads following and threatening me because they recognized me from the internet was weird, but it was true. Rather than put me off from continuing my work, however, it motivated me to carry on. I started to see just how nasty the other side could be, and it reinforced my belief that the BNP and the people I'd found myself associating with were indeed being smeared and slandered by the press. If the media had never reported on left-wing violence, but I was experiencing it at my own university, why should I ever believe what they say about the far right?

And if the far left didn't want to engage but threaten me instead, then I wasn't going to back down. That's when I decided to start distributing leaflets on campus. Up until then I'd only attempted to recruit online, but I decided to step things up a bit. I organized a leafleting session during a freshers event on campus with some friends I'd made from university, and some others I knew in the city. I even arranged to have a bodyguard for the day, which ended up being a wise idea.

We started in the center of the campus, where other university societies had set up stalls to recruit. The Marxist societies were there. The Labour Party society was there. The feminists with the green armpit hair were there. And so were the protesters who had heard I was going to turn up, ready to start screaming. Scream they did.

The minute the protesters saw me turn up with leaflets in hand, they started chanting something about racism and Nazis. At first, they didn't stop me from handing leaflets to anybody, and I attempted to ignore them. Every time I handed someone a leaflet, they'd tell the person who took it that I was a neo-Nazi and an extremist. There I was, a teenager who was otherwise shy and mild-mannered, handing out leaflets with a bodyguard to my left and a crowd of socialists chanting behind me.

It would have been one thing if the leaflets I was distributing were calling for violence, or for terrible things to happen to gay people and immigrants, but that wasn't the case at all. My leaflets were decidedly *culturist*. They told students to be proud of the British identity, to embrace what makes us British, and to reject political violence. Having heard horror stories about people on my side of politics getting bricks through their window and clawhammers to their head (yes, clawhammers), I was genuinely passionate about stopping political violence.

The chanting started getting a bit much, and the crowd was getting bigger, so we gradually started walking to a quieter part of the campus. I'd fully expected to be treated like this, so as I walked away and led the protesters further away from the main hub of activity, I sent a text message to a secondary team that was waiting around the corner. As the enraged Marxists and "anti-fascists" continued screaming at me, a team of two others went back to the student union building and plastered the notice boards with leaflets and distributed as many as they could without getting caught again.

The thugs who were chasing me at this point weren't all students. Many of them were fully grown men covered in Communist badges. One was a lanky young lad who was literally foaming at the mouth while he screamed, "You're a fascist piece of shit" in my face. His eyes were pinholes, so I assumed he was high on some kind of drug. There were some young girls there who lingered behind the men, shouting at me. They asked the man acting as my bodyguard who he was and why he was there. He was a biker, and an old family friend, so he wasn't the kind of guy people would want to mess with. When he told them he was family, at least two of them told him, "You should disown him."

It took me a while to give in and go home. At this point, no leaflets were getting distributed. I was surrounded by a gang of thugs who kept trying to find the perfect moment to grab the leaflets from our hands. They managed to grab some off my friend Craig and throw them over a fence. They then started taking photographs of us to upload to their "Liverpool Antifascists" blog, in which they declared great victory over us.

Media reports from the time[86] note that the police briefly got involved, which I had forgotten until I read them. The police turned up, asked what was going on, told the protesters to leave us alone and then…left. The protesters continued screaming, "Nazi scum off our streets!" and one older gentleman very politely informed me that if I ever stepped foot in Toxteth (a region in Liverpool), then he'd shoot me dead.

We hailed a cab and left.

It's pretty much only white boys who are treated like this by other students. We are the Devil incarnate to these insane ideologues, and their completely unhinged behavior does its job. They put off a vast majority of young white lads from speaking their minds at university. My recruitment on campus ultimately came to nothing, but not because people weren't agreeing with me. I was receiving emails every day from other young men who had read about me in online magazines and news reports (I'd started attracting the attention of the national press at this point). They told me that they supported what I was doing but couldn't risk their education by standing up and getting involved. They recognized the likelihood that they would be dogpiled by far-left extremists on campus and maybe even get kicked off their cause. There were a few lads on my own campus who I used to meet for a quiet pint every now and again, but who wouldn't commit to

86 Jack Robinson, "'Nazi' Society Hounded Off Campus," *The Liverpool Tab*, October 1, 2012, https://thetab.com/uk/liverpool/2012/10/01/controversial-society-meets-violent-resistance-at-freshers-fair-335.

getting involved because they didn't want to become the target of abuse. And who could blame them?

I did see a lot of the young men I knew get increasingly angry at the situation, though. I met with one young guy who had contacted me through my website in Liverpool city center one afternoon. We went for a pint and a sandwich, and he didn't strike me as insane or irrational. In fact, he was pretty boring. He agreed with everything I'd said, was supportive of the work I did, and told me he wasn't planning on getting active himself because he knew how the far left behaved.

Within a year or so, someone sent me photographs of him wearing a KKK hood. There's something particularly crazy about that, given the KKK is nonexistent in the UK and pretty much a laughingstock to everyone, the far right included. But there he was, Sieg Heiling and wearing white robes. He would later go on to join the terrorist organization National Action and ultimately be arrested and sentenced to prison.

To be clear, not everyone ends up like that. Most of the young lads I knew at this time have kept their heads down and gone on to finish their studies and establish a career. They're not extreme and never became extreme because they stayed out of this grand old mess. I envy them, in a way. While I know my experiences in this bizarre world have allowed me to impart important knowledge on the wider public, my life would have been much easier if I'd ignored the injustices I'd seen around me and got on with my education. By now, I wouldn't be a struggling author, still branded a racist by the left and right alike. I'd be settled and comfortable. C'est la vie.

Honestly, I think it's a miracle I didn't end up radicalized in the same way many other young men I knew were. The hatred and abuse I faced at a young age just encouraged me to be more radical and say more extreme things, but somehow, I… stopped. I wonder whether the people who chased me through campus and distributed posters comparing me to Breivik realize that their actions were, from the start, more likely to make me angrier and more extreme?

Do they not realize that by shutting down students who ask questions or stray from the conventional progressive path, they are lending credibility to far-right extremists who warn working class boys that this is exactly what's going to happen if they speak out? The far left falls directly into this trap and push the young men and boys they ostracize right into the arms of the far right.

The rejection of the study of Western culture, the refusal to accept or celebrate any form of unique British identity, and the claim that there is no such thing as "British culture" does exactly the same thing. This is true in the United States, too. Sure, the US is a melting pot, but it's generally a melting pot of Europeans. The nation was founded by Europeans, it is based on European political systems and concepts, and its people are mostly European. At least for now. When far-left activists on campus deny the existence of a British people, and a unique British or American culture, they are denying young men an identity. That's a very dangerous thing to do.

Just like young girls who have been told to reject femininity turn to radical feminist politics, stop having kids, and start hating men, young men who have been told they simply *don't exist* will turn to whatever group tells them they *do exist.*

VIOLENCE, STRAW MAN ARGUMENTS, AND SELF-FULFILLING PROPHECIES

The reason why I struggle believing that most far-left ideologues and activists don't realize what they're doing is because so much of what they do appears to be calculated. Sure, it's entirely possible that the straw man arguments so often used by far-left campaigners could be the result of them just not listening to the other side, but I think it's far more likely that they're used to help them "win" the argument. Truth doesn't matter if you can just win the argument by attributing invented beliefs to your opponents. With the media and politicians behind you, it's possible to get away with pretty much anything.

Why does the absurdity of calling millions of modern-day Europeans and Americans "Nazis" seem to pass everybody by?

A 2017 survey found 91 percent of American students believed "words can be a form of violence." Why and how do so many people accept this as truth without even thinking twice about it?[87] Even words inciting violence are, by definition, not violence. But in a world where words can be violence, millions of normal people can be Nazis.

We're told these untruths are truths by some who believe it, and others who know they're not true but recognize the power of embracing them *as* true.

Perhaps one of the best examples of the power of straw man arguments is the use of the term "anti-fascists." By labelling

87 David French, "New College Student Survey: Yes, Speech Can Be Violence," *National Review*, October 11, 2017, https://www.nationalreview.com/2017/10/college-students-speech-can-be-violence/.

themselves "anti-fascist" and "anti-racist," the most extreme left-wing activists have granted themselves the power to attribute terrible labels to anyone they don't like, legitimized and reinforced by the number of people they get to turn up to a demo. If enough people brandishing anti-fascist literature and placards turn up to protest an organization or a person, that organization or person is now a fascist. If anti-racists protest against you, you are a racist. The more this happens, the more the legitimacy is reinforced, and it's extremely powerful.

It's so powerful that Antifa, a section of the "anti-fascist" movement that favors violence over regular protest, is widely defended by the politicians, the press, and left-wing activists and commentators. These are the people who don't just call your boss and get you fired. They wear masks, take to the street, set cars and buildings on fire, and use weapons to physically attack any conservative or nationalist they come across.

A 2019 study by academics from the University of Bristol, Goldsmiths, and University of London detailed the violent extremist tactics and ideology of the sectarian far left extremely well.[88] It notes that violence is most commonly endorsed by "revolutionary socialist" activists, which is true. It is a minority of left-wing activists who go out and commit these crimes, but a minority of a huge section of society is a lot of people. The rest? They either stay quiet or perpetuate the false narratives and

88 Daniel Allington, Siobhan McAndrew, and David Hirsh, "Violent Extremist Tactics and the Ideology of the Sectarian Far Left," Kings College of London, University of Bristol, and Goldsmiths University of London, July 2019, https://assets.publishing.service.gov.uk/government/uploads/system/uploads/attachment_data/file/818862/Allington-McAndrew-Hirsh-2019-Jul-19.pdf.

straw man arguments that allow the far left to get away with committing acts of violence.

On August 17, 2019, in preparation for a protest by the Proud Boys in Portland, an Antifa group distributed a poster that claimed "armed violent white supremacists" were gathering in the city to attack minorities.[89]

The Proud Boys are a Western chauvinist group of young men, of different racial backgrounds, who assert that the West is the best. They're boisterous and laddish, but they're not white supremacists and they certainly weren't out to target ethnic minorities. Sure, the Proud Boys are no angels and I'm not a fan myself, but that shouldn't cloud people's fair judgment. I don't doubt for a moment that these young men were willing to fight, but it is categorically untrue that they were there to beat up or target minorities. If anything, they were delighted that Antifa were showing an interest, and were ready to brawl in the streets with left-wing activists.

Just reading the poster boils my blood. It reads, "BE SAFE, AUGUST 17TH" and goes on to say, "Armed violent white supremacists" are coming to town, targeting "Black/indigenous/Latin American/Asian/Pacific Islander/immigrants/religious minorities/disables/houseless/LGBTQ people." It even advised local people to "establish a safe place that you can be on this day. Protect yourself, your family, and your community,

---

89 Andy Ngo (@MrAndyNgo), "Flyers are posted around Portland saying that 'armed violent white supremacists' are here to target black, indigenous, Asian, Pacific Islander, Latin American, immigrant, religious minorities, disabled, houseless ^ LGBTQ people. It calls for organizing 'self defense' groups," tweet, August 17, 2019, https://twitter.com/MrAndyNgo/status/1162628462433071105.

and organize community self defense groups. Talk to your neighbors, coworkers, and friends. Travel with a buddy, or let someone know where you are."

The whole thing is a lie. There was no risk of disabled people and immigrants being targeted or hurt—but they don't let that get in the way of their narrative. If they say it with enough conviction and enough fake emotion, they know enough people will fall for it. The whole damn thing is completely fabricated, but these far-left extremists have the temerity to behave as if they're acting in the best interest of the local community. They're "*protecting minorities.*"

When you realize there are real extremists out there who want to do people harm, you see just how insulting and vile this is. The Proud Boys might not be to everyone's taste—understandably so—but there was virtually zero risk of the Proud Boys orchestrating violent attacks against nonwhite people and bystanders in Portland. That didn't stop the local Antifa group insincerely encouraging people to "find a safe place" to be on that day, to "protect yourself, your family and your community," and to "organize community self defense groups." This is the most significant part of the poster for me.

The suggestion that the Proud Boys were out to cause violence was the first part of the deception. Once Antifa had expressed their fake concern about minorities in Portland, they went on to pre-contextualize the violence that would come the next day.

What happened that day was interesting. Antifa rioted, but so did the right-wing protestors. Left-wing activists putting up these posters foretold a self-fulfilling prophecy. They predicted violence and boy, did it happen. Just not in the way they predicted, or for the reasons they predicted. Antifa threw concrete bricks into the crowd, hammered at vehicles, and laughed as an older man was beaten to the ground unconscious. The Proud Boys and other right-wing activists seemed perfectly willing to engage in violence that day, too. Footage published by journalist Andy Ngo showed the extent of the violence from Antifa but failed to detail the violence directed back at them. In fact, footage from the day shows that Ngo failed to film (or publish) many examples of violence committed on behalf of right-wing activists who had decided to turn up specifically for a confrontation with *Antifa* (not innocent bystanders).

There was no need to propagandize the violence that took place that day. It is symptomatic of the violence promoted by Antifa all over the Western world, but it also represented the problem of reciprocal extremism that the West faces. It's one thing defending yourself against left-wing violence, but carrying hammers and weapons in anticipation of a fight is not good. Provocation like this from Antifa is not helpful, and honestly, we should be glad that the right-wing men fighting back that day haven't become even more radical. They're still accepting of people of all races and are in many ways perfectly normal populists and conservatives. But they're angry, riled up, and ready to fight back and defend themselves.

The left's violent proselytizing is the straw that broke the camel's back for many young Western men.

My first experience of left-wing violence was during a BNP protest in Liverpool sometime around 2011, when a member of Antifa punched an older woman square in the face. It shocked me then and it still shocks me now. It's not a new thing, though it has definitely become more organized over the last decade.

In 2018, an Antifa website called for the "slaughter" of "fascistic border patrol dogs and their bosses."[90]

In 2019, Antifa also threatened to burn down a theater in New Jersey for hosting a debate about political violence.[91] The planned discussion was called "Ending Racism, Violence and Authoritarianism," but the presence of some men's rights activists was enough for Antifa to deliver credible threats of violence and arson. They also hacked the Twitter account of the venue and promised to occupy the place until they cancelled the event. The event was cancelled.

Antifa has been punching its way through the opposition for decades in the UK, and while it's mostly true that revolutionary socialists have been doing the same in the US for a similar period of time, it seems that it's only recently become a "phenomenon" in the States. I think it was the case of Yvette Felarca that really raised the profile of left-wing violence back in 2016. The Berkeley teacher was seen punching right-wing activists in the street, as part of her radical activism with the group By Any Means Necessary. Eric Clanton, an East Bay college professor, also used a bike lock as a weapon, striking a man over the head

---

90 Debra Heine, "Antifa Website Calls for 'Slaughter' of 'Fascistic Border Patrol Dogs and Their Bosses,'" PJ Media, September 21, 2018, https://pjmedia.com/trending/antifa-website-calls-for-slaughter-of-fascistic-border-patrol-dogs-and-their-bosses/?fbclid=IwAR1i57EhZSquxOas8IBJR5stFgMN119AuX0i5q6d9oytFhSwhA_JHsBUPmk.

91 Allum Bokhari, "'Minds' Event Organizers: Antifa Threatens to Burn Down Theater Hosting Debate on Political Violence," Breitbart, August 19, 2019, https://www.breitbart.com/tech/2019/08/19/minds-event-organizers-antifa-threatens-to-burn-down-theater-hosting-debate-on-political-violence/.

during a free speech rally in Berkeley in 2017. Years later he took a three-year probation deal for the attack, but his and Felarca's actions exposed their radicalism to the country.

Since then, Antifa has violently protested everything from moderate conservative events and protests to neo-Nazi gatherings. They make no distinction, and while they're throwing bricks, bottles and bike locks, Democratic senators are supporting them.

Representative Debra Haaland of New Mexico in 2019 refused to even acknowledge the violence associated with the organization, describing them as "peaceful protesters" who are just trying to "safeguard their city."[92] This is verifiably untrue.

The media will defend you, like CNN's Chris Cuomo did when he said Antifa is wrong to hit people, police, and reporters, but "right" to fight "hate." He said, "All punches are not equal morally."[93]

Representative Maxine Waters also endorsed Antifa's tactic of making the lives of political opponents miserable through constant harassment, calling on supporters to "create a crowd" and "push back" against anybody from Trump's cabinet.[94]

---

92 Mike Brest, "Democratic Congresswoman Calls Antifa 'Peaceful Protesters,'" *The Washington Examiner*, December 11, 2019, https://www.washingtonexaminer.com/news/democratic-congresswoman-calls-antifa-peaceful-protesters.

93 Schwartz, "CNN's Chris Cuomo Defends Antifa: Attacks on Police, Journalists 'Not Equal' to Fighting Bigots," *RealClear Politics*, August 14, 2018, https://www.realclearpolitics.com/video/2018/08/14/cnn_chris_cuomo_defends_antifa_attacks_on_police_journalists_not_equal_to_fighting_bigots.html.

94 Jamie Ehrlich, "Maxine Waters Encourages Supporters to Harass Trump Administration Officials," CNN, June 25, 2018, https://edition.cnn.com/2018/06/25/politics/maxine-waters-trump-officials/index.html.

Left-wing violence is either ignored or excused depending on how the politicians and members of the press are feeling on a particular day. The use of straw man arguments, the suggestion that they are "fighting bigots," and the self-fulfilling prophecies have meant far-left activists have been able to go about physically attacking and destroying the lives of decent American and British people for years.

When these ideologues are not directly committing violent acts themselves, they're establishing shaky narratives that put lives in danger. Far-left activists frequently tell the world that words cause violence, while failing to recognize (or pretending to fail to recognize) that their words and actions are inciting violence. When these people lump conservatives, nationalists, and populists in with neo-Nazis and the very worst of the worst, they are perpetuating the nonsense narrative that half the general public are neo-Nazis and extremists. In America and the United Kingdom, there is a very natural and universal hatred of neo-Nazis. We won the war for a reason, we're proud of winning that war, and we (on the most part) maintain a natural aversion to fascism and blind hatred of people based on their race or religious views.

Honestly, even with the growth of the real far right in recent years, it's difficult to find people that support that kind of hatred. Regardless, Antifa pushes the narrative that minorities are frequently endangered by the mere presence of conservatives, while at the same time encouraging violence against Nazis. The "Punch a Nazi" campaign hasn't stopped since the time white nationalist Richard Spencer was sucker punched on camera. Attacking Spencer was clearly wrong (and if anything, validated the message of his most extreme followers), and it has put everyone who rejects the extremist thinking of the radical left in danger. Disagree with open borders? You're a Nazi and it's reasonable to punch you. Support free speech, even for racists? You're literally Hitler, and breaking your nose is a righteous and just act.

Activist and advocacy groups like HOPE not hate and SPLC also use their platforms and funding in a way that, I believe, puts targets on the backs of people and organizations they take issue with. Having the ear of the politicians and the press, and having ample funding that allows them to spend every waking moment obsessing over the "far right" and how they can destroy their political opponents, has resulted in countless hit pieces and smears against thoroughly decent, normal people. The case of the Family Research Council is a particularly troubling example.

In this instance, the SPLC labelled the activist group Family Research Council as a "hate group." Their religious views relating to homosexuality earned them the label, despite never advocating violence against homosexual people (they are, after all, Christian). In 2012, Floyd Lee Corkins II stormed into their offices with a 9mm pistol and a backpack full of Chick-fil-A sandwiches. He shot an unarmed security guard in the arm before being wrestled to the ground. The shooter admitted he had planned to smear the sandwiches over the lifeless faces of his victims, in reference to the "homophobia" of the fast food chain's chief operating officer Dan Cathy.

The presence of an extreme and violent contingent of activists in progressive circles, labelling every organization that disagrees with them a "hate group" is a very worrying thing indeed.

This conflating of real neo-Nazis with normal people is extremely dangerous. For a start, punching (or murdering) real neo-Nazis doesn't solve a damn thing. It reinforces their belief that the odds are stacked against them, and that "ZOG" (Zionist Occupied Government) wants them silenced for speaking the truth, etc. But conflating these conspiracy theorists and racists with normal people creates a self-fulling prophecy.

There's something that Professor Jordan Peterson once said in one of his lectures that stuck with me, and it fits this context. He said that the best way to torture somebody is not to punish them when they do wrong, but to punish them when they do something right. Naïve, working-class young men like me want to speak up when we hear about the grooming and rape of young girls. We want to shout from the rooftops when we see all kinds of injustices in our communities, and we don't yet realize just quite what we're up against. So, when we speak up about these things only to find ourselves punished, violently attacked, or harassed and smeared to the point that we'll enjoy no meaningful employment ever again, it is certainly a punishment.

There is no better way to radicalize a generation of new far-right extremists than to punish them for speaking out about injustices and conflating their legitimate concerns with neo-Nazism.

What these far-left ideologues do is not just calculating, it's evil.

This is particularly true when they follow up by labelling resistance to their violence, extremism and sly tactics as "trying to make it a crime to oppose fascism."

Just by calling themselves "anti-fascist" and "anti-racists," ideologues have set the scene to make opposing any of their actions a detestable offence. Writing for Truthout, Shane Burley claimed, "Conservatives in the U.S. have long sought to reframe grassroots political activism as dangerously radical," seemingly missing the point that it's the *violence and extremism* that is being considered "dangerously radical." He bemoaned the moves made by Senators Bill Cassidy and Ted Cruz to label the violent and extremist organization "Antifa" a "domestic terrorist organization."

Let me be crystal clear about this: Antifa is a terrorist organization. Any organization that endorses and encourages violence, commits serious acts of violence, threatens to burn down buildings, and actually does set cars and buildings alight to assert political dominance is quite clearly a terrorist organization.

Their straw man arguments are working because most normal people have no idea that politics has become this extreme. When people see a poster saying that neo-Nazis are in town and you should be scared, they'll probably believe it. Why would somebody lie? Far-left ideologues are getting away with murder, attributing extreme beliefs to verifiably moderate people, and doing their damned best to make it impossible for roughly half the population to express their views or promote their worldview.

By shutting down every possible avenue for white, working-class, conservative, and Christian people to express themselves, far-left ideologues have created a self-fulfilling prophecy. In the public consciousness, the far right is lurking around every corner. *Every Trump voter wants gay people closeted and Mexicans detained and killed.* In reality, more young men (because let's face it, it's the young men doing this and not the young women) are turning to the real far right because their access to moderate conservative and populist outlets has been completely shut off. The Proud Boys that Antifa fought in Portland are cute little puppy dogs compared to the neo-Nazis that Antifa's antics are creating behind the scenes.

When you've been ignored by the politicians and smeared by the press, this final assault from far-left ideologues is enough to make the most mentally stable person crack. In many cases, it's enough for vulnerable, angry, and lost young men to find kinship and support from a small, but growing neo-Nazi fringe.

CHAPTER SEVEN

DRIVEN TO EXTREMISM

Consider the naïve, working-class young men in Britain who want to (and believe they can) speak up when they hear about the grooming and rape of young girls. Think about, in the United States, the young lads in towns and cities affected by mass immigration and huge demographic shifts who know in their hearts that it's right to speak out and say something. They don't realize what they're doing, in the eyes of the established media and political elite, is worthy of punishment. It took a while for me to realize that, too.

When these young lads (or people, generally) speak up about injustices only to find themselves violently attacked, harassed, and smeared to the point that they'll enjoy no meaningful employment ever again, that punishment comes as a genuine surprise. The British white working class and Christian middle America are being punished for speaking out about very real injustices. It starts with a negligent political class that creates the issues and then ignores them. It is aided by a complicit media, completely unwilling to represent the views of huge sections of society accurately and perfectly willing to smear them as racist and extreme. The icing on the cake is the violence, smear campaigns, and bullying from far-left ideologues who know the politicians and the media have their back.

There is no better way to radicalize a generation of new far-right extremists than to punish them in this quite extraordinary way, for simply trying to speak up about uncomfortable truths. And that's what they're doing. I know it's easy to assume that this is all hyperbole, that working-class lads are actually lashing out because they're genuinely racist, but overall that's just not the case. People who lash out at society because of deep-rooted racism they've felt from an early age are rare. Racists who have been radicalized by this three-pronged attack, however, are becoming increasingly common.

Conflating legitimate concerns with racism, far-right extremism, and neo-Nazism drives many people, mostly young men, to real neo-Nazi groups or to online forums that spout conspiracy theories and offer easy, over-simplistic answers. This is a problem we as a society need to face. It's not about left fighting right, or right fighting left.

In spring 2019, I wrote an article setting out the basic concept of the three-pronged attack. I contacted every outlet I could think of that is usually willing to publish pieces from controversial thinkers and writers. I reached out to conservative news outlets (in the UK and the US) and pitched to as many magazines as I could. Nobody was interested. I wasn't surprised, if I'm honest. I have been sidelined, ignored, and smeared for many years by people on the left and right, because of my former association with the BNP. Despite those days being a decade behind me, I'm still considered the "Boy Wonder of the

Far Right," but nobody ever seemed willing to listen to why I (and a million others in 2009) turned to the party in the first place.

So, when I published two articles on this matter on my own website, I was surprised to begin receiving mail from people who had taken the time to read them. Some were conservatives who had never quite realized why that bizarre phenomenon happened back in 2009, some were liberals who agreed with my analysis of the modern left, and others were self-described fascists. I sought permission from one person who contacted me to share his message with you. What he wrote reaffirmed my belief that the system is stacked against normal working-class lads, forcing them into the arms of extremists. His message was troubling too, because while he accepted what I said was true, he also made it clear he didn't plan on changing.

> I just wanted to drop you a line and let you know how much your far right article resonated with me. I'm also a thirtysomething from Lancashire who somehow started out being a lentil eating lefty and have recently become "radicalised" towards the far right view. I'm not really sure how or when it happened to be honest but I've gone from a federalist/globalist to something resembling a fascist or national socialist in the space of a few years. I think what you said about dissatisfaction with Government/democratic process to affect real change in the lives of the working class is a strong point that more need to contend with. I just wanted to let you know that as somebody whose pathway mimics the type of person in your article, I felt like you'd explained the problem better than I've ever read before. I do hope the Police and/or Government reach out to you in order to help those who are much more violent than myself.

I encouraged him to "reconsider the fascist/national socialist thinking," advising it's neither healthy nor helpful. He politely declined, telling me:

> Perhaps it's the ideals of unity and togetherness of the nation that appeals to me, or perhaps I just enjoy how it is unabashed in pointing to the hypocrisies around PC culture at present.

This isn't a unique line of thinking. I've heard it many times before. An American neo-Nazi once asked me if I believed the obsessive, revolutionary Communists and social justice warriors would ever change their minds. When I told him that in many cases I don't think it's likely they will, he told me, "That's why they have to be sent to the chambers." The talk of "chambers" is largely just a meme, but scratch the surface and there's some real meaning to it. Many 4Chan dwellers and online neo-Nazis aren't kidding when they say the radical left need to be killed.

Often, they care more about killing and removing the radical left than they do the Jewish people, setting somewhat of a distinction between this new far right and the neo-Nazis and white supremacists of the past. In fact, many have resigned themselves to the fact that the presence of nonwhite people in Europe and America (or, in fact, the presence of so many migrants) is the fault of the people who encouraged them to arrive in the first place. That has created huge discontentment. Some just keep their head down and complain that the politicians ignore them, but others become radical.

Unity is a driving factor, too. Seeing this kind of extremism in real life is particularly tragic when you consider both the fact that there are many innocent nonwhite people who can be targeted by these politics, as well as the many young white boys who have been enveloped in this hatred too. Born from a love of their own culture and people, and radicalized by a political establishment that tells them they're evil, these young boys are finding their own kind of unity in a society that has become deeply divided.

The way I was treated at university went a long way in my own radicalization, if I can call it a radicalization. I was never a neo-Nazi or an anti-Semite, but I did find myself parroting many of the talking points of the extreme right, including using racial language. The more I saw people incorrectly calling me racist, the more I was demonized during college and university, and the tougher they made my life, the more I found kinship and unity among the extreme right. I would use language that, just the thought of using today, makes me feel sick. I would make extremely offensive posts online just to give those people something to be really offended by, and I would purposely use offensive racial slurs in private messages or even on public forums either to get a rise out of people or to mock the very idea that people called me a racist in the first place.

For instance, I once tweeted a poster made by a neo-Nazi group known as the National Alliance, which advocated for white people to refrain from having sex with blacks or bisexuals. The justification was the statistical fact that people from these communities were more likely to have AIDS, and from what I knew at the time, it was technically correct. What I didn't think to do was research who the National Alliance was or consider the fact that it is a completely inappropriate thing to say in the first place. I wrote "We need these posters on campus," knowing very well it would cause offense. That was the point, though.

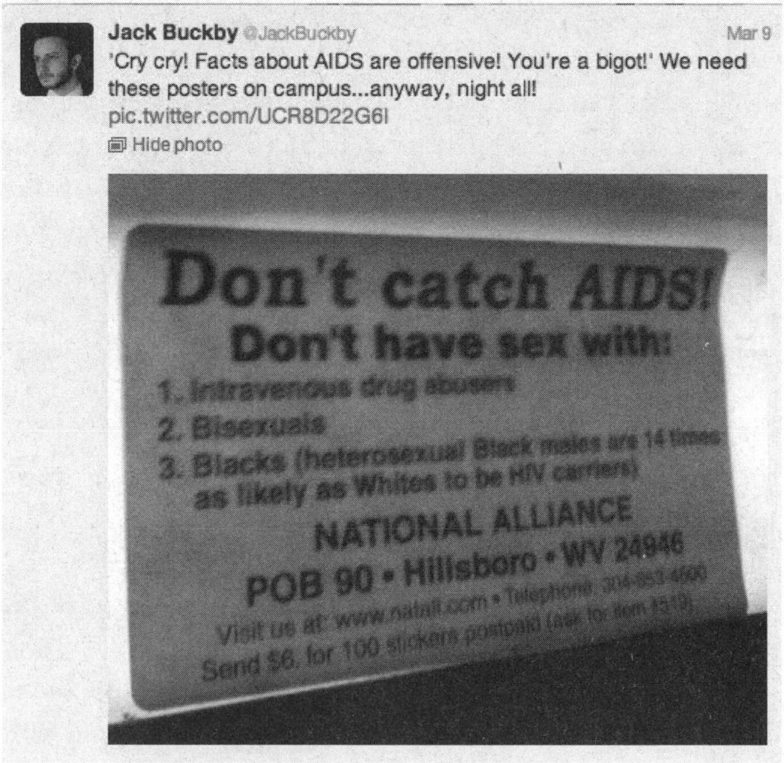

I had been treated with such disdain for expressing some fairly moderate views. The more I was sidelined, the angrier I became. The answers the far right offered me felt more and more accurate. At this point, the politicians had completely ignored me, the media had smeared me multiple times and were contacting my university for comment, and far-left ideologues were taking to the street to physically oppose me. Why wouldn't I believe someone when they told me the entire establishment was stacked against me, that I would always be hated for being white, and black and Asian people were always going to do better than me because the politicians didn't want me to succeed? What evidence, at this point, had I seen to suggest that this wasn't true?

It causes a massive amount of resentment. It can take me, someone who had never felt much hatred toward anyone in his life, someone who was bullied relentlessly at school for being the smart kid, and someone who was extremely shy, and turn me into a loud-mouthed political activist who was perfectly willing to say disgustingly racist things.

TWO BOYS FROM SKELMERSDALE

Growing up in Skelmersdale was mostly uneventful. It was a very ordinary town. I was from a working-class background, my friends were working class or at most, lower middle class, and most people I knew lived entirely normal lives. If you didn't work in a factory, you worked in a call center or an office. I was a bit of an oddball, to be honest. I was the weird kid who didn't like football, wrote the school newspaper, and hung round with the goths and the other rejects. It's pretty remarkable that I went from being shy and studious to vocal, active, and radical within the space of a few years. It all happened pretty quickly, and my own case is unquestionably extreme compared to most other young men who have been at the receiving end of the three-pronged attack.

Unlike most other young lads in this political scene, I was quickly picked up by the leaders of the BNP and given a platform. Most of the young people in the movement were the kind of boys who were good with their hands, liked football, and didn't particularly care for the news or the inner workings of politics. I was the perfect fit, so I experienced the three-pronged attack at an accelerated rate. By the time I got to college I'd already experienced political negligence, by the time I'd gotten to university I was being mocked and attacked by international news and media outlets, and at the same time, I was being physically attacked in the street and hounded by far-left ideologues and activists. It took a huge toll on my mental health, and sent me spiraling into what I could only describe as a mental breakdown. Multiple issues in my life compounded to cause extreme mental strain, though the experiences I was going through in this bizarre political world were a significant part of it. I was ostracized, I couldn't get regular work, I couldn't live a normal life, and I was losing friends one by one. I became extremely ill, I was forced to leave my studies for a year before returning (as I alluded to earlier in the book), and my lifestyle became erratic and unhealthy.

The things one can do and say while in this mindset are shocking. When you're backed into a corner, the only thing you can do is lash out in the least dignified way possible. And that's what I did.

My conversations with Jack Renshaw, another young man from Skelmersdale whom I have previously discussed, show that. As I write this book, I have found myself sifting through hundreds of old text message exchanges between Jack and me. These were from a time when Jack was preparing to go to university and was beginning to experience the third element of the three-pronged attack—the attacks from the far left. He'd been outed as a nationalist in college, and after a series of confrontations, the things he'd say became increasingly radical.

People who read about Jack in the newspapers so often fail to realize that he wasn't always a Neo Nazi terrorist. In fact, I remember the days he and I would mock the anti-Semites and extremists in the BNP.

In one text, Jack asked to arrange a meeting for him, me, and Nick Griffin to discuss "getting rid of the type of people that foam at the mouth when thinking of Jews and Gays." In another, he told me he was "having to defend the Jews against a nazi [sic]...Again!" He told me about how another member of the BNP was having it out in a Facebook comments argument about the Jews and asked me, "Why are people that stupid alive?"

Much like me, Jack found himself butting heads with anti-Semites and questioning how people could be so hateful.

His radicalization was gradual, and I can unequivocally say that the older men in the BNP were the ones that pushed him in that direction. The older nationalists, Nick Griffin in particular, had a lot of influence over him and other young men. Whenever they came out with a great line on TV, Jack would parrot it. I suppose I did the same for a while, too. We looked up to these men because they'd welcomed us into their movement, offered us answers that explained why we were being targeted, and were eager to train us to become their eventual replacements.

Jack and I might well have mocked neo-Nazis, but that didn't mean we didn't say terrible things in private. For me, it was largely a self-deprecating joke—though not entirely. In moments of anger, it was all very real, but I would also often use racial slurs in private conversation to mock the idea people had about me being a racist. I knew many nonwhite people, I was polite to every person I ever met, but in private chats with other young men like Jack, I would say things that I wouldn't dream of saying now.

It's hard to tell what was and wasn't a joke when talking to Jack. We'd go from using racial slurs to mocking neo-Nazis and extremists in a message or two. After sending me a text asking, "is it me or has racism only become an issue in football since they started letting the wogs play?" Jack then messaged me to say a prominent member of the BNP was tiring him out with his "irrelevant nazi drivvle."

It's not even a kind of cognitive dissonance, but more of a transitional state of mind. One minute you're using racial slurs as part of an in-joke, mocking those who think you're really a racist. Next minute, it all seems real and your friends are neo-Nazis. What other people say about you can have an effect on young, vulnerable, angry, or impressionable boys.

Jack was definitely experiencing his own troubles. I had been downtrodden and cornered until I'd reached thc point of mental breakdown, and from what I knew, Jack was going through family problems. He knew he was going to face trouble at university, and he knew he was probably never going to have any semblance of a normal life. Most men in the nationalist movement, unless they were already retired, had serious issues in their lives and didn't fill us young men with much optimism. All we saw were tired, middle-aged blokes who were being evicted from their homes because they couldn't pay rent, sacked from their jobs because they'd been exposed as a BNP member, or fighting in the streets every chance they got because it was the only way they could feel alive.

This three-pronged attack is wasting the potential of so many young white men across America, the UK and Europe.

It is creating monsters, and for what? For the sake of ignoring some socio-economic issues that could be resolved if the politicians actually put some effort in?

Some young men get so sick and tired of hearing that they are a neo-Nazi that they just become one. Venture into the world of extreme-right politics online, or even just regular old conservative politics, and you'll eventually be approached by people who tell you, "They'll call you a neo-Nazi whatever you do, so it's pointless trying to prove you're not." I couldn't tell you how many times I've had to tell people that just because people call me a neo-Nazi doesn't mean I have to become one. Evidently, I'm not representative of all young men.

Almost everything was in place for me to become radicalized in the same way Jack Renshaw eventually was, but for one reason or another, I wasn't. I left. And, when I did leave, I tried to write about it. Nobody wanted to listen to me, of course. I wrote a piece titled "The BNP Danger" which was briefly published on a Conservative Party-supporting website and promoted by a university friend who was an active member of the Liverpool Conservative branch. She was not only reprimanded by her party, but by activists online who thought even listening to a *former* member of the BNP was reprehensible. I felt terrible for the abuse she received, and it was at this point I realized I would *never* be forgiven.

I think I can probably actually thank the neo-Nazis in the nationalist movement in Britain for pushing me away and ensuring I didn't end up down the same path as Jack Renshaw and others. The rumors of me being Jewish that started from the very beginning of my experience in nationalist politics were ultimately what ensured I didn't become one of them. During my time at university, the abuse I received from neo-Nazis became quite extreme. At a time when I was being harassed and even stalked by far-left extremists, I had the far right on my back too.

The two men from the first BNP meeting I attended in St. Helens were from Liverpool, and very active in the city. One of them threatened on social media to stab me, and another nationalist group he was associated with announced on Facebook that I had been placed on their "hit list." It became increasingly evident to me that the "small minority of crazy people" in the party and wider nationalist movement were more common than I'd initially thought.

In fact, the threats became so bad that the police reached out to *me* about it. I would meet with police officers in Liverpool who warned me about the danger I was in. It was in the library café on my university campus where I sat with a police officer that I realized what had happened. I'd spent years of my young life trusting people I should never have trusted, amongst many other naïve and decent people who had been hoodwinked in the same way. It's a hard pill to swallow, and I wonder what might have happened if these gangs of neo-Nazis hadn't decided to target me.

Could I have been another Jack Renshaw?

JOINERS AND POLITICAL CULTS

Politics has separated into two cults. People may well exist outside of the far left and the far right, but their inability to effectively challenge these competing extremist factions means they don't stand out. Far-left progressivism is mainstream, and far-right extremists are fighting back hard. There are people who have wised up to the threat, namely populists and some libertarians, but the extreme right is increasingly the most attractive option to young men for a multitude of reasons I have already explained, and which I will build upon throughout the rest of this chapter.

At this point, we are dealing with two major political cults with multiple divisions inside each one. Those who join these cults, mostly young people, do so as part of their need to be a part of something bigger. Life in the twenty-first century is all fur coat and no knickers. Young people try to make their life look as interesting and blissful as possible on Instagram, while they actually spend most of their time locked in their dark bedroom, playing video games, consuming popular media, mindlessly scrolling social media, and longing to be part of something more important.

When Western identity has been boiled down to little more than pop music and having the freedom to wear booty shorts without getting stoned to death, many find themselves turning to one of the two major political cults to fill the gaping hole where their national identity could once have been found. The rest just continue to read *People* magazine, swipe Tinder, and watch TV talent shows.

For some, they find real purpose and belonging in their cult and they'll never leave. Mark my words, in fifty years we'll see seventy-year-old blue-haired feminists with armpit hair still fighting the good fight. Many are not truly committed or loyal to their cause; instead, their cult is interchangeable and the only thing that matters to them is being a part of something.

I saw this play out in real life with a young guy I met at university called Craig. Like Jack Renshaw, he had his own vulnerabilities. He had Asperger's syndrome, was a bit of a loner, but seemed to be a nice guy. We met through my attempt to create a youth society for culturists, and we would get together in Liverpool to drink. He was kind of weird, but no weirder than many of the other people I had met throughout my time in the movement. In fact, the youth wing of the BNP (which I was never actually involved with, despite media saying otherwise) was full of troubled young men, nerds (for want of a better word), and outsiders. Out of all of them, Craig honestly seemed the most normal and I found his quirks funny. I'm a weird guy myself.

It eventually turned out that Craig was really just a joiner. He lived at home, lived off welfare because he couldn't get a job, and was seeking a home in the nationalist movement. He found me, but he never really found a *family* in the movement—and he soon left. Once he began posting more radical content online, I made my excuses and stopped contacting him.

Years later, while I was drinking at a friend's house in Skelmersdale, Craig showed up at the door. It was a particularly creepy moment for me, because Craig had no connections to Skelmersdale and didn't know any of my friends. It turns out he was in a relationship with the brother of one of my friends, and he didn't know I'd be there either. An awkward exchange followed, along with another awkward explanation to my left-wing friends as to how we knew each other. He took me to one side and told me, "I'm a Communist now."

Sure enough, when I checked his Facebook the next day, he was posting far-left material and had a hammer and sickle in his profile picture.

He didn't really believe in anything; he was just a joiner.

He was looking to belong to something, and I don't think he ever found it. Last I heard, Craig had been arrested and later imprisoned for plotting to throw a Molotov cocktail through his former lover's window.

From the start, Craig was vulnerable. Top it off with an immigration policy that makes finding a low-skilled job more difficult than it ever should be, and his life spiraled out of control. Rob young people of their identity and set them up for failure, and it should come as no surprise when things like this happen.

A broken society has created a generation of joiners, and right now, not enough is being done to stop these joiners walking into the ranks of the far right—or far left, for that matter.

SHUTTING DOWN MODERATE OUTLETS PUSHES PEOPLE TO THE RADICAL FRINGE

Joiners find themselves among the far left because not only do they lack any sense of national pride or identity, but they don't miss it or desire it either. These people intend to fill that hole with revolutionary politics and pursue a life of contrarianism. Joiners who find themselves amongst the ranks of the far right, however, do so because they realize they feel like they've lost that identity and want to maintain it. And they're not wrong, are they? Young Europeans, in Europe and America, are told to embrace every culture except their own, and every moderate outlet through which they can express their concerns is being shut down.

Moderate conservatism or nationalism is being condemned on the world stage, with the president of the United States regularly condemned as a "white nationalist" and critics of radical Islam accused of hating an entire race of people. This mobbish, cult-like behavior from far-left "progressives" and revolutionaries is playing right into the hands of the real far right. When the Democrats in the US and Labour in the UK are so committed to state-sponsored multiculturalism, the concept of "white privilege" and the demonization of young white men as rapists, racists, and the purest embodiment of evil, they are declaring war on white people. When the only people who seem to be saying this are far-right extremists, where should we expect young men to turn to?

The far right relies on the radicalism of the left to recruit young men, and that is amplified by the silence of the moderate political right. For some, acknowledging the war on whites is just more trouble than it's worth. For others, it's just impossible to make a difference. Moderate outlets are being smeared and silenced all the time, whether it's small and insurgent political parties in Europe, columnists, media personalities, or even celebrities. When Morrissey, the former front man for The Smiths, a committed vegan and life-long lefty, is condemned as a racist by the international media for supporting a small culturist political party in Britain, it's pretty clear that far-left ideologues are not going to let any moderate voice get away with challenging their agenda. If you're willing to ask questions about mass immigration, radical Islam, or transgenderism, then you should expect a retaliation proportionate to your fame or influence.

For the average young man, you might expect rumors to circulate around your school or university about your racism. You might experience some violence on campus or receive complaints from students who say your presence makes them feel "unsafe." If you become politically active, you can expect that retaliation to get increasingly worse until you are totally ostracized.

The likes of Morrissey can expect something much worse. After he announced his support for For Britain, the international press proclaimed him to be "far right"[95] and took delight in backlash from the outrage mob. The Council on American-Islamic Relations urged people to boycott his US tour, his record was banned from sale in the world's oldest record store, and progressives even took to the streets to protest him.

Far-left radicals have ensured that any moderate voice criticizing their new worldview will be shut down. Moderate political parties and groups that embrace people of all races but propose strict measures to tackle Islamic radicalism are hounded so much that it's impossible to host public events or hold gatherings without facing violence and protest. In the UK, it is now virtually impossible for any political group that wants to tackle mass immigration and take on Islamic extremism to hold any public event. I should know; I've been hosting and arranging events like that for years. Every single one was marred by violence or protest or cancelled because the venue received death threats and constant phone calls from far-left radicals who called us neo-Nazis. Conservatives and moderate leftists in the United States have repeatedly faced this same problem when trying to host public events in which speakers are willing to challenge the narrative of the extreme left.

95 Roisin O'Connor, "Morrissey Reaffirms Support for Far-Right Party and Claims 'Everyone Prefers Their Own Race,'" *Independent*, June 25, 2019, https://www.independent.co.uk/arts-entertainment/music/news/morrissey-interview-far-right-for-britain-racist-brexit-nigel-farage-a8973276.html.

If an organization persists even after protests and harassment campaigns, bigger far-left organizations with lots of money to throw around tend to take control of matters and ensure smear campaigns are so effective that their targets can simply never recover. Morrissey, for instance, should only expect his critics to become more vocal and to eventually be shunned from the music industry entirely.

Meanwhile, many moderate organizations and political parties should expect to fall victim to the far left's ability to establish self-fulfilling prophecies that ensure neo-Nazis are attracted to organizations to which they never belonged in the first place. A moderate, multiracial, culturist political party can incorrectly be labelled a far-right, racist hate group, which in turn attracts far-right extremists looking for a new home. Once the organizations and outlets who originally made those false claims get the first whiff of extremists being active in the groups they smeared, they'll use that evidence to perpetually demonize every single moderate conservative, nationalist, populist, or even liberal who is also involved.

This happened to For Britain. The moment the party was formed by former Labour Party member Anne Marie Waters, HOPE not hate and all the other usual far-left groups in the UK classified it as a racist hate group. Perhaps some people would find what the party says reprehensible. To be honest, more people would probably just find themselves uncomfortable with the *way* in which they say things. To label the party a racist hate group is a stretch, but that's exactly what happened. Media coverage labelled Waters a racist following a high-profile race in 2017 to become the next leader of the United Kingdom Independence Party. As a result, the party was infiltrated by neo-Nazis and extremists who obviously believed what the press had written. Despite nonwhite people joining the party and forming branches, and many former Labour members jumping on board and getting active, members of the illegal terrorist group National Action also joined and managed to pass through vetting and run for election under the party name.

After smearing For Britain, which made it clear they disavow violence and race hatred, HOPE not hate reported the following in Summer 2016:

> "HOPE not hate can reveal that Sam Melia, a candidate for Anne Marie Waters' For Britain Movement, was also active in the nazi [sic] organisation National Action, now banned as a terrorist group."[96]

No matter what you think of For Britain and its policies or the way in which it campaigns, this is a shocking and clearly deliberate tactic of creating neo-Nazi hate groups. When neo-Nazis are sparse (or hard to find), far-left groups have to invent new monsters to justify their existence. And the formula is simple.

1. Find a political organization that you oppose, and which may pose a threat to your narrative, and call it racist. Spread the message as far as your funding will allow, and ensure the press make the same claim.

---

96 Right Response Team, "Exposed: Ex-National Action and BNP Members Active in Anne Marie Waters' for Britain Movement," HOPE not hate, June 6, 2018, https://www.hopenothate.org.uk/2018/06/06/exposed-ex-national-action-bnp-members-active-anne-marie-waters-britain-movement/.

2. Watch as extremists, racists, and neo-Nazis looking for their next political home flock to the organization that the media suggests they'd be welcomed into.

3. Expose the organization you lied about for accepting racist members.

In For Britain's case, nobody in the party's leadership was aware of this particular candidate's political history or beliefs because he didn't reveal them or disclose it during vetting. The moment the leadership became aware of the issue, Melia was permanently expelled from the party. This is a simple observation of fact.

The press didn't report that, though. Multiple national outlets, as well as HOPE not hate, produced substantial reports and opinion pieces centered around For Britain being a new far-right threat. It's utterly *ludicrous.* While I am no longer politically active, I was for some time very friendly with members of the party. That's not to say, of course, that I was happy with or supportive of all the decisions that party made. But many of the members in the party whom I was personally friendly with were immigrants, nonwhite, or homosexual. The decision makers and the activists in that party were about as "far right" as the Green Party. A new BNP it was not.

I tell you this story for a reason. It's all part of the way in which the established "anti-racism" campaign groups and media outlets create the monsters they claim to fight. For the papers, it makes for a good story. For the "anti-racism" campaign groups, it gives them a reason to exist.

It also serves to shut down moderate outlets for concerned middle America and working-class Brits. Oh, how the progressives tried to shut down Trump's campaign the minute he started talking about radical Islam. They didn't succeed, but they weren't far off and they're going to start winning this battle soon.

When concerned citizens have no moderate populist/conservative/culturist party or organization to turn to (because it has been shut down and smeared relentlessly), where will they go? When young men can't celebrate their own culture and heritage at university, who will they turn to? And when it's impossible for even left-wing activists and personalities to assert their concern about mass immigration and state-sponsored multiculturalism, did anyone ever stop to think that it might benefit the far right as well as the authoritarian far left?

Far-left ideologues in the press and radical "anti-fascist" groups have ensured that politics is no longer divided down the traditional right/left lines. Instead, you're either left or you're far right. Conservatives cannot exist, populists cannot exist, and culturists cannot exist. Only racists.

And when no moderate outlets exist anymore because they've all been smeared as racist, where will the angry young men go? The real far-right radicals offer all the answers, lift up these young men, and give them reason not just to live, but to fight back too. Shutting down moderate outlets for people to voice their concerns and labelling anyone to the right of Stalin a racist is shepherding otherwise normal people into the pits of racist extremism.

FAR-LEFT PURITANISM MAKES NEO-NAZIS COOL

Enough people have written about far-left puritanism now, and there really isn't much I can add in terms of commentary. The never-ending alphabet stew that is the LGBT+ movement, the trans rights activists, the intersectional feminists, and their friends in the revolutionary Communist movement have become trendsetters in popular youth culture. If you thought the 1960s was a radical decade, the 2010s have effectively brainwashed a generation of young people into believing that there are hundreds of genders, "xe" is a pronoun, and that words are violence. These people are the new church ladies, dictating what can and cannot be said, and while for the most part young people seem to be buying into it, the kids who in the past might have been punks, goths, and geeks are turning their noses up at it.

Far-left puritanism is so tedious and absolutist that the most vocal opponents are the cool guys now. While mainstream and moderate voices are either drowned out or encouraged not to say anything at all, far-right ideologues and shock jocks are cashing in. If there's one thing we can learn from the 1960s, it's that the youth like to rebel. Breaking free from the rules at home and going to university only to be met by a new set of rules that you must follow or face ostracism doesn't fly with an increasingly large number of young people.

That's why a female neo-Nazi sympathizer who attended Charlottesville cashed in to the tune of more than $30,000 during one livestream, and several thousand more during another livestream in which she recounted her experiences at the white supremacist rally. Other young YouTubers and streamers draw thousands of young viewers on their nightly shows, in which they rail against PC culture and far-left puritanism, spout conspiracy theories about Jewish people, and offer easy answers that explain why white people are so hated by the extreme left.

Far-left puritanism made neo-Nazis cool.

EXTREMISM BREEDS EXTREMISM

In her book *The Rage: The Vicious Circle of Islamist and Far-Right Extremism,* researcher Julia Ebner argued that modern politics is defined by the simultaneous equilibrium and conflict between far-right extremism and Islamist extremism. In an interview with *Vox*, Ebner said:[97]

> The main argument is that far-right extremism and Islamist extremism feed off one another, and that if we don't combat both of them, the situation will deteriorate because they create a vicious circle of escalating divisions.

Respectfully, I disagree. Ebner has spent years trying to understand the far right and how people are driven to extremism, but I'm afraid some of her conclusions are entirely wrong. As someone who has lived through the kind of extremism she has attempted to study, I would argue that modern politics is not defined by an interdependency between far-right extremism and Islamist extremism, but between the far right and the far left. Islamist extremism is a unique problem that sits between

97 Sean Illing, "Reciprocal Rage: Why Islamist Extremists and the Far Right Need Each Other," *Vox*, December 26, 2018, https://www.vox.com/world/2017/12/19/16764046/islam-terrorism-far-right-extremism-isis.

the two. It is a nuisance that has been imported and which has an odd relationship with both the far left and the far right. The far left seems to maintain a bizarre relationship of convenience with Islamists when it comes to issues like Israel and minority rights. The far right battles Islamism, though then again, so do millions of normal British and American people who see a very clear threat to their Western civilization and want to stop it.

Ebner suggests that we must fight far-right extremism and Islamism at the same time, while failing to recognize that tackling Islamism would go a long way to solving far-right extremism without much additional effort. Of course, I'm sure Ebner and I also define far-right extremism differently. She falls into the trap of putting the far right and Islamists on the same playing field. This is the kind of demonization I talked about in chapters four, five, and six. It is true that many regular people across the UK and America might not express their concerns about radical Islam in the most polite or academic way. Sure, they take to the street and sometimes end up in brawls (this is particularly true in the UK counter-jihad protest movement). But does that make them far right? Well, unless they're advocating genocide against Jewish people, pushing white supremacist conspiracy theories, or advocating the most extreme racial nationalist policies, I would argue that no, they are not. Ebner suggests otherwise, and because she does so, her entire theory collapses.

However uncouth a right-wing protestor might be, it is categorically *wrong* to put them on par with Islamist extremists unless they are terrorists. Protesting against Islamism—even if that involves swearing, vulgar jibes about pigs and pork, or ungracious jokes about burkas—is just not the same. It is a reaction to a problem, and an entirely different reaction to those on the *real* far right who see Islamism as a symptom of a wider problem—namely, a Jewish conspiracy that spans the whole of the Western world.

Reciprocal extremism is a real thing, but it starts with the radical left and the interdependency doesn't directly involve Islamism. It is strictly between the far left and the far right. I would also argue that the spark that initiated the conflict between these two sides came from the left/progressive side, too.

As I briefly referenced at the end of Chapter Four, Andrew Neather, once a speech writer and advisor for former prime minister Tony Blair, admitted that the Labour government's policy of open-door immigration to the United Kingdom was a plot to engineer a "truly multicultural" nation and to "rub the right's nose in diversity."[98] It is not a conspiracy theory or a well-hidden scheme. These people have been quite open about their intentions to provoke the right for a long time, and their schemes have worked.

Without the three-pronged attack, would there be a growing far-right movement in the West to oppose an increasingly militant left?

The attack on decency and moderance is extreme. In what world is harassing and smearing people *not* considered extreme? An emboldened radical left is using vast resources and influence to provoke political opponents and sustain a vicious cycle of political extremism that has normalized one side and ostracized the other. It has facilitated the growth of the extreme right, guided vulnerable and angry young men right into the arms

98 Whitehead, "Labour Wanted Mass Immigration to Make UK More Multicultural."

of dangerous radicals, and used the monster they created to establish their credentials as the voice for anti-extremism and anti-racism campaigning. It's one of the biggest cons of the twenty-first century.

DIVISIONS WIDEN AND THE LEFT (LITERALLY) DOESN'T UNDERSTAND THE RIGHT

Politics is nastier and more hostile than ever before. The partisan divide in the West is getting wider while the Overton Window shifts. What is considered "extreme right" by much of the press and politicians is really just normal conservative thinking that has been shifted right, making it practically impossible for anybody to consider themselves a moderate conservative. Meanwhile, the center is being pushed further left, making Democrats like Nancy Pelosi look right wing compared to her younger counterparts, Alexandria Ocasio-Cortez and the rest of the squad. Pelosi, along with every Democratic presidential candidate for the 2020 election, has compensated by shifting left on immigration and healthcare. The Democrats now support universal healthcare for illegal immigrants because if they didn't, they would face accusations of being right wing.

You've heard this argument before, but multiple studies show it to be completely true. A 2017 study by the Pew Research Center, titled "The Partisan Divide on Political Values Grows Even Wider,"[99] found that Republicans and Democrats are now

---

99 Pew Research Center, "The Partisan Divide on Political Values Grows Even Wider," October 5, 2017, http://assets.pewresearch.org/wp-content/uploads/sites/5/2017/10/05162647/10-05-2017-Political-landscape-release.pdf.

more ideologically divided than any time in the past. Their data showed that the median Republican in 2017 was pretty much the same as in 1994, in terms of their values—but with more people leaning further right (which is how Trump's populist campaign generated so much steam). However, their data also showed that the median Democrat had shifted significantly left, as you can see in their graphs below.

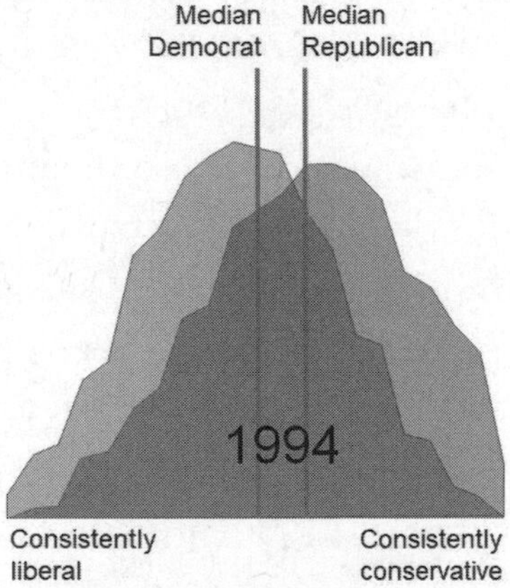

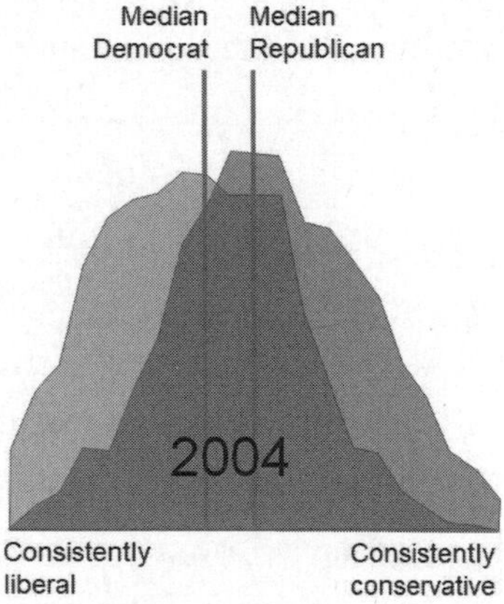

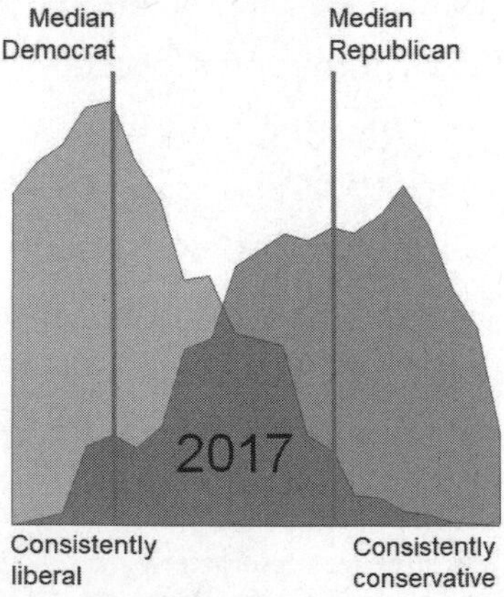

Data from Pew Research's report "The Partisan Divide on Political Values Grows Even Wider"

The data also shows how the median Republican and Democrat were relatively close in terms of their ideological and political positions in 1994 and even 2004, with things taking a drastic turn left in the years up to 2017.

A study by the Higher Education Research Institute (HERI) at UCLA also shed light on how the Overton Window has shifted, courtesy of the influence of university professors. Their research found that the number of professors who identified as "liberal" or "far left" jumped from 42 percent to 60 percent between 1990 and 2014.[100]

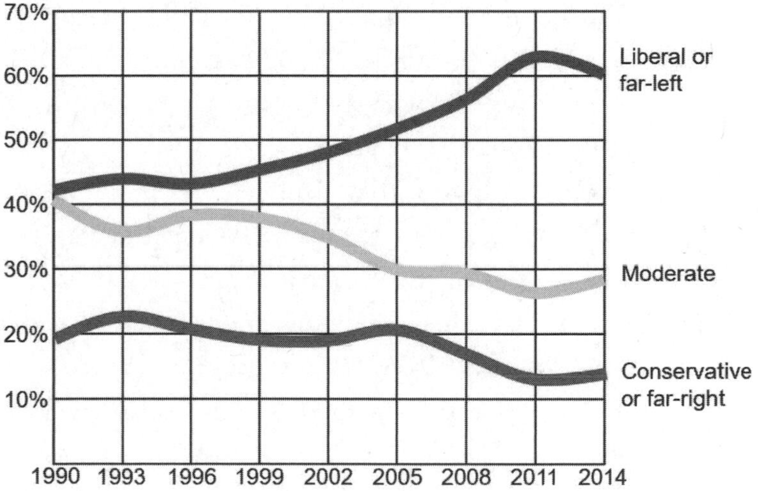

100 Christopher Ingraham, "The Dramatic Shift Among College Professors That's Hurting Students' Education," *The Washington Post,* January 11, 2016, https://www.washingtonpost.com/news/wonk/wp/2016/01/11/the-dramatic-shift-among-college-professors-thats-hurting-students-education/?noredirect=on.

Conservative professors are virtually nonexistent, and those who do exist keep quiet because they know they'll get the Jordan Peterson treatment if they utter a word about it. You'll also see in the graph that professors who identified as moderate declined by 13 percent, once again demonstrating the widening of the political divide in society.

Left-wing media bias is well documented, too. A study for Indiana University's School of Journalism in 2014[101] noted that the percentage of Republican journalists has decreased from 25.7 percent in 1971 to just 7.1 percent in 2013. 50.2 percent in 2013 claim to be moderates, and 28.1 percent are Democrats. Further research from Arizona State University and Texas A&M University found that 17.63 percent of journalists called themselves "very liberal" and a further 40.84 percent called themselves "somewhat liberal."[102]

The Overton Window has shifted left because the institutions have shifted left. The United Kingdom has seen this exact same pattern in the universities and the media, and political divisions have been growing wider since, I would argue, the Iraq War and Tony Blair's decision to open the borders to mass immigration in the late '90s. Those divisions have been widened further not because of the referendum decision to leave the European Union, but the years of delaying

101 Lars Willnat and David H. Weaver, "The American Journalist in the Digital Age: Key Findings," Indiana University School of Journalism, 2014, http://archive.news.indiana.edu/releases/iu/2014/05/2013-american-journalist-key-findings.pdf.

102 Andrew C. Call et al., "Meet the Press: Survey Evidence on Financial Journalists As Information Intermediaries," December 27, 2018, https://papers.ssrn.com/sol3/papers.cfm?abstract_id=3279453.

and bickering between the politicians that didn't want to implement the decision.

I have already argued that this partisanship can be a driving factor behind the radicalization of the most ignored people in society, but I have yet to discuss the very real problem of people on both sides of the political aisle not understanding what it is that the other side has to say. Research from the US and the UK shows that both of our countries experience this phenomenon, and in both cases the progressive left is the worst culprit for it.

In 2018, nonprofit group More in Common launched a study called "The Perception Gap" that analyzed how Democrats and Republicans view each other.[103] The findings are incredible, and whenever I discuss partisanship and political extremism, I encourage everybody to read the report. As part of the research, a sample of 2,100 Republicans and Democrats was taken during the week following the 2018 midterms and asked what they understood about their political opponents' platforms. The findings reveal that Republicans have exaggerated and inaccurate views of most Democrats, and vice versa.

According to the data, Republican respondents believed that only half of Democrats are "proud to be American." The findings show that eight out of ten Democrats are proud to be American. Similarly, Republicans believed that only three in twenty Democrats opposed open borders. In reality, seven in ten Democrats said that they oppose open borders.

---

103 Daniel Yudkin, Stephen Hawkins, and Tim Dixon, "The Perception Gap: How False Impressions Are Pulling Americans Apart," More In Common, June 2019, https://perceptiongap.us.

Democrat respondents said that they believed only half of Republicans believed racism still exists. Eight out of ten Republican respondents said that they believe racism still exists. Democrats also believed that just half of Republicans believed that "properly controlled" immigration can be positive for America. In reality, nine in ten Republicans believed that "properly controlled" immigration can be positive for the country. The study finds many other examples of this and makes the point clear that American society is divided, but nobody is entirely sure *why*.

The slanging matches that started during Trump's 2016 presidential campaign and continued ever since are a good example of this. It is sheer insanity for Democrats to scream "racist" and "white supremacist" at black Trump supporters, but they still do it. This is the perception gap in action, with a dash of willful ignorance thrown in for good measure.

Amazingly, though, these findings weren't the most fascinating part of the study. It gets way more interesting. What the researchers also discovered was that the media and universities were playing a significant role in creating the perception gap. According to the report, those who said they read the news "most of the time" were actually almost three times more distorted in their perceptions of political opponents than those who said that they only read the news "now and then." Republicans might find the rest of this section of the report to be uncomfortable reading, but it's still important. It found that the news outlets who contributed most to creating the perception gap were the hyperpartisan outlets on the left and the right. We're talking online magazines and outlets without a presence on traditional networks. The likes of Fox and CNN still feature, but the research finds their contributions to the perception gap are lower than their online counterparts. This makes logical sense, as television channels and shows are more heavily regulated. The media, therefore, is contributing to the American people misunderstanding what the other side has to say. However, that's not to say it's all the media's fault. Online media outlets are driven by clicks and traffic, and in order to get clicks and traffic, they need to offer something that traditional outlets can't and which their audience wants to see, read, and hear. If the people weren't already looking for hyperpartisan content, there would be no reason for these websites to produce it. The same is true for traditional TV networks and shows.

So why are the people divided? I think it goes back to the politicians. Clearly there has been an issue with illegal immigration at the US-Mexico border, but president after president has failed to do anything about it. Meanwhile, American families have suffered the consequences. In the UK, majority-Muslim grooming gangs have been swept under the rug by the authorities and mass immigration encouraged by a Labour government to "rub the right's nose in diversity." Negligent and self-absorbed politicians created this mess, and the media outlets are just filling gaps in the market.

I think we can also lay blame on our schools and university professors. "The Perception Gap" findings support this hypothesis. To explain this, I will quote the report exactly:

> Education is intended to make us better informed about the world, so we'd expect that the more educated you become, the more you understand what other Americans think. In fact, the more educated a person is, the worse their Perception Gap—with one critical exception. This trend

> only holds true for Democrats, not Republicans. In other words, while Republicans' misperceptions of Democrats do not improve with higher levels of education, Democrats' understanding of Republicans actually gets worse with every additional degree they earn. This effect is so strong that Democrats without a high school diploma are three times more accurate than those with a postgraduate degree.

The more a Democrat is exposed to Higher Education, the more their views of Republicans are distorted.

Separate research in the UK indicated that the same perception gap exists here. As part of the Party Members project,[104] a series of reports funded by the Economic and Social Research Council, three British academics conducted surveys in conjunction with YouGov to see how political activists perceived themselves and their political opponents.[105] It isn't dissimilar to "The Perception Gap," but it works slightly differently.

Enthusiastic supporters of six major political parties in the UK were asked to rank themselves between zero to ten, with zero representing "very left wing" and ten representing "very right wing." They were asked to rank the five other political parties using the same system. For those who aren't familiar with British politics, the six major political parties chosen included the Labour Party, Greens, Scottish National Party (SNP),

---

104 "Project," ESRC Party Members Project (PMP), 2019, https://esrcpartymembersproject.org/project/.

105 Tim Bale, Paul Webb, and Monica Poletti, "Ideology Is in the Eye of the Beholder: How British Party Supporters See Themselves, Their Parties, and Their Rivals," London School of Economics and Political Science, January 8, 2016, https://blogs.lse.ac.uk/politicsandpolicy/ideology-is-in-the-eye-of-the-beholder/.

Liberal Democrats, UKIP, and the Conservatives. The Labour Party is Britain's socialist party, and at the time of the writing this book, it is the official opposition party in Parliament. The Greens are exactly what you'd expect, the Scottish National Party is a left-liberal party that wants Scotland to secede from the United Kingdom, and the Liberal Democrats are capitalists with left-wing social values. UKIP is the United Kingdom Independence Party, the original pro-Brexit party. The Conservatives are conservatives (or, at least, they claim to be).

UKIP and the Conservatives are the most right-wing parties represented in the study. Labour, Greens, SNP, and Liberal Democrats are all on the left in different ways. What the research showed was that those on the left believed they were less left wing than the researchers' objective analysis suggested. Similarly, those on the right believed they were more right wing than they really are.

	Green	Labour	SNP	Lib Dem	UKIP	Con
Where they place their party	2.3	3.44	3.55	4.63	7.28	7.82
Where they place themselves	2.4	2.97	3.65	4.4	6.77	7.53
Objective measure by researchers	1.65	1.6	1.86	2.88	2.62	5.08

Data from "Ideology Is in the Eye of the Beholder: How British Party Supporters See Themselves, Their Parties, and Their Rivals"

They also found that while the most right-wing activists could predict how left-wing their opponents are fairly accurately, the most left-wing activists significantly overestimated how right wing their opponents are.

Supporters	Left (0) - Right (10) scores given to parties by supporters					
	Green	Labour	SNP	Lib Dem	UKIP	Con
Green	2.3	4.67	3.46	5.16	9.04	8.37
Labour	3.23	3.44	3.75	5.35	8.21	8.36
Scottish National Party	3.14	4.77	3.55	5.57	8.18	8.42
Liberal Democrat	2.74	3.4	3.27	4.63	8.46	7.94
UKIP	2.3	2.21	2.06	3.52	7.28	7
Conservative	2.26	1.98	1.37	4.12	7.52	7.82
Mean	2.73	3.41	2.78	4.74	8.28	8.02

Data from "Ideology Is in the Eye of the Beholder:
How British Party Supporters See Themselves, Their Parties, and Their Rivals."

UKIP members estimated Labour supporters to be 2.21 on the scale, and Conservative members estimated they were 1.98. That is less than one point of difference from the objective measure offered by the researchers.

Labour supporters, on the other hand, estimated UKIP supporters to be 8.21 on the scale—almost six points more than the objective measure. Green members were the worst for this, predicting UKIP supporters to be 9.04 on the scale. Labour supporters also estimated that the Conservatives were even further right wing than UKIP.

This is significant. UKIP supporters are an interesting combination of former Conservatives and former Labour Party supporters. They are disillusioned Conservatives who want to get Brexit done, as well as working-class former Labourites who want to see immigration cut. Neither of these things make those people explicitly *right wing*, but Labour, the Greens, and the other left-wing British parties call them far right to suit their own political agenda.

When the ideological left doesn't understand the right, why should we be expected to consider them an authoritative voice on the far right? They don't know anything, and everything they tell us is politically motivated.

Both sides of the debate don't understand each other, and while it's true that the left appears to have a bigger problem than the right, that doesn't mean we should just give the right a free pass. In my years since leaving the BNP, I have been personally friendly with many right-wing political commentators who have endorsed the use of far-left tactics as a method of fighting back against their lies and smears. I have been told several times that I should be taking to the streets, engaging in street warfare, trying to get left-wing people fired, and spreading misinformation in the same way they do. This is what I've seen happen in right-wing and populist circles since 2016. It is an ineffective method of fighting back against far-left ideologues, but an extremely effective way of creating a never-ending circle of violence, misinformation, extremism, partisanship, and sensationalism. The perception gap, in this time, has just gotten bigger.

It's time to start talking again. I'm often told that it is impossible to create better dialogue and talk through our issues instead, and people who say that are right—but the far-left ideologues aren't the people we need to talk to. A discussion must be opened up between the moderate left and the populist right. While it is unlikely these talks would result in any kind of meaningful agreement on the big political issues of our time, it could go a long way to clarifying political differences, narrowing that perception gap, and encouraging more people to fight back against extremism on both sides. It's more important than ever for moderate left-wing activists to stand up to far-left bullies in the Democratic Party or the Labour Party, and it is essential for right-wing populists and nationalists to get off the defensive, accept that the far right is real, and start owning the problem.

In the last two chapters of this book, I will explain how I believe it is possible to reclaim the narrative on extremism from far-left radicals, and how we can obliterate the far right.

CHAPTER EIGHT

RECLAIMING THE EXTREMISM NARRATIVE

Anti-racism groups have lost their way. The days of lynching are long gone, laws that stop racial segregation and discrimination have been in place for decades, and in many ways, they are no longer even necessary. Laws apply equally to everybody, and opportunities are not denied to a person on account of their race (unless they're white and trying to get an internship at the BBC). Instances of real racism in everyday life are met with derision and contempt from most normal people.

Anti-racism groups today resemble the last of the gold diggers in California in the mid-to-late 1800s, searching desperately for the last remaining nuggets of gold and ore they can sell and make a buck from. Groups like the SPLC now serve a substantially reduced role, and instead of tackling the challenges that I would argue they legitimately have a responsibility to tackle, they desperately seek big stories that suggest white society continues to oppress black and ethnic minority people.

This shift in focus has encouraged and invigorated far-left extremists all over the West, and even promoted racism against white people—that is, a hatred for white people and white society.

Why, then, are we allowing these extremists and frauds the luxury of dominating the narrative on political extremism?

THE EXTREMISM NARRATIVE IS CONTROLLED BY EXTREMISTS

Far-left extremists have established themselves as the custodians of the issue of extremism and the narrative surrounding it. Conservatives and moderate liberals alike have utterly failed to respond to this, with conservatives assuming a defensive stance and liberals ignoring it completely. It is insane that far-left extremists in the UK and the US are allowed take to the streets in violent protest and create hate and harassment campaigns against political opponents under the guise of "anti-racism" while so few people challenge them on their claims.

The media never asks whether their reasoning is sound. Nobody seems to even consider the possibility that these people might not be telling the truth. Just the fact that they assert themselves as "anti-racist" makes the matter extremely difficult to talk about. Of course journalists don't want to ask them whether what they are doing is right or whether their intentions are pure; they would just accuse the journalist of being a racist. It's not a position anyone would want to be put in.

In the United States, the SPLC is one of the largest and most influential groups that campaigns against racism, hatred, and bigotry. It is joined by other organizations like the

Anti-Defamation League (ADL) who use their considerable funds and sway to set narratives in the television, media, film, and arts industries.

The SPLC was founded in 1971 and existed initially to file civil suits for monetary damages for the victims of the Ku Klux Klan and similar white supremacist organizations that were terrorizing nonwhite people. It was a noble cause, but with the Ku Klux Klan so small in 2019, the SPLC has turned its focus to politically charged court cases against right-wing political activists. Either the SPLC doesn't realize that initiating court cases like this and smearing the wrong people as "far right" is actually creating the monster they purport to fight, or they're doing it on purpose precisely *because* they want and need somebody to fight. With over two hundred employees and hundreds of millions of dollars crossing their palms each year, there is certainly an incentive for these people to maintain their control over the extremism narrative.

In fact, since the election of Donald Trump as president, the organization has seen its Twitter following double, and its Facebook followers increased from 650,000 to over a million. President Trump has not been the driving force behind this growth. Instead, it's the repeated and false claims that the president and his supporters are neo-Nazis and white supremacists. If there is a new white supremacist threat out there, the people are obviously going to turn to the organization that straightened out the KKK back in the day. The constant smearing of regular people as neo-Nazis is abhorrent, but for the SPLC it's all just good business.

Could that be why the SPLC has labelled over 1,000 organizations in America as "hate groups"? The levels to which these people will stoop are shocking, and their tactics were exposed to more people than ever when they labelled Maajid Nawaz an "anti-Muslim extremist." Nawaz has spent years educating the public about Islamic extremism through his think tank Quilliam and his national radio show. If anything, he is often criticized by the conservative right for not being honest *enough* about Islam, so what exactly makes him an "anti-Muslim extremist"? Well, nothing, it turns out. Nawaz sued and won $3 million in settlement, along with an apology from the SPLC.

In the UK, HOPE not hate and a plethora of far-left extremist groups work alongside each other to promote the narrative that everyone to the right of the Conservative Party's most "moderate" MPs are "far right." I put "moderate" in quotes because, in reality, the most moderate Tory MPs are very socially liberal. The Conservative Party does maintain some truly conservative MPs, though even they are regularly referred to as the "far right" of the Tory party by the official opposition and mainstream press.

HOPE not hate enjoys support from the Conservatives, Labour, and a number of other political parties elected to Westminster here in the UK, but their extremist and radical roots seem to be consistently ignored by their signatories. The organization was established in 2004 by Nick Lowles as a project of *Searchlight*, an "anti-fascist" magazine in the UK for which Lowles also worked as an editor. Searchlight was founded by Gerry Gable, a veteran far-left activist who has spent his life chasing neo-Nazis, making false claims about conservatives, and committing crimes—all in the name of extreme-left convictions. Gable is notorious for his obsession with his cause and has spent the last decade or more bickering with other factions of the "anti-fascist" movement.

Gable was a member of the Communist Party of Great Britain, worked on the party's *Daily Worker* newspaper, and later become a trade union organizer for the Communist Party. He even stood for election as a Communist, and only left the party because of their opposition to Israel's existence.

Searchlight was and is one of the worst examples of "anti-fascist" activism. Its influence on the modern Antifa movement should not be downplayed or forgotten. Gable's extremism and the criminal activity in which he and his followers engaged was motivated somewhat by delusion, but also by a genuine desire to defeat Nazism in all its forms. Gable was Jewish, and having been born in 1937, the horrors that the Jewish people suffered during the twentieth century were more relevant to him than they are to most people today. Perhaps his commitment to the movement really was an honest desire to defeat the extremism that murdered millions of Jewish people, but that doesn't mean we should forget his own extremism. His righteous quest for justice never came to an end, and like the SPLC, I believe he and his followers continue fighting for a combination of financial reasons, delusion, and a desire to completely crush their political opponents. This is extremism.

I believe Gable is an unstable man, and while his influence in the "anti-fascist" movement has dwindled as years have gone by (he is now in his eighties), his tactics are still extremely popular and his protégés have gone on to run some of the biggest extreme-left "think tanks" and campaign groups in the country.

HOPE not hate appears to be, for all intents and purposes, a rehashed *Searchlight Magazine* that has been more successful in terms of fundraising and its ability to appeal to a mainstream audience. The organization has obtained the support of all sorts of celebrities, has the ear of many Parliamentarians, and throws annual events with high-profile speakers and attendees in which it reveals the previous year's research. The annual "State of Hate" report reads like a personal blog written by activists expressing personal grievances to members of the far right. They include real neo-Nazis, but they also include disparaging remarks and personal attacks on people who could more accurately be described as democratic populists, culturists, and civilizationists, i.e., people who wish to maintain the freedoms we enjoy in our Western civilization.

What's interesting is that HOPE not hate does seem to understand what most of the country is thinking; it's just that they seem to think most people in the country are racist. In a report titled "Modernising and Mainstreaming: The Contemporary British Far Right," HOPE not hate researcher Joe Mulhall makes the first mistake of conflating angry populists concerned about radical Islam and immigration with neo-Nazis and far-right extremists. Interestingly, his own report admits that most of the British public seem to agree with the policy proposals and convictions of what he calls the "British far right" but doesn't question his own hypothesis based on the information he presented. In the concluding paragraph of his report, Mulhall admits:[106]

---

106 Joe Mulhall, "Modernising and Mainstreaming: The Contemporary British Far Right," HOPE not hate, https://assets.publishing.service.gov.uk/government/uploads/system/uploads/attachment_data/file/816694/Joe_Mulhall_-_Modernising_and_Mainstreaming_The_Contemporary_British_Far_Right.pdf.

> What this polling worryingly shows is that much of the platform of the contemporary British far right chimes with wider societal beliefs. Whether it be Islam and Muslims, free speech, or a sense of betrayal by an "elite," the central campaign points being used by the far right have widespread support.

Concluding that much of the platform of the modern "British far right" chimes with wider societal beliefs logically means this organization believes (or should therefore believe) that much of the UK supports extreme politics. This is clearly not the case. Any rational person of sound mind would conclude that the British public is looking for something new in politics and searching for an answer to a problem. If so many people are searching for a solution to a problem, would it not be more productive to examine the problem, rather than condemn millions of people as racists and extremists?

The fact that this report was commissioned by the British government under the Commission for Countering Extremism is even more concerning. The British government asking left-wing radicals for their objective views on the far right is like asking a vegetarian for their objective views on the best cut of steak. It is utterly farcical.

The research produced by organizations like HOPE not hate and the SPLC is not just used by our governments, but also by left-wing talking heads in the UK and US media to push a false narrative about extremism. This compounds the problem and makes it even more difficult to challenge these activists and commentators without also being condemned as racist. With an army of political commentators and activists pushing biased reports (or written propaganda pieces) and false narratives professionally published by far-left organizations, the boundaries of what constitutes "extremism" have been changed and set in stone.

In the UK, columnist Owen Jones leads an army of online activists and street protesters who wave Communist flags[107] and sing "The Red Flag"—just like Labour Party leader and veteran socialist Jeremy Corbyn. His friend and fellow political commentator, Ash Sarkar, proclaimed live on ITV's *Good Morning Britain* "I'm literally a Communist!" as if it was the most normal and acceptable thing in the world.

In the US, Linda Sarsour is considered by many to be a strong voice against extremism, bigotry and hatred, despite her very clear links with the Muslim Brotherhood.

Meanwhile, Antifa runs amok, beating people up in the streets, shutting down events, and behaving just like the neo-Nazi skinheads of the 1980s—though arguably even worse. For some reason, the media and the politicians are perfectly willing to consider this street militia an authority on extremism, while people like me who have seen far-right extremism up close and personal are sentenced to a life of mockery, derision, and exclusion. So much so, that the process of writing this book has been, while somewhat cathartic, rather depressing. I want to make a difference on this issue, but I fully expect to continue to be sidelined and ignored by conservatives as well as liberals for my unforgiveable sin of joining a radical political party as a teenager.

---

107 Claire Anderson, "Diane Abbott and Owen Jones Caught Red-Handed Speaking Metres Away from Communist Flags," Express, July 23, 2019, https://www.express.co.uk/news/politics/1156622/Diane-Abbott-Owen-jones-latest-labour-news-communist-london-Boris-Johnson-protest.

The narrative on extremism must not be controlled by extremists. We cannot expect this extreme political partisanship and radical, often violent, politics to go away any time soon as long as the far left is given free rein to define the parameters of extremism and continue to provoke the far right.

WE MUST RESET AND REGAIN CONTROL OF THE NARRATIVE

If anything is ever going to change, far-left progressives must be stripped of their dominance over the extremism narrative. We must not allow ideologues to control what is considered political extremism or define the parameters within which we are allowed to speak. There are multiple truths that must be reasserted and re-established by sane-minded people, both liberal and conservative.

We must assert that the far right does indeed exist, that it is small, but that it has huge potential to grow. The definition of "far right" used widely by the media, the politicians, and far-left activists is misleading and demonizes huge sections of society. Should the smearing of millions of decent British and American people continue, the far right will continue to capitalize on the discontent of these people and grow in size, significance, and influence.

We must assert that much of the so-called far right are in fact democratic populists, most of whom are not driven by race hatred. These democratic populists and culturists exist because of a fundamental and seismic shift in politics in the West that dragged centrism quickly and stoutly to the left, leaving ideological and political wreckage in its wake. These populists share as many characteristics with neo-Nazis as the far-left extremists who accuse them of extremism. These ideological crossovers should not be used as ammo in political debate for the simple reason that ideological crossovers happen all the time. A staunch Communist may support the same animal rights policies as a the most stalwart conservative, but it is simply insignificant. It is unreasonable and unfair to compare democratic populists of the twenty-first century to twentieth century fascists and race haters.

We must also be willing to admit that state-sponsored multiculturalism has not been a total success. Former British Prime Minister David Cameron and German Chancellor Angela Merkel, both advocates of multiculturalism, have admitted this in the past—and more people must be willing to accept this. Admitting that state-sponsored multiculturalism has failed is not merely a talking point of the right, but an entirely logical conclusion to make when one considers the widespread dissatisfaction with the policy amongst the general public. This is particularly true in the United Kingdom, where polls continue to show the public are not hopeful for the future.

A YouGov poll commissioned by HOPE not hate (ironically) discovered that 43 percent of the British public believed relationships between different ethnic communities in the UK will deteriorate in the coming years.[108] In the US, the rise of democratic populism under the Trump administration has made

108 Townsend, "Multiculturalism Has Failed, Believe Substantial Minority of Britons," *The Guardian*, April 14, 2018, https://www.theguardian.com/world/2018/apr/14/multiculturalism-failed-substantial-minority-britons-integration-rivers-blood-enoch-powell.

it extremely clear that the American public is ready and willing to defend their cultural identity. This political shift should make it absolutely clear to everybody regardless of their political opinion that there must be an open and honest conversation about multiculturalism, and it must happen very, very soon.

In a similar vein, we must be willing to discuss the widespread discontentment with Islamic immigration into the West. When candidate Trump announced, "Donald J. Trump is calling for a total and complete shutdown of Muslims entering the United States until our country's representatives can figure out what the hell is going on," he was met with enthusiastic praise and extreme anger in equal measure. Half of the American public who turned out to vote for Trump in the 2016 election are quite clearly not neo-Nazis, but that's exactly what the media and political class appear to be implying when they call the president a racist, white nationalist, and extremist. Tens of millions of American citizens must have a point, so let's instead listen to them and be open to the possibility that Islamic immigration may pose some legitimate issues for the American people. Equally, when a third of Britons say they believe Islam threatens their way of life,[109] we must be willing to ask *why*.

Finally, we must be willing to accept that far-right extremists are not the only political radicals we should be concerned about. Liberals and conservatives must be united in their condemnation of far-left extremists under their many

---

109 Frances Perraudin, "Third of Britons Believe Islam Threatens British Way of Life, Says Report," *The Guardian*, February 17, 2019, https://www.theguardian.com/world/2019/feb/17/third-of-britons-believe-islam-threatens-british-way-of-life-says-report.

different banners. From Antifa to revolutionary Communist organizations, these political radicals pose a violent threat, a political threat, and an ideological threat. With influence in Congress and Whitehall, these extremists have spent decades twisting the arms of politicians and using popular culture to normalize radical ideas. We cannot be silent about this.

Extremism is not created in a void. Far-right extremism can only be effectively tackled if we are first willing to accept it exists, and second are willing to define it accurately and honestly.

FIGHT PARTISAN SENSATIONALISM

The way in which media companies make money is changing. Just a few years ago, it was possible for right-wing websites to make large sums of money by posting propaganda videos on YouTube. Today, with the crackdown on "hate speech," hyperpartisan right-wing websites resort to producing increasingly sensationalist content that drives people toward websites that feature ads or encourage people to donate or sign up to a mailing list. This isn't exclusively a right-wing tactic, of course. There is a multitude of radical left-wing websites that do exactly the same thing. Partisan sensationalism is a big industry, but also an industry that is scrambling to survive. Moderate, level-headed, and honest content doesn't sell, so videos and op-eds become increasingly controversial.

I've worked in political media, and I can't say I enjoyed it. Partisan sensationalism is a dangerous game. It exacerbates the perception gap that we know to exist in the UK and the US, and it discourages open and honest discussion between moderates on both sides of the political aisle. This kind of media only exists, however, because there are hundreds of thousands (if not millions) of people out there who *want* it. If the hyperpartisan media outlets of the left and right that we know today simply ceased to exist, they would quickly be replaced by new outlets established by former consumers. Those new outlets would then quickly find themselves competing in the same race to the bottom, whereby the content they produce becomes increasingly radical, provocative, and sometimes completely dishonest in an attempt to gain (or keep) viewers.

This hyperpartisan media exists because there is demand for it, and there will always be demand for it for as long as there are two competing extremist cults. While liberals and moderate leftists continue to be passive about the influence radical progressives have on mainstream politics and popular culture, there will be an equally extreme reaction from the right. If this battle continues, we will see a steady and regular influx of new self-serving, egotistical, famous political activists created on the back of outrage, shock tactics political activism, and vanity protests. Surely this isn't a future any of us want.

It is hard to expect the media (or at least, the hyperpartisan media) to change the way they operate without a fundamental shift in how our society works and thinks first. If there was any value in truth at this point, the media would be quite different—but the division between left and right has grown deep and volatile. The only way this can be resolved is if liberals become more willing to tackle extremism on their own side, and conservatives become more willing to admit that the far right *exists*.

Conservatives who are willing to engage in sensationalist media or politics must also recognize that their actions do nothing to change the divisive and violent political landscape they claim to oppose. One cannot disavow left-wing political violence or media smears if one is willing to do virtually the same thing back at them.

A tweet by conservative political commentator and author Dinesh D'Souza sums up what I mean very well. On September 22nd, 2019, D'Souza published an image of young climate change activist, Greta Thunberg, next to a picture of a Nazi propaganda poster that featured a young white girl with similar blond, braided pigtails, holding a Nazi flag. In his tweet, he wrote:

> Children—notably Nordic white girls with braids and red cheeks—were often used in Nazi propaganda. An old Goebbels technique! Looks like today's progressive Left is still learning its game from an earlier Left in the 1930s.[110]

Making comments and comparisons like this is a popular tactic in the sensationalist war against sensationalism. It is completely unhelpful, and it is not based on any kind of truth. I'm no fan of using children as part of a political campaign and I am certainly no fan of the radical left, but the use of Greta Thunberg as a political figure has nothing to do with Nazism or Joseph Goebbels. Climate activists do not use Thunberg to promote racial purity. Instead, Thunberg is used because her age and her Asperger's syndrome make her a difficult target for political opponents. Accusing left-wing activists of secret Nazism is as ridiculous as accusing many right-wing activists of hidden Nazism.

---

110 Dinesh D'Souza, Twitter, September 22, 2019, https://twitter.com/dineshdsouza/status/1175848457191510016?lang=en.

It might seem impossible to win the war against political extremism with open dialogue, but when was the last time we tried? Have we *ever* tried? Far-left progressivism has been seeping into the public consciousness for decades, and for as long as that has been happening, there has been a far-right response. In Britain, we had the National Front and the skinheads. In the US, there was the KKK. In between the extremes, we have had a sorry succession of "moderate" politicians who have done nothing to solve this problem. Either they ignore it, or they misunderstand it completely. I can find no solid example of moderate liberals being willing to engage with populists on the defining issues of the late 20th and early 21st centuries. It simply hasn't happened and, as the radical left has gained ground, populists have grown louder and political debate more muffled.

I say this as somebody who is guilty of perpetuating this exact hyperpartisan sensationalism just a few years before writing this book. I was invited to appear on a live television segment for a national news channel, in which I was to debate the emergence of a young right-wing movement in the West. Still an angry young man who believed shock tactics drew attention to important political issues, I handed the radical left-wing activist sitting next to me an application form to take a Syrian refugee into her home. Citing the migrant rape crisis sweeping Europe at the time, I told her "I hope you don't get raped." I stand by the validity of my argument, but I sigh just thinking about it as I write this. I achieved nothing other than getting myself effectively banned from appearing on live television again any time soon. It wasn't helpful, and it didn't achieve anything other than a few laughs from other angry young men like me.

Another good lesson for conservatives—on the matter of partisan sensationalism—is to stop blaming everything on the left. It is possible to recognize the dangerous behavior of far-left radicals without attributing inaccurate (or exaggerated) labels to them. Just like claiming climate activists are using an "old Goebbels technique," it is not helpful or responsible to claim Democrats are the real racists because historically many members of the KKK were Democrats, or that the Democrats once supported slavery. Far-left radicals use the crimes of our European forefathers as a stick to beat us with all the time, and I won't ever use that same dishonest tactic. Nor should any conservative who is interested in restoring sensible political discourse. Conservatives must be better than this.

Tit-for-tat political jibes and arguments offer the two big political cults fresh sources of drama on which they can establish new online hate campaigns, new narratives, and fresh ways to insult their own political opponents. While this kind of endless, ruthless fighting goes on, it can be hard to see a light at the end of the tunnel.

A refreshing source of optimism, I think, comes from liberal US Supreme Court Justice Ruth Bader Ginsburg. An idol for liberal feminists and radical progressives, Justice Ginsburg takes a notably different approach to political disagreement. Although her supporters consider the late Justice Antonin Scalia to have been the Devil incarnate, Ginsburg often speaks fondly of her friendship with the staunch constitutional conservative. She laughs about how Scalia would pick up on grammatical errors she would make, but only ever do it in private to save her the embarrassment before her colleagues. The eighty-six-year-old Supreme Court justice also told an audience, as part of the

2019 92Y Recanati-Kaplan Talks, that on occasion she would politely advise Scalia that his opinion was so "strident" that he might be more persuasive if he "toned it down."

"That was advice he never, never took," she said, smiling.

The way in which Justice Ginsberg has maintained collegiality and even friendship with those with whom she strongly disagrees should be an inspiration to everybody in politics. In the fight against partisan sensationalism, I think her friendship with Justice Scalia should be the example we all try and live up to.

Conservatives and liberals need to do better.

CONSERVATIVES MUST GET OFF THE DEFENSIVE

Conservatives are perpetually, and understandably, on the defensive over the issue of the far right. Every time there is a terror attack committed by a white nationalist, conservatives begin jumping over one another to be the first to explain why the person who committed the atrocity isn't actually right wing or conservative.

This is a terrible tactic, and it is morally questionable. The first feeling any decent person should have is sheer horror and pain. Terror attacks, no matter whom they are committed by, are terribly tragic things and it is abhorrent to start politicking or defending oneself the minute something like this happens. Although at this point it might be instinct for conservatives to immediately start defending themselves when something like this happens, it doesn't change how the far left views them. To radical progressives, conservatives will always be monsters and far-right terrorists will always be representative of the average conservative.

Conservatives, if they want to get past this hurdle, must think differently about the far right. They have effectively been lulled into a trap by the far left. By expanding their definition of "far right" to include the average conservative, nationalist, or populist, progressives have tricked many of those people into believing the far right simply "doesn't exist." Ever since I have been outspoken about the real far right, I have been bombarded with tweets and emails telling me that I'm wrong, and that the far right simply isn't a thing. "But they call you far right, Jack!" They have told me, while failing to recognize the existence of many neo-Nazi groups across the UK and the US, and a loosely aligned online network of white supremacists. Denying the existence of the far right feels like the natural defense mechanism when radical progressives tell you *everyone* is far right, but that is an indefensible position.

Equally, it is a terrible idea to try and attribute far-right attacks to the far left. Just because a far-right terrorist believes in social healthcare doesn't mean he is a progressive in any meaningful sense. It might *technically* be true, but ask yourself whether a neo-Nazi school shooter would be welcome at an intersectional feminist rally and the ridiculousness of the claim becomes clear. That's not to say he would be welcome at a conventional conservative rally, but it is obviously true that ultra-conservative, ultra-nationalist, white separatists fit more neatly into the extreme fringes of the right than the progressive left. Accepting that this is true does not mean accepting that far-right terrorists are representatives of conservatism, and instantly puts conservatives in a better place to offer advice on how to solve the problem.

Taking back control of the far-right extremism narrative is an extremely valuable tactic for conservatives, which is why I hope Republicans in America and populists in Europe will consider taking my advice. If the right can take back control of this narrative, it puts them at a political and tactical advantage. Suddenly, it is possible to (rightfully) turn this back around on far-left radicals who caused this bloody mess in the first place.

Conservatives can stop taking a defensive position every time an atrocity occurs and start drawing attention to the fact that far-right radicals are being created by the negligence of our politicians, the smearing by the international press, and the extreme policy proposals and street activism of radical progressives.

In doing so, "the right" can redefine what it means to be a nationalist in the face of this ugly far-right extremism. Only in being willing to recognize this problem can they effectively fight back against the smears and the lies told by far-left progressives and reassert the real values of democratic populism and nationalism.

LIBERALS MUST BE BRAVER

The role of conservatives in reclaiming the extremism narrative is important, but it will only solve half of the problem. Unless liberals are willing to face down the extremists on their side too, the madness will simply continue. Much of this problem has been driven by a great fear of being labelled racist or simply right wing by the most radical factions of the political left.

Liberals must put aside their fear of being called racist or right wing. For too long, they have been browbeaten by their own people, like the owners of an unruly dog who can't even navigate their own house without risking being mauled with their companion's sharp and unforgiving teeth. Liberals should be under no illusion that radical progressives feel any more affinity to them than they do conservatives or populists. Radical progressives will be as ruthless with moderate liberals who step a foot wrong in their new, complicated world of controlled speech as they will be with conservatives and even other radical progressives. They are perfectly happy to eat their own and to destroy the lives of people they once considered allies. There is no good reason for moderate liberals to stand by and watch as extremists take their place and standing up to them now will be infinitely easier than it will be in another ten years. By then, the dogs will well and truly have taken over the house and the owners will be in the kennels.

Left-wing moderates would be right to expect backlash from the radicals if they stand up to their extremist agenda, but if they are under the impression that a great many members of the general public would be hugely offended, they're just plain wrong. There's a whole world outside of politics, and those normal American and British citizens are not sitting at home worrying about misgendering a work colleague or pondering whether the steak they had for dinner had too large a carbon footprint. If anything, the average person is totally confused by all the new rules they have to abide by, and a shift back toward the center-ground would be welcomed by them. It might even re-engage some people with politics.

The average man or woman wouldn't make a liberal's life hell if they took a stand against political correctness and the social justice mob, and they certainly wouldn't accuse left-wing people of being right-wing.

Just look at the huge success of Titania McGrath, a character invented by British comedian Andrew Doyle. On the parody Twitter account, McGrath describes herself as an "Activist. Healer. Radical intersectionalist poet." Before revealing that Doyle was behind the character, McGrath fooled many activists from the far left and far right who found her ramblings believably insane. McGrath has been one of the most effective and notable forms of resistance to the tyranny of far-left social justice warriors, and the character has been met with rave reviews and packed audiences when the role was taken up by a professional actress. The success of this unlikely and bizarre Twitter parody account should be an example to moderate liberals that fighting back can be as simple as laughing at the insanity of their extreme politics. Sometimes all it takes is stepping into No Man's Land with a smile on your face to facilitate change. But Doyle and others like him can't be left out there alone.

Once moderate liberals are willing to open dialogue with conservatives and populists and denounce the extreme left in the same way that they denounce the extreme right, we can make real headway in solving this problem. If we speak in unison about extremist politics, united by a common vision, we can remove the power from the radical progressives and reclaim the extremism narrative that they have maintained a stranglehold over for too many decades.

If we reclaim the narrative, we can more accurately establish what exactly is happening to young, working-class white men. We can identify the real enemies and stop the smearing of innocent people, and we can see who does or does not pose a danger to society. People will also no longer be afraid to be honest, which in itself is a catalyst for meaningful political reform.

Ideologues cannot be trusted to be objective in matters as important as political violence, extremism, and terrorism—which is why open dialogue between the left and right is essential for political extremism to be truly dealt with.

Conservatives, you must be honest. Liberals, you must be braver.

CHAPTER NINE

HOW TO DEFEAT THE FAR RIGHT

The most effective lies are based on a modicum of truth. When far-left ideologues, the media, and the politicians tell you to beware the violence, extremism, and bigotry of the far right, they're warning you of a monster they created. They are telling you the truth, but they're also misrepresenting huge sections of society and attributing the "far right" label to people who hold perfectly normal views.

They're lying without lying.

There is a far right in Britain, Europe, and the United States. It is small, but it is growing by the day, and it is gaining influence every time establishment media and political figures demonize the views of half the population. Attempts to disparage good people are not only scaring people into submission, but rightfully enraging millions of people. Some of those who are left angry and feeling so desperately betrayed are finding themselves welcomed into the arms of some of the most dangerous right-wing political ideologues, and it is having the opposite effect to what left-wing and far-left activists are trying to achieve.

We must stop this attempt to control political discourse and shift the boundaries of acceptable speech if we are to preserve our own sanity and safety. While I see more people from the right and left joining together in their efforts to protect freedom of association and speech, I am disappointed that so many fail to see the link between the emboldening of the far right and the power that has been granted to far-left extremists.

Perhaps my unique experiences, which I have shared with you throughout this book, are what allow me to see this link so clearly. It is my sincere hope that these experiences could be put to some real use, and that you the reader may understand why I feel it necessary to discuss the far right in more open and honest terms. I have been down the path of radicalization, I have seen young men become terrorists, and I know better than any political commentator, politician, or journalist why young men turn to the real far right in the first place.

We can defeat the far right, and we can curtail political extremism. It's just going to take willingness from those who are currently silent to make that change.

POLITICIANS MUST ADDRESS DIFFICULT ISSUES

Had a single US president gone down to the southern border, taken the time to learn what was happening to American citizens in those border towns, and actually taken some action on the problem some decades ago, Donald Trump would not have been elected president and the 2016 race would have been decidedly less divisive. Had Republicans and Democrats been willing to take control of the immigration issue some years ago, had they been willing to address far-left political extremism, and had they been willing to address globalism's impact on the job prospects for the average American, then the political system would look a lot different today.

Similarly, had British politicians been willing to reverse former prime minister Tony Blair's extreme open borders policy and stand up to the bureaucrats and wannabe dictators in Brussels sooner, politics wouldn't be anywhere near as divisive and vicious as it is now. As I write this, our Parliament returns from a prorogation initiated by Prime Minister Boris Johnson (a perfectly normal function of government) that the Supreme Court, incredibly, ruled unlawful. Johnson faces accusations of lying to the Queen, Labour Parliamentarians are literally screaming at members of the government in the chamber, and activists fight and shout at one another on the grounds of the Palace of Westminster over ongoing Brexit indecisiveness. The British people voted to leave the EU precisely because the politicians hadn't been listening to them for decades, and even after they told the politicians to listen, it took three and a half years to even come close to Brexit *possibly* happening. Who knows if Brexit has even happened by the time this book is published?

Incredibly, left-wing British politicians seem so completely ignorant to the role they play in the emboldening of the far right that they seem to think they are the victims of the Conservative Party's "dangerous" language. On September 25, 2019, Boris Johnson faced MPs for the first time since he prorogued Parliament. Those opposition MPs were taking all measures they could to stop the prime minister from leading the UK out of the European Union on October 31 with or without a deal, and their primary line of attack was what is known as the "Burt/Benn Act"—a piece of legislation that requires the prime minister to seek an extension to Article 50 (the mechanism by which the UK leaves the EU) so that we do not leave the EU without a deal. The legislation meant that the prime minister's hand in negotiations was severely weakened, as the EU knew he could not simply leave without an agreement (something the EU would also like to avoid). Johnson repeatedly referred to the legislation as the "Surrender Act," much to the disgust of parliamentarians who seemed shocked that their attempt at subverting the will of the people was being challenged by the prime minister.

The following day, Labour MPs took turns to express their disgust at the language used by Johnson. In weepy tones and with sad faces, they repeatedly decried the prime minister's willingness to fight back against their constant disruption of the Brexit process. They even referenced the murder of Jo Cox, whose killer labelled her a traitor, and expressed their concern of being called traitors on social media by voters.

What, exactly, were left-wing MPs who have spent years trying to stop Brexit expecting? Of course the public is going to be angry at them, and of course they are going to be called traitors, charlatans, and enemies of democracy. The tragic murder of Jo Cox cannot be invoked as a means of stopping criticism or public anger. Behaving in this way, and expressing faux outrage in emotional rants in Parliament, signifies that many left-wing MPs are more than just moderate leftists who unknowingly enable the far left. They *are* the far left.

Had Western politicians been willing to address difficult issues from the start, the divisiveness would not have begun in the first place and the far left would not have had the opportunity to get a foot in the door of mainstream politics. This lack of action, and the neglect of average working citizens, has pushed people to the edge. Some keep quiet and get on with their lives, some become the consumers of hyperpartisan sensationalist media, some dedicate their lives to an uphill battle against serious injustice, and others find themselves surrounded by neo-Nazis and white supremacists as if it's the most normal thing in the world.

I never would have joined the BNP if the politicians had just listened to the very real concerns of working-class people, and I know that most of the young men from my home county who became terrorists would probably have gone on to lead perfectly normal lives too. If only the politicians had done what they were elected to do from the start, which is to represent the people, then the world we know today would be a very different place. Perhaps if the politicians were exposed to the bad parts of town that working class people are forced to live in, were made to listen to the Angel Moms who lost their kids to illegal alien criminals, or sat down and heard the horror stories of Muslim grooming gangs from heartbroken families across England, they might realize the harm they have done.

To politicians, it's easiest to take the path of least resistance. If they can bank their salary, keep the special interests happy, and retire with a healthy pension, then they'll have succeeded. Who cares about the people who put them there?

The politicians hold the key to curtailing extremism. They just have to do their job and *represent the people*. If the people tell them to do something about an issue they care about, they should not be dismissed with the use of buzzwords. If they tell the politicians they want to leave the EU, the politicians should facilitate Britain's exit from the EU. If the people say they're concerned about illegal immigration, they should not be told they hate all Mexicans and that illegals should be given free healthcare.

Dismissing real concerns backs desperate people with no power into a corner. It has to end, and the politicians must face up to the reality that their wishy-washy idealistic view of the world isn't shared by all (or most) of their constituents.

THE MEDIA MUST REPRESENT THE AVERAGE PERSON TOO

It is also incumbent on the media to stop bowing down to the radical left as if they are in the least bit representative of the people that read their newspapers and watch their news shows. Opinion pieces about gender and pronouns appeal to a niche audience, but the vast majority of the public never think about these things. The average reader or viewer might never meet anybody who identifies as a genderfluid intersectional feminist lesbian, and they'll likely have zero interest in learning what that is supposed to mean even if they did.

If 2016 taught us anything, it is that the media completely misunderstands their readers and viewers. The Brexit vote came as a surprise to pretty much every major newspaper and news outlet. You could see the shock on the faces of the television news reporters as they were made to announce that Britain had voted to leave the EU.

Similarly, much of the American press spent the latter part of the 2016 campaign predicting that Trump had an almost 0 percent chance of winning the election. I will never forget watching the election of Donald Trump in the early hours of the morning in New York City, seeing joy in the faces of the people around me and the shock of the people on the television screens.

Mainstream media outlets believe what they want to believe and keep getting proven wrong. Are they really this blind? Do they really believe that most people are interested in the extreme ideological goals of revolutionary Communists and social justice warriors? Or do they say these things in the hope that average people will follow suit? Let's not forget that the main culprits of this are the commentators and the journalists who are hired by mainstream outlets like CNN and the BBC. These commentators publish extremely radical ideas in the form of op-eds, accusing millions of people of racism, bigotry, xenophobia, and a bunch of other new buzzwords we hadn't heard of ten years ago.

How complicit are their bosses? I believe it is likely that, in a world that's turning to the internet and hyperpartisan online outlets for their news, the big bosses are simply chasing the last remaining clicks they can get as they watch their empires slowly die. They think that the hip, young journalists with their man buns and Apple Watches know how to reach new audiences, but the reality is that the audiences they think they're reaching are more interested in far-left, hyperpartisan news sites and blogs. The obvious audience the mainstream outlets seem to be missing is simply *the vast majority of normal people*. Outside the world of politicos and commentators are millions of people who don't particularly care all that much about politics and still get their news from the television, the radio during their drive to and from work, and even from the newspapers.

By turning its back on normal people, the media is playing a critical function in the three-pronged attack I have described in this book. Their desperate chasing of a younger, cooler audience also illuminates how this three-pronged attack has occurred organically and not through conspiracy. I don't believe this attack on the working class is a conspiracy, but rather, the result of the snowball effect initiated by the radical nature and relentlessness of far-left ideologues who have infiltrated the institutions over a period of decades. They have shouted so loudly for so many years that activists, commentators, authors, politicians, and other people with influence have kept their mouths shut for fear of falling victim to the venom and vengeance of the radicals. The politicians have moved to the left, the far-left ideologues have infiltrated popular culture and overrepresented their extreme ideas, and the media has simply followed suit.

The way in which the media behaves has a material impact on the radicalization of white, working-class people—though most commonly, young men.

A journalist friend of mine, whom I consulted during the planning stages of this book, reminded me from the start that the mainstream news outlets say what they say and do what they do because they are appealing to the audience that tunes in. This person told me that working-class people typically do not engage with the mainstream media anymore, to which I responded, *"Can you blame them?"*

It is true, I am sure, that white, working-class young men are not engaging with mainstream media outlets in the same way that many other demographics are. But that doesn't mean they have simply turned their backs on those outlets in favor of something new. Some turn to hyperpartisan media outlets, of course, but many simply *tune out of the news altogether*. Young men are likely to learn of significant world events through their social media (though the posts they read will be links to mainstream news outlets like Sky, BBC, or CNN)—and when they really do need to see what's going on, they are still likely to turn on their satellite television and tune into the news.

The mainstream news and media outlets cannot use the excuse that the white working class is tuning out to justify their lurch to the far left. It is their lurch to the far left that has forced many people to tune out in the first place, and the normal people they have left only continue listening, reading, and watching because they have found no better alternative.

The media's complicity in the advancement of radical progressivism, and policies that have disadvantaged the working class for decades, have fueled the far-right fire. Have many journalists ever stopped to think why the far right, the neo-Nazis and white supremacists, are almost entirely working class? When people see the national press so clearly out of touch with normal thinking, they look for answers. I know that's what I did as a young adult, and what every young far-right terrorist from my home county did too. We couldn't understand why the politicians didn't want to listen to us, and why the media wasn't interested in representing (or even fairly covering) our concerns either.

For those who can't understand what is happening, the far right often provides a very simple answer; it is a Jewish globalist conspiracy to undermine white people. It's a strikingly effective lie, and ingenious in that it is only reinforced when the media come out in force against the far right.

First, the media smears the white working class for their alleged bigotry and racism. Then, some of the most vulnerable, angry, and desperate members of the white working class find answers from the far right. Neo-Nazis offer a detailed explanation for why the Jews want to destabilize the West and profit from war, and how the media will stop at nothing to defend them and continue demonizing the white working class. Naturally, the media maintains and intensifies their assault on the white working class as this sentiment grows, and the prophecy is fulfilled. The more the media attacks the white working class for their racism, the more legitimacy the far right can claim.

When so few people are willing to stand up for the interests of the white working class, the media should not be shocked when angry young men join the ranks of far-right extremists who defend robustly the rights of white men.

Mainstream media outlets still hold an awful lot of power. Should these outlets choose to better represent the interests of working-class people and stop chasing far-left ideological and political fads, then they could capture the anger of young white men and channel that emotion into something more productive. Just imagine how powerful the media could be in changing public discourse if it brought millions of young, disadvantaged white men from the brink of extremism and showed them how to *really* put the politicians under proper scrutiny.

The media must be a voice for working-class people, and for young white men, too.

END THE FUTILE CRACKDOWN

Academics and politicians keep getting their approach to tackling the far right completely and utterly wrong. Every single initiative created to tackle the growing threat of far-right extremism in the US and the UK has failed miserably because they do not recognize *how* and *why* young white men fall into the ranks of the far right in the first place.

Instead of reconsidering their tactics, those who initiate futile crackdowns on the far right double down on their insane attempts at curtailing the speech of people who are committed to speaking despite the onslaught of restrictions they face.

Attempting to stop the far right from speaking or organizing does not work and will never work.

Banning neo-Nazis from Twitter does not stop neo-Nazis from existing, nor does it stop them from recruiting. Stopping the far right from organizing, deplatforming them, and labelling them hate groups does nothing to deter these people. If anything, it motivates them to continue fighting back against the system and even lends credibility to their argument. When you attempt to silence the far right, you give them the evidence they need to claim their message is being silenced because what they say is true.

The current methods for cracking down on the far right are merely reactionary and do not offer any kind of long-term solution to the problem. Anti-extremism researcher Julia Ebner, whom I have already referenced in this book, gets some things right and some things wrong about the far right. In a piece for the BBC, Ebner explains how she infiltrated online far-right groups and flags any talk of committing violence to the security forces and tech firms.[111]

111 Julia Ebner, "Infiltrating the Far-Right," BBC video, 02:17, July 9, 2019, https://www.bbc.co.uk/news/av/world-48829930/infiltrating-the-far-right.

Although flagging these communities and online discussions to the authorities could assist in the prevention of more far-right terror attacks, this is not a long-term solution. Much of what Ebner says in the piece about the far right is accurate; she suggests that far-right propagandists have a "very well thought through strategy of step-by-step radicalisation." She also explains how they tap into real grievances and tailor their message to the grievances of certain target audiences. This is entirely accurate and a conclusion I have already drawn in this book. But can't we look beyond reporting these people to the police? Can't we ask why there are grievances to be tapped into in the first place?

In August 2019, a report from the Tony Blair Institute for Global Change attempted to define the far right in the UK and propose measures to curtail their influence.[112] "Narratives of Hate: The Spectrum of Far-right Worldviews in the UK" sparked quite a big debate about freedom of speech here in the UK, and not surprisingly. The report not only totally misunderstood what it means to be far right, but it also attempted to conflate organizations with wildly differing views and suggested new laws should punish organizations and people for violent crimes *they haven't committed and may never commit.*

As somebody with more experience with the far right than any of the authors of the report, I took the time to read the entire thing and I was shocked at how much they got wrong. First, for a report about the *modern* far right, I was surprised to

112 Narratives of Hate: The Spectrum of Far-right Worldviews in the UK," Tony Blair Institute for Global Change, August 27, 2019, https://institute.global/news/narratives-hate-spectrum-far-right-worldviews-uk.

see how heavily they referenced the BNP. The BNP ceased to be an influential political force in the UK in 2014 when Nick Griffin failed to defend his seat in the European Parliament, though the party's influence had been dwindling since the 2010 General Election. Today, much of the BNP has moved on to other things. The most radical found themselves in National Action and other far-right terrorist groups, while most of the membership moved on to vote for UKIP or the Brexit Party.

The report focused on four political groups in the UK: Britain First, the BNP, Generation Identity, and For Britain. Britain First is a political party that appeared as the BNP died, and although it briefly gained some momentum and coverage in the national press, today it is little more than a website that peddles Britain First merchandise. For Britain, as I have mentioned previously, is a political party with diverse membership united behind a common cause of wanting to curtail radical Islam.

Generation Identity, an ethnopluralist organization with an extremely small presence in the UK, was the fourth group that the report focused on.

Had any of the researchers working on this project had any understanding of the far right in Britain, they would have focused on the organizations that have formed since National Action was prescribed as a terrorist organization. They would have done what Julia Ebner did and opened their laptops and found the real far-right extremists in dark corners of the internet. Instead, they decided to focus on practically defunct political groups in the UK, a multi-racial political party that rejects violence, and an ethnopluralist group with practically no influence in the UK at all.

Are these people completely incompetent? Or could they be ideologues?

Consider their opportunistic use of the death of Jo Cox and intellectually lazy comparisons to murderer Anders Breivik, and I think it's fair to conclude that these people are ideologues. In the report, researchers point to ideological overlaps between British political groups and the Norwegian far-right terrorist. In their key findings, the authors write:

> Most of the nonviolent activist groups studied promote a worldview that significantly overlaps with Breivik's. It describes a world where the white race and Western civilisation are under threat from the growing influence of Islam, a religion they present as inherently barbaric. This indicates a thread linking the messaging and narratives of these activist groups to those of a convicted extremist, which can be difficult to delineate. These narratives form building blocks to promote some version of a shared divisive worldview that believes in the victimisation of white populations, and seeks to create a chasm between Islam and the West.

This is the second indicator that the researchers behind this report, and the people funding it, are ideologically motivated and not interested in tackling the far right at all.

The report proposes that legislation must be put in place that would make political groups illegal if they share any views with Breivik. It attempts to draw a comparison between the beliefs of nonviolent political groups and activists in the UK, and Breivik. Should any such legislation be implemented, the government would be given the power to decide which groups share suitably similar views to Breivik and ban them on those grounds. That would mean proscribing nonviolent political organizations that have committed no crimes, and even *political parties*.

Besides the obviously troubling proposal to make opposition political parties illegal, there are multiple flaws with this. For instance, the researchers did not recognize that Breivik admitted he had purposely misrepresented himself as a counter-jihad activist. I detailed this in chapter three. In reality, he was an anti-Semite and would be categorized as far right under the definition I have proposed in this book. This immediately sets him apart from at least one of the groups outlined in this report: For Britain.

Furthermore, even if Breivik was indeed motivated by the same ideas as the groups outlined in their report, what significance would this have? Breivik isn't the only terrorist in history who shares some political beliefs with completely nonviolent political activists and groups. The Earth Liberation Front, an ecoterrorist organization founded in the early '90s in the UK, has been responsible for a multitude of terror plots all over the world. If we follow the logic of this bonkers report, environmentalist teenager Greta Thunberg might soon start brandishing knives and blowing up federal buildings.

This is not an honest attempt to stop the far right. It is the culmination of a futile crackdown on what is perceived to be the "far right." It is terrifying and Orwellian. Whether you like For Britain or not—or even Generation Identity—it is wrong to even *consider* the possibility of proscribing political parties and groups on a hunch that they might one day become violent.

This futile crackdown must end. It has not changed anything and is counterintuitive in that it provides the far right with the proof they need that there is a conspiracy trying to silence them. Attempting to shut down the speech and the reach of conspiracy theorists lends credibility to their argument that what they have to say poses a threat to the establishment.

It's also a fight that will never end. Rather than continuously plugging holes, academics and politicians might instead spend their time better by trying to understand what the far right really is and why young men are turning to these extreme politics in the first place.

STOP SMEARING AND BULLYING YOUNG WHITE MEN

We can't bully young men out of the far right. Take it from someone who spent his teenage years being viciously attacked by the media (that's tough enough for grown adults, let alone a confused teenager), ostracized from pretty much every social group I was involved in, sneered at, physically assaulted, and flat-out bullied. I started out in politics as a teenager with all the right intentions. I was compassionate and I wanted to fight injustices—but within a few years, I was filled with rage and to this day I'm surprised I didn't end up more radical than I did.

I was known as a fascist in college, I was spat at when people walked past me, I've even had people in the center of London shouting "Racist!" from the top of an escalator while I was running to catch the Tube. Viciously berating young men and attempting to browbeat them into rejecting their political views doesn't work precisely because that intimidation is the kind of thing young men join the far right to fight in the first place. As is most often the case in life, the best solution is compassion and understanding. While it's hard (if not, impossible) to feel sympathy for far-right murderers and terrorists, we must not forget about those who have never committed a crime and may not ever commit a crime.

Conservative and right-leaning journalists are to blame for this as much as their left-wing counterparts. For a brief time, I became a target for conservative writers who were trying to make a name for themselves by ripping on me and using it as evidence that they were as against extremism as the next person. I think back to when a relatively well-known conservative journalist wrote a piece about me in one of the major right-leaning newspapers in the UK. I was so angry at the time that he would write the things he did about me and misunderstand what I was saying so badly. I knew that he would agree with most of what I said if he'd just spoken to me and heard me out. His main point of contention was the simple fact that I was a member of the BNP, and it was something that I'm sure could have been worked out had he made an effort to reach out to me rather than just use me as a talking point in his newspaper column. I don't know what his goal was, but all it did was make me focus my aim on mainstream conservatives whom I considered as much an enemy as the far left.

A left-wing journalist reaching out to me, or any other young man who had found himself in the far-right scene, wouldn't really mean much. These people are so different from us that alarm bells instantly ring, and for good reason. Had a conservative, male journalist reached out to me to talk, however, that would have been quite different. Personally, I had no moderate right-wing role models. All the older men in my life were nonpolitical. As far as I know, I'm the only politically active person in my entire extended family. An email from a conservative journalist, or an offer to meet up for a coffee and a chat when I was eighteen years old, could have turned my life around. I needed that guidance, but conservative writers and journalists chose to lambaste me as much as the left did. I could have learned something from them, and crucially, I'm sure they could have learned something from me too.

STOP TRUSTING "ANTI-RACISM" GROUPS

Misidentifying the far right is as dangerous as emboldening the far right through the silent endorsement of far-left progressive ideology. When moderate liberals idly stand by as radicals on their own side dominate the extremism narrative, they are giving their consent to dangerous ideologues to misrepresent a political threat to our society for their own gain. The bombardment of "anti-racism" propaganda into popular culture, and the use of far-left think tanks to disseminate false information about the far right, is making it impossible to tackle extremism. It creates a vicious cycle of *reciprocal* extremism, pitting two cults against each other and pushing the center of politics further left all the time.

Anti-racism groups, as I have discussed, have lost their way and fail to identify the real far right. If we are ever to tackle far-right extremism, we must first be able to define it. To do this, anti-racism organizations would either have to accept fault and be willing to change, or moderate liberals must join with conservatives in the total condemnation of Communists and far-left radicals who claim to offer all the solutions to far-right extremism.

The media must stop using extreme left-wing organizations as sources. CNN and similar outlets should not promote any work by the SPLC until they prove that they are willing to accept that conservatives and populists can exist without posing a threat of racial violence. Until the SPLC is willing to focus its efforts on the real far right—the neo-Nazis and white supremacists—and stop demonizing the white working class with legitimate concerns, their work should be considered without merit.

Equally, in the United Kingdom, organizations like HOPE not hate must not be considered an authoritative voice on extremism. Often accused of unprofessional and unlawful behavior, HOPE not hate has consistently proven (in my opinion) that it is unwilling to identify the real far right and instead prefers to focus its efforts on delegitimizing and smearing anyone it considers a threat to their political agenda. I must make it clear that I am not making any accusations about HOPE not hate; I am merely acknowledging that many other people have made accusations about them relating to improper behavior in the years since its founding. Our BBC and newspapers must stop turning to HOPE not hate for answers when they misidentify the far right at every turn. Should a member of their team ever read this book, I am quite confident they will make some kind of personal dig about my writing ability before moving on to calling me a crypto-fascist or a far-right extremist who is simply trying to hide his racist views.

Similarly, our politicians must rely more on the wisdom of their constituents than the propaganda produced by "anti-racism" organizations. Speaking to the people whom they represent will offer a more accurate insight into political extremism, why people feel left behind, and what can be done to tackle the problem. Furthermore, people like myself who have seen the far right from the inside can offer a more accurate analysis of the problem we face. Why trust a middleman motivated by financial gain and a desire to crush right-wing or even moderately conservative opponents who threaten their extreme-left agenda?

Practically every "anti-racism" organization out there has been infected by far-left bias. Their purpose is not to stamp out racism, but instead to use the term as a weapon to crack down on speech they don't like and political activity that poses a threat to their dominance over political discourse. This must end.

The politicians, the journalists, and the moderate left must be willing to acknowledge the failings of these organizations who contribute to the radicalization of young white men. Only once these organizations are challenged can we cool down our political climate, restore some normality, and stop giving people a reason to listen to the far right in the first place.

STOP DESTROYING EVERYTHING WE LOVE

As if calling everyone a racist wasn't bad enough, radical progressives have embarked on a mission to destroy everything that most normal people love. Whether it's popular culture, education, or even our diets, we are being forced to live our lives differently and screamed at if we protest.

The treatment of Professor Jordan Peterson shows the world that if you don't accept dozens of new pronouns, you're a transphobe. The rebooting of hugely popular movies with all-female casts demonstrates that everything we used to love is sexist and must be remedied. The overrepresentation of the LGBTQ+ community on televisions teaches us to stop being bigots.

Normal people's lives are being impacted by a radical ideology that seems to have almost totally crept up on them. It is vicious, it is relentless, and it is unforgiving. Everything you love will be changed and you will be forced to accept it. If you don't accept it, you'll be subject to abuse like you've never experienced before. Everything is fair game to these people. They're the reason why Gamergate happened, and subsequently why a movement called Comicsgate has appeared. Characters in famous, longstanding comic book franchises are being changed to suit a new progressive agenda, but the readers aren't buying it. They're angry, and they're fighting back with their own independent comic books that raised millions of dollars in 2018. Their fight against the bastardization and politicization of comic books has put them in direct competition with DC and Marvel.

Beyond popular culture, our education system has been infiltrated by a political agenda that the vast majority of normal people would consider extreme. It is not only dictating what our children are taught (and not taught), but it is also telling children under ten that they can change their gender, choose their own pronouns, and take hormones to block puberty. This is insane.

They're robbing children of their personal identity as well as their cultural identity. In 2016, the National Union of Teachers in the UK voted against a proposal from the government to teach British values in school. The union claimed that teaching British values at school would be an act of "cultural supremacism" and instead proposed teaching "international rights" instead.[113]

Any reasonable person would consider this extreme. What nation in history has been so self-hating that it considers teaching its own history to be *cultural supremacism?* Why must we be expected to forget our past, and what makes it acceptable to study the history of other peoples? This is an assertion of dominance by ideologues who are committed to destroying any semblance of national pride. They're not just denying our children an understanding of their own history, but they're tainting whatever pride we have left with their own politics.

In the UK, classical music concerts are held daily in central London in an event known as The Proms. People from all over the country gather in London to embrace this tradition that dates back to 1895. The Last Night of the Proms is perhaps the most prominent event of the whole summer season, bringing people together with patriotic songs that celebrate Britain's cultural and historical significance. It is a chance for the British people to gather at the Royal Albert Hall, at other screening events throughout London, and even in their own homes to wave the Union Flag, sing the national anthem, and feel an emotional connection to our beloved country and Queen. It is one of the few remaining events that allow the British people to feel truly proud of who they are, but in 2019, that changed.

---

113 Javier Espinoza, "Teaching Children Fundamental British Values Is Act of 'Cultural Supremacism,'" *The Telegraph*, March 28, 2016, https://www.telegraph.co.uk/news/2016/03/28/teaching-children-fundamental-british-values-is-act-of-cultural/.

Once an event that could bring people together despite their political views, the concert was hijacked by a self-described "queer girl with a nose ring," Jamie Barton. As the American mezzo-soprano sang "Rule, Britannia!" she decided against the traditional waving of a Union Flag and instead held an LGBT flag high in the air. Singing one of the most recognizable patriotic British songs, this American far-left ideologue ruined the entire event for a significant section of the British public. This flag represents far more than just equality for gay people, but an ideology that continues to change the parameters in which we are allowed to speak. It represents a forceful left-wing movement that seeks to rewrite history and rob us of our pride.

These people are taking away our favorite TV shows and movies, rewriting our history, denying our children the chance to learn about their ancestors, and robbing us of the few opportunities we have left to celebrate who we are.

The destruction of everything that most people love or hold dear is done purposely to provoke by some, or as an ill-thought-out exercise by followers who genuinely believe they are doing good. It is divisive in that it may attract some who have already decided to abide by the new rules of political correctness and social justice, and make others harbor deep resentment and hatred for the provocative nature of those implementing the changes. The most ideologically driven activists take joy in provoking those who hate their new interpretations on popular franchises and their rewriting of history—but do they realize that their actions are creating far-right terrorists?

Injecting far-left progressive agendas into everyday life and making it impossible to avoid politics in the most normal of activities is a sure-fire way to create mass shooters and far-right murderers. It pains me to say this, but forcing people to interact with a political agenda they find repulsive and wrong will only ever result in violence. One cannot simply trap millions of people inside of an ideological cage and not expect them to revolt, get angry, and fight back against the people who put them there. It also pains me to say that I believe many of the ideologues who entrap normal people with their sick ideological talking points know this to be true and yet go ahead with it anyway.

Knowing full well that the politicians refuse to listen to anybody who is concerned about immigration and that the media will always defend the latest advancements in progressive thinking, far-left ideologues have set about destroying the lives of normal people who don't abide by their rules. Not only are they forcing normal people into a cage, but they're poking them with sticks every time they release a new "woke" version of a classic movie and dogpile you if you say it's bad.

Let me tell you, I could have become a very different person than I am today. When I see the absolute takeover of far-left progressivism, the silence of moderate liberals who are too afraid to stand up to it, the strict control over what we can and cannot say, the destruction of everything we love, and the condemning of everyone who doesn't agree to these new rules to a lifetime of harassment and misery, my blood boils. Every cell in my body becomes enraged, and I feel a wave of hatred flow through me that I typically never feel. Believe me, this is true for many other people too.

I have felt this anger since my teenage years, and what's so disturbing about it is that this extreme emotion I experience is completely warranted. I am not irrationally angry about a minor inconvenience in my life, but incandescent with rage about major injustices that go ignored while I am subject to the most authoritarian social activism that the West has ever seen.

I could have easily gone down the same route as the far-right terrorists in Britain. Had the circumstances been right, perhaps I would have ended up just like Jack Renshaw. Perhaps my rightful anger might have driven me to seek answers in conspiracy theories and lash out at the people who have enabled this all to happen. But that didn't happen. Instead, I am here, writing this book. I have spent enough years consumed by anger, and I have seen far too much neglect in working class communities, to simply throw that away with pointless street activism, violence, or reciprocal extremism.

Take it from someone who truly understands the far right; injecting a political agenda into every aspect of normal life and destroying our culture along with it is the most effective way of creating a new generation of far-right extremists who will risk losing everything to fight back precisely because they have nothing to lose.

CONSERVATIVES MUSTN'T MISTAKE IDEOLOGUES FOR FOOLS

Conservatives are complacent. Seemingly content with "owning the libs" with facts and logic, many on the ideological right believe that their ultimate purpose is to just *be right.*

This sentiment has culminated in political activists across the Anglosphere mistaking dangerous ideologues for fools. Prove Owen Jones, Chelsea Handler, or Alexandria Ocasio-Cortez wrong in a sternly worded tweet and you'll gain thousands (if not tens of thousands) of followers overnight. Owning the libs has become an industry in itself, and conservatives are falling into the trap of assuming many of their political opponents are fools with no real idea of what they're doing. They believe that a Republican president is sufficient to fight back against them and that alternative media will ultimately reverse the influence that the radical progressive left has on our culture and society.

Meanwhile, immigration trends are changing the makeup of Western populations, children are being indoctrinated in schools, and the people who remember how society was before are dying. In no time, owning the libs will be exposed as the money-making, self-absorbed ego trip it has always been. It has created some minor right-wing celebrities, but it has changed nothing and allowed dangerous progressives to shape the world into what they want it to be without being sufficiently challenged. Soon enough, their electoral success will be guaranteed every election year.

It is easy to call political opponents idiots, but it isn't always true. Conservatives should complacently mock Alexandria Ocasio-Cortez at their own peril. Laugh all you like, but she won an election and more people like her will win elections too. Everything is working out for these ideologues, and if they are not taken seriously—and their policy initiatives taken seriously—they will continue to push the dangerous narratives I have outlined in this book. And, as I have already detailed, their ongoing commitment to enforcing a new, strict far-left code of conduct for living will continue pushing young white men into the arms of the far right.

Mocking far-left ideologues may serve a purpose in that it can give some power back to normal people who have their lives impacted by extreme-left politics. However, conservatives must realize that not everything these ideologues say is wrong. Notably, their claim that the far right is dangerous and growing is *not actually wrong*. They might not understand what the far right really is and what these people believe, and they might not realize that their existence and growth is directly connected to their own far-left radicalism, but their analysis that the far right *exists* is not in itself inaccurate. Conservatives too willingly believe that the far right *simply doesn't exist* because they assume far-left ideologues to be fools. They are not. They are ideologues, and they are dangerous.

Therefore, conservatives have a duty to take these people seriously. Stop assuming everything they say is wrong and instead be willing to fight back and reclaim the narrative they stole. The far right does exist, and it is not a weakness to accept that the far right exists.

Accepting this can instead be a strength. If conservatives are really interested in political point scoring and owning the libs, then let this be the way to do it. Analyze the threat of the real far right, learn to communicate the reality of this problem back to the public, and be willing to point the finger back at far-left ideologues and prove that *they* are the ones causing this problem. Do this, and they'll be winning more than just the argument; they'll be exposing one of the greatest deceptions of this century and helping defeat political extremism before it destroys our entire political system.

REFORM PREVENTION SCHEMES, AND LET PEOPLE BE CONSERVATIVES/POPULISTS

At present, the deradicalization of far-right activists is focused on encouraging people to see beyond their political influence, envision a life outside of politics, and to accept the established order. This system is built on the assumption that multiculturalism, mass immigration, and social liberalism are the default values of most people, and that these values must be instilled in those who have become far-right radicals. Every report I have read from various pro-multiculturalism think tanks, many of which are commissioned by the EU and Germany, get as much right as they get wrong. They correctly identify that racist values typically come *after* joining far-right groups, as recruits are typically initially attracted by the strong sense of community they offer. However, they incorrectly assume that every recruit is devoid of any true ideological values and would be willing to completely change the way they see the world.

This isn't always the case.

While there are many people who are attracted to the strong sense of identity and community in the far right—who I have previously described as *joiners*—there are also plenty who join the ranks of the far right as a result of an accurate observation of the radical shift leftwards of the political center. For some, the far right is the natural antidote to the far left, and they see no other option than fighting back with the same level of extremism that has been imposed on them by ideologues in their everyday life.

I call these people *principled fanatics*.

These are the people who know young girls have been raped by mostly Muslim gangs while the police and politicians ignored it, who recognize that mass immigration has transformed communities and initiated new waves of violent crime and general criminality, and who struggle to see any way of maintaining their national culture without reversing the trend of immigration and establishing white ethnostates in Europe and America. I would be inclined to call these people *righteous fanatics*, though I have hesitated to do so for fear that some may assume I believe their cause is righteous. I believe that principled fanatics are drawn to far-right extremism because they recognize many real problems.

Deradicalization programs cannot therefore be one-size-fits-all operations that assume everyone will be willing to completely change their worldview and go on to become multiculturalist liberals.

In the UK, the Prevent Strategy is a government operation designed to stop people from becoming terrorists or supporting terrorism. It's intendeds to "Prevent, Pursue, Protest, and Prepare" against terrorist threats, and in recent years the number of people admitted to the program for being involved with the far right has increased. Drastically.

1,312 people were referred to Prevent in the years 2017–2018, but this number by itself doesn't really tell us much. Anyone can be referred to Prevent, and it doesn't necessarily mean these people pose a real risk (or are even legitimately far right). What we do know, however, is that 174 of those referrals were moved on to the Channel scheme, which aims to stop people from becoming terrorists. It was an increase of

40 percent over the previous year.[114] Clearly, there are more people becoming vulnerable to this problem, showing that the crackdown on the "far right" isn't working. To this day, practically nothing is being done by any major political party or politician to address the issues that push people toward far-right terrorism in the first place.

The Channel program "provides tailored support for a person vulnerable to being drawn into terrorism," offering "theological or ideological mentoring."[115] Not only are the root causes of this problem not being addressed, and not only does this entire scheme not recognize that some people are driven by real ideological purpose, but it also offers ideological mentoring. I suspect it does not involve encouraging right-minded people to become more moderate conservatives or populists.

I met a journalist in London who doesn't share my politics but was interested to understand what it is I want to achieve with my counter-extremism work. She detailed an example of success in the Prevent scheme whereby a former far-right activist had become an ardent supporter of multiculturalism, rejected all right-wing politics, married a black woman, and had mixed-race children. It is wonderful to know that there

---

114 "Individuals Referred to and Supported through the *Prevent* Programme, April 2017 to March 2018," Home Office, December 12, 2018, 16, https://assets.publishing.service.gov.uk/government/uploads/system/uploads/attachment_data/file/763254/individuals-referred-supported-prevent-programme-apr2017-mar2018-hosb3118.pdf.

115 HO News Team, "Factsheet: Prevent and Channel Statistics 2017/2018," Home Office, December 13, 2018, https://homeofficemedia.blog.gov.uk/2018/12/13/factsheet-prevent-and-channel-statistics-2017-2018/.

are success stories from this program, but we must recognize that for somebody to drop his neo-Nazi beliefs and become a multiculturalist liberal implies there was little devotion to ideology to begin with. Changing one's worldview so drastically and so quickly means not much thought went into it in the first place, and therefore I would conclude that this man is a *joiner.* This is a man who became entangled in the far right for the sense of community and belonging it offered.

In many cases, Channel doesn't work.

In an interview with *The Financial Times*, a mentor for the scheme revealed that one teenager he worked with, who they believed had relinquished his extremist tendencies, was later found to be sharing photos on WhatsApp glorifying jihad.[116] It shows the fragility of the program and the inability to effectively predict who is and isn't safe, and who has been "converted." It is extremely difficult to deradicalize people who are motivated by ideological conviction, whether that's an Islamic terrorist or a far-right extremist. This is why the scheme needs to change, and the approach to deradicalization must change too.

Governments across the Anglosphere, whatever side of the Atlantic, must be willing to recognize that their failure to act on major political issues is creating this mess to begin with. It is extremely difficult to know when someone really has relinquished their extremist tendencies, but initiatives like

116 Helen Warrell, "Inside Prevent, the UK's Controversial Anti-Terrorism Programme," *Financial Times,* January 23, 2019, https://www.ft.com/content/a82e18b4-1ea3-11e9-b126-46fc3ad87c65.

Prevent might not need to worry about this all that much if fewer people are coming through their door.

Secondly, people generally must become more accepting of conservatives and people with culturist, traditionalist, or generally "right wing" ways of thinking. It should not be assumed that most people are multiculturalists and that this view is the "standard" in a normal society. It isn't, and it immediately puts a target on the back of culturists (normal people who believe in their own national culture). It has become so prevalent that deradicalization schemes attempt to convert neo-Nazis into multiculturalists, rather than setting the much more achievable and sensible goal of repositioning these people as moderate conservatives or populists.

Converting a joiner into a multiculturalist might not be all that difficult a task, particularly if there is a new community for them to become a part of. I've seen many joiners leave the ranks of the English Defence League (an anti-Islam street movement in the UK) and become supporters of multicultural groups that oppose "Islamophobia." It's an easy task and something Prevent and other deradicalization schemes count on. But how do they handle a principled fanatic? How likely is it that someone committed to an ideological cause, whether far right or Islamic, will reject the values that define them and join the ranks of their opponents?

It is not a reasonable expectation. Consider the man whom I described in Chapter Seven, who contacted me to say he had joined the far right and that my analysis of why people do so is accurate. He clearly stated that it was the "ideals of unity and togetherness" that attracted him, but that he was also drawn in by how the far right is "unabashed in pointing to the hypocrisies around PC culture." This man is not a joiner, but a principled fanatic. He saw real problems caused by the radical left and decided the best way to counter it is with an equal measure of extremism.

Will a man like this be willing to embrace multiculturalism and join the side that pushed him to the far right in the first place? I don't think so.

Combined with efforts from politicians to address the root causes of this problem, deradicalization schemes should work with far-right radicals to bring them back to a more moderate position *on their own side*. Far-right extremists, particularly the principled fanatics, don't typically come from the far left. They are born of a more conservative, populist, and culturist inclination, and have been pushed further to the right by their environment.

This would first require action from politicians, as well as a willingness from the moderate left to accept that roughly half the population is always going to disagree with them. This means engaging with conservatives and populists and accepting that they exist and will always exist. In turn, a new-found acceptance for conservatives will allow for deradicalization schemes and "ideological tutors" to encourage far-right radicals to realign to more moderate conservative values, rather than adopting the impossible task of turning far-right extremists into multiculturalists.

Furthermore, Western governments must be willing to engage with people who have real experience of the far right and the political issues that cause radicalization to begin with. I don't mean left-wing political campaigners who think anybody right of Paul Ryan or Theresa May is "far right," but people like me who have been vulnerable to radicalization and who have seen first-hand how it happens.

There is also much to be learned from principled fanatics who have seen the light and moved toward the moderate center. Deradicalization schemes regularly use former members of the far right who had a change of heart and became multiculturalists as examples of how people can be changed. Right now, there are former far-right activists working alongside the Prevent scheme, trying to win over young principled fanatics. This will not work.

Western governments, charities, and counter-extremism organizations must understand the difference between these two distinct kinds of far-right extremists, and they must account for it in their deradicalization program.

Deradicalization programs must be reformed, and there must be a fundamental shift in how society views conservatives and populists.

WE HAVE TO START TALKING AGAIN

We must never underestimate the power of dialogue and decency.

Having a sensible conversation with far-left radicals is typically impossible. Those who have tried it have been met with boycott, mockery, and when their attempts at shutting down the conversation fail, violence.

It is deeply sad that we are met with such hostility and vindictive behavior whenever we simply try to talk, but if that is how we're going to be treated, then I guess we don't have to speak to them at all.

The power, after all, lies mostly in the hands of the moderate liberals. These are the silent people who refuse to publicly acknowledge that their side of the political debate is now dominated and controlled by radicals with whom they share very little in common. They don't realize it, but their silence is considered their consent, and every day they keep quiet, the more dangerous it will become to finally speak out. But they *must* speak out.

Now is the time to reopen the dialogue, push the far-left radicals aside, and engage in productive, honest discussion that could deescalate much of the political tension we see on both sides of the Atlantic.

I'm reminded of a discussion I had over a beer in London one summer with a documentary maker I had previously worked with. She isn't really political but definitely fits the bill of a left winger. Our discussions are always fascinating when we meet because we live such different lives. I'm always intrigued to hear the stories from her most recent films, and she has taken a great interest in my political progression over the years. I won't put words into her mouth, but I know from our conversations that she has always believed that the things I say are not motivated by hate, but by an honest desire to tackle injustice.

I value friendships like this a lot. Not only is it good for the soul, but the conversation can be genuinely insightful and present ideas you might never have thought of otherwise. I find that it is always possible to discover areas of mutual understanding and agreement when the conversation comes from a good place. A constant desire to prove the other side wrong is not conducive to solving problems because it requires there to be disagreement. The worst thing we can do in politics, and in our own lives, is to eschew open dialogue and instead opt for hyperpartisan sensationalism.

During our conversation in London, we talked about Brexit, Trump, and the growing divide between the two political camps. On the issue of the US/Mexico border and illegal immigration, we agreed that there absolutely *is* a problem, and that not all of those illegal immigrants arrive in the US with pure intentions. As "The Perception Gap" showed, liberals often are not as extreme on immigration policy as the far-left radicals shouting on the streets, so it is no surprise to me that two people from different sides of the debate can agree on the basics. We discovered that our biggest disagreement was simply the language being used by President Trump to describe the issue. She understood Trump's comment, "some, I assume, are good people," to mean that he believed most Mexican people were in fact rapists, criminals, and drug dealers. I understood his comments to be explicitly referring to illegal aliens who cross the border.

While I don't find Trump's comments to be offensive (particularly given that his claim that many of the illegal immigrants coming over the border are criminals and rapists is true), I can understand why some people see it differently. I can see why people are instantly turned off by the language, and I can understand why people interpret the quote so differently. Of course, the media has a huge part to play in this given the way in which they reported the story, but perhaps the media shouldn't have been given that low-hanging fruit in the first place.

I do believe these comments were important at the time. It showed people he was serious about solving the problem, and it brought him the vote of the angry people who might have lost faith in politics completely. For that reason, I think the anger and the radicalism that came with the Trump campaign was cleansing. However, as divisions grow wider, I wonder if now is perhaps the time to be more tactful in the way we present our arguments.

If moderates in the Democratic Party were willing to talk to conservatives and escape the stranglehold that the AOC-like radicals have over them, then maybe something could finally be done about that porous southern border. Maybe if moderate liberals were willing to put some differences aside and work with conservatives and populists, something might actually change.

The same would be true for moderate progressives in the UK. Our situation here is slightly different in that most of the Conservative Party doesn't subscribe to many conservative ideas anymore, so in which case it would be necessary for both conservatives and the moderate left in Parliament to start listening to populists who have lost faith in politics completely.

Political point scoring and the mad desire to constantly prove one's political opponents wrong seeps into the media, too.

In 2016, I appeared on a documentary for the BBC. I was initially told it would be about British culture, but I learned that wasn't really the case when I met the presenter, data journalist Mona Chalabi. It was a setup to talk about race and racism.

In the first few seconds of filming I shook hands with Chalabi, to which she responded "Ouch, that really hurt!" Off camera, I told a self-deprecating joke that I thought she, as a left-wing journalist, would appreciate. I told her, "Sorry, I'm only used to shaking old white men's hands." She smirked.

Chalabi was born to Iraqi immigrants in England, and the theme of the show was British identity. She asked me repeatedly whether I considered her British, and I told her the truth; yes, she is British, but she is not *ethnically* British.

This is true. It is not an opinion, it is not an ideological talking point, it is not an insult. It is simply true that Chalabi, born to Iraqi immigrants, is civically and legally British but she is not ethnically British. My wife was born to two Croatian immigrants and is visibly of Eastern European ancestry. She is an American citizen, but she is ethnically Croatian. I myself am a British citizen, so I am civically British (or English!). Ethnically, I am also British. I am a mix of English, Scottish, Irish, and Welsh ancestors.

These are facts, and race hatred doesn't come into it. Nor does it mean I wish to expel nonwhite people from Britain.

I never once told Chalabi she wasn't British, nor that she didn't belong in the country; but that didn't stop her ending the segment by calling me racist and telling the camera I denied her British identity. I did no such thing.

After the documentary aired, Chalabi also tweeted that I had told her off camera that I "only shake hands with white men." I couldn't believe it.

It is quite a stark contrast to the experience I had with the documentary film maker I mentioned earlier. With her, our conversation was productive and interesting, and it offered me a line of thought to use in this book. With Chalabi, our conversation achieved nothing…other than allowing her to grandstand on national television and use the experience to elevate her profile and get more TV work.

If the purpose of dialogue is not to understand what the other side is saying but to portray that side in a pre-determined way, then the conversation is not worth having. It is pointless debating ideologues like Chalabi, and it is pointless even talking to them. Their worldview is fixed and cannot be changed.

I have met hundreds of people like her. It is one of the reasons why I spent much of my youth so angry. I have been guilty of the kind of hyperpartisan sensationalist behavior I have condemned in this book. I have used shock tactics to draw attention to issues I believe are important, and it has *never* worked. It might have gotten me into the newspapers a few times, and it briefly brought attention to the issues I talked about, but nobody took me seriously because I was just another angry young white man.

This has to end. Conservatives must encourage and seek open and productive discussion with moderate liberals, and those moderate liberals must be brave enough to stand up to their radical left-wing oppressors.

If conservatives, democratic populists, and moderate liberals can come together and reclaim the narrative on extremism, we will take away the power from the far left immediately. We will make the politicians listen, and we will begin once again to represent the entirely decent, moderate, and sensible people of Europe and America. We will reset our political landscape and make popular progress as a society. Once the politicians and the media realize that the vast majority of the public reject far-left radicalism, then those radicals will lose their power. They will no longer dominate every media platform, they will no longer get to decide who can and cannot speak, and they will not get a free pass to warp popular culture to fit their agenda.

Very little can be achieved through blind anger, and we've had more than enough time to get that anger out of our system. This is a turning point in history.

Civilized and open political discourse will pull the rug from underneath the radical progressives, make the politicians deal with difficult issues, and encourage the press to more accurately represent the people.

STOP PROVING THE FAR RIGHT RIGHT

All of the arguments I have presented throughout this book, and particularly in this final chapter, can be summed up by simply saying we must stop proving the far right, right. Politicians neglecting their constituents, the media misrepresenting the people, and far-left ideologues being given a free pass by moderate liberals has created the perfect storm. While people search for meaning in their lives and ask why the political establishment seems to hate them so much, the far right uses the internet to appeal to disaffected young people and provide the answers they're searching for.

We can revert the arguments of the far right back to pure conspiracy theories if we can remove the circumstances that lend them credibility in the first place.

Had I been given any reason to trust the media in the first place, then would I ever have trusted far-right extremists instead? Had the media not offered such a negative portrayal of people with real concerns, had the politicians not neglected working-class communities, and had far-left extremists not made me a target, I may not be telling this story today.

I fear that I may never be allowed to move on from my past, and over the years I have come to terms with that. In the age of the internet, it is easy to perpetuate myths about a person. The unforgetting and unforgiving nature of Google and social media means that I will likely always be known as that kid who was "tipped to be the next Nick Griffin." But, if this book helps shift the extremism narrative and offer conservatives, liberals, and populists a new perspective on this issue then at least I will have been able to put my experiences to good use.

My involvement with the far right in the UK came to an end many years ago. I eventually realized that the people I had trusted had abused my naivete. The more I saw, the more it became clear to me just how big a mistake I had made. The people who told me the party I had joined had modernized were in fact still pushing anti-Semitic conspiracy theories online. I was at the receiving end of vile abuse from those who believed I was a "Jewish state agent" and a "shill." I saw multiple other members of the BNP leave the party as its polling numbers collapsed and much of the leadership was slowly revealed for what they really were.

I had been taken in by a community of many decent people who had nowhere else to go, but moved up the ranks by a more extreme leadership team that saw potential in me. I was young, outspoken, intelligent, and could deliver a half-decent speech. If it wasn't for the dedicated neo-Nazi activists in the party who had targeted me so viciously, who knows how deep into that world I might ultimately have found myself.

I am thankful to be telling this story now, and thankful my involvement ended when it did.

I sincerely hope that the story I have shared with you has offered a valuable insight into this problem and perhaps made you think differently about this issue.

Whatever side of the political aisle you might be on, I believe there are lessons we can all learn, and steps we can all take, to make politics less divisive and extreme.